GIVING BACK

GIVING BACK

Research and Reciprocity in Indigenous Settings

EDITED BY RDK HERMAN

OREGON STATE UNIVERSITY PRESS *Corvallis*

Library of Congress Cataloging-in-Publication Data
Names: Herman, R. D. K., editor.
Title: Giving back : research and reciprocity in indigenous settings /
    edited by RDK Herman.
Description: Corvallis : Oregon State University Press, 2018. | Includes
    bibliographical references and index.
Identifiers: LCCN 2018037751 | ISBN 9780870719370 (paperback)
Subjects: LCSH: Indigenous peoples—Research—Social aspects—Case studies. |
    Indigenous peoples—Research—Moral and ethical aspects—Case studies. |
    Indigenous peoples—Research—Methodology—Case studies. |
    BISAC: EDUCATION / Multicultural Education. | SOCIAL SCIENCE /
    Ethnic Studies / Native American Studies.
Classification: LCC GN380 .G55 2018 | DDC 305.8/00723—dc23
LC record available at https://lccn.loc.gov/2018037751

⊗ This paper meets the requirements of ANSI/NISO Z39.48-1992
(Permanence of Paper).

Oregon State University
OSU Press

Oregon State University Press
121 The Valley Library
Corvallis OR 97331-4501
541-737-3166 • fax 541-737-3170
www.osupress.oregonstate.edu

Front cover photo credits (left to right):

Row 1: Allen Payne, Maria Fadiman, RDK Herman
Row 2: Maria Fadiman, Clare Colyer, RDK Herman, RDK Herman
Row 3: Maria Fadiman, Matthew Reeves (The Montpelier Foundation),
    Roxanne Ornelas, RDK Herman
Row 4: Chie Sakakibara, Chie Sakakibara, RDK Herman, RDK Herman
Row 5: Allen Payne, RDK Herman, Chie Sakakibara, Roxanne Ornelas
Row 6: RDK Herman, RDK Herman, Clare Colyer, RDK Herman

CONTENTS

Introduction

Why "Giving Back"?

RDK HERMAN

THOSE OF US WHO HAVE BEEN in the field in Indigenous settings—whether for scientific data collection, medical research, or ethnographic work—know that our success depends on the assistance, cooperation, and even aid of peoples in those communities. As I discuss in chapter 1, and others touch on throughout this volume, the framework and methods of academia have historically encouraged an extractive approach to data collecting: the researcher goes in, obtains the data, and leaves, returning nothing to the community and sometimes even publishing or patenting knowledge and "discoveries" derived from the local informants, to the detriment of the local people. Although newer research methodologies recognize that this is exploitative, and have developed approaches to at least engage the local communities as partners in research projects, the notion of *reciprocity* in research is slower to take root.[1] Especially for those of us who engage closely in the lives of the peoples we work with—building relationships for the short, medium, or long term—we have to negotiate these relationships constantly. And, particularly in Indigenous communities, that involves *giving*.

But the act of reciprocity in Indigenous research involves a cross-cultural encounter wherein two (or more) sets of values, senses of obligation, social rules, and ritual protocols collide. Western notions of individual ownership and intellectual property come up against Indigenous notions of collective ownership—or no ownership, for how can certain things be owned by anyone?—and responsibility. Research ethics coming from a purely Western approach do not suffice to deal with this encounter. Nor do government and university guidelines and the oversight of research review boards. Such research guidelines focus on mitigation of research abuses, but do not otherwise call for giving back.

The growing field of Indigenous studies recognizes that as scholars—whether Native or non-Native—we are entering into a relationship with a community and its members that is rooted in trust, responsibility, integrity, and genuine concern for the well-being of that community and its knowledge and traditions. The days of "parachute" scholars, who descend into communities with their research agendas already in hand and expect to get the data they want before they disappear—perhaps never to return, and with no intent of bestowing any benefits on the community—are becoming a thing of the past. Not only has the advent of feminist and postcolonial theories illuminated the exploitative nature of that approach, but Native communities themselves are increasingly demanding more say over or about the nature of research projects in their communities and on their lands, and are willing to say no to projects that do not clearly serve their interests. Meanwhile, a number of guidelines for conducting research in Indigenous communities have proliferated, and they call for a much more inclusive and reciprocal approach to such work.

The present volume was sparked by a symposium titled "Geographies of Hope," organized by the Indigenous Peoples Specialty Group of the Association of American Geographers, for the 2013 meeting of the association. The symposium included eleven different panel and discussion sessions, all with a common thread of addressing geographies of hope—both the means (struggles and activism) and the ends (social and environmental justice)—across a multiplicity of scales and dimensions and forms, contingent on the theoretical framework, the positionality, and/or the cosmovision of the researcher.

Within that symposium were three sessions on the topic of "giving back." The aim was to discuss how research with communities can better accomplish reciprocity with those communities. Recent university and professional-association ethics policies have been revised to address that most research has not reflected pluri-ethnic worldviews and has not been premised on reciprocity. Principles of respectful relationships, consultation, and collaboration have been incorporated into research protocols. Still, individual researchers must define for themselves what the quality and nature of their relationships will be with the communities with whom they work. They must ask themselves, What does reciprocity look and feel like in my working relationships with communities? What institutional barriers must be navigated in efforts to develop reciprocal relationships with community partners? How do you know when the outcomes of a research project have upheld your ethical obligations or goals of reciprocity? How do you navigate the unequal power relations inherent in academic research with Indigenous and "other" communities, in defining appropriate ways of "giving back"? How can research be mutually beneficial, given the historical and ongoing relationships of power in centers of knowledge production? How are the multiple perspectives within an individual community navigated in efforts to ensure positive outcomes for research partners? Even for researchers who are members of the communities with whom they work, giving back may present unique challenges and opportunities. Can research itself be a form of giving back?

As scholars in these panels discussed their struggles with the question of how to give back to their communities of research, it became clear that more guidance on this matter was needed, and a call went out for participation in the present volume.

For me, this undertaking follows on fieldwork with eight communities, mostly in the American Pacific, on projects that documented and presented Indigenous knowledge on the web. As I discuss in chapter 9, though the project design described there served the interests of the communities involved, some turned the project away, stating that more tangible benefits to the community should result—a clean water source, for example. Some noted that previous (for-profit) researchers to their communities had paid them money, and why wasn't I? Meanwhile, there were struggles with everyday reciprocity: how to return the time, support, food, and gifts provided? To whom does one give? The effects of our attempts to "give back" may not be the ones intended, and may even cause unintended and unexpected consequences or problems.

Many of us are never sure whether we get it right in our attempts at reciprocity, so this volume turns to those who have had more experience in this matter, or given it more thought, or engaged in innovative practices to create different paradigms from that of extractive research. There is much more that can be said on this topic, but in this limited space, it is hoped that some maps to this complex territory may emerge.

Researchers and Indigenous Communities

There is a good argument that Indigenous peoples should be able to develop their own capacities such that they would never need outside researchers. From that point of view comes the criticism that this volume runs contrary to the goal of Indigenous-led work. My contributors and I recognize that Indigenous-led research is increasing, and we hope and expect to see that trend continue. But we disagree that the work herein is therefore unnecessary or even colonizing.

Part of research ethics should be that researchers don't work where they are not wanted. The researcher/community dualism, however, is not an accurate reflection of the reality for many people. Rather, as the chapters herein show, a relationality of researchers and reciprocity exists to the extent that the researcher can be considered an "insider" of the community (Sharp and Dowler 2011). Reciprocity is one aspect of an "ethical" rather than structural or ethics-based practice on which researchers must constantly reflect with a view to a more ethical engagement with all research subjects or co-participants.

As Jennifer Carter, a coauthor of chapter 2, points out, relationships between researchers and communities form for a range of reasons. Indigenous communities may seek additional expertise in bid for commercial viability (as might any new business), or seek to strategically align with a scholar-activist, or may simply be seeking additional resources or people working toward their aspirations. In some cases, communities approach researchers or universities, either directly or through representative individuals and bodies. The Australian case study in chapter 2, for instance, provides two examples wherein individuals from Indigenous communities approached their representative body, who then found researchers to work alongside the community, and another example in which the researcher was asked to completely change a project that someone had previously approached the community about, in order that the project (which had to be formally renegotiated) achieve community aspirations. That chapter also provides an example from Australia in which the researcher siphoned money to Indigenous communities to undertake aspects of the research they wished to (leaving the researcher to undertake aspects of the project they didn't want to work on), and another example in Canada wherein the entire grant was received and administered by the community who undertook the work they wished to, alongside an "outside" researcher of their choosing. In these cases, there was a problem in presuming that all or even some Indigenous community members want to undertake some or all of the research themselves rather than working in partnership with a researcher who helps to achieve their outcomes.

In other words, there is much to suggest that Indigenous peoples should document their own knowledges, undertake research projects, receive funds, and so on. But for now, in the majority of Indigenous communities, the internal capacity to undertake all the research the community needs is simply not there. Where I work, in the Hawaiian Islands, new Native Hawaiian MA and PhD graduates emerge every year, but they are still spread far too thin to cover the work needing to be done. Many Indigenous communities also want the value-added that a researcher may bring. In this way, Indigenous peoples exert their agency in choosing whether to hire or engage with a researcher or, indeed, to undertake the research themselves, and as such, undertaking research "on their terms" is different from undertaking research themselves.

There are also the ever-slippery questions of "Who is the community?" and "Who speaks, or decides, for that community?" Even without the presence of an outside researcher, this can be fraught. As Gwyn Isaac, coauthor of chapter 3, states,

> Every tribe, group and community I work with has different ideas about and approaches to negotiating power relations, especially when it comes to research. I have groups that say they will decide everything as a community-based decision with no input from curators and my institution, and I have groups that want to have total collaboration, which they see as research methods and institutions bringing a 50 percent investment and therefore resulting in 50 percent research-based institutional voice. I also have groups that want each of their clans to be in charge, so there is in fact no central authority. And I have communities that want religious leaders or elders to be in charge. So the authority is often distributed in complex ways. Repatriation also deals with these concerns, arguing for a case-by-case basis because of the myriad of authorities that have to be taken into account. While this does not address that the "West" has concentrated and centralized powers that dominate Native communities, over-simplification of power relations is not helpful for community members or Native scholars, or researchers who want to work in these areas.[2]

Therefore this volume looks at where factors—communities, methodologies, and schools—intersect in the research realm; the present state of these intersections is the topic of interest for this volume. The authors represented are trying to understand this space where different knowledges and values intersect, and this is one of the first steps to understanding power relations writ large. If a power-relation model is transposed onto every colonial, postcolonial and settler environment, it hides the inner workings of the local knowledge and value systems at play. The point of this volume is that each case study is *emergent*—meaning that the collaborative groups and researchers are having to find their way dependent on each context.

The Organization of This Volume

This volume is loosely organized into four sections. I say "loosely" because some themes cut across these sections: advocacy, repatriation, and struggles against the dominant research paradigm are among these. Part 1, "Considerations on Research and Reciprocity," begins with my review of the history of research regulations and points to where, at the time of this writing, those regulations may be going and how Indigenous peoples, at least in the United States, are responding on their own. It also reviews the directions for reconsidering research that have been elucidated by Indigenous scholars. For some readers this is a review, but it is important to delineate the historical, institutional framework in which we scholars function and the current trends that are working to shift that paradigm.

In chapter 2, Jennifer Carter, Tristan Pearce, and Chris Jacobson take on the university context, arguing that working beyond the community to shape our academic institutions brings reciprocal benefits to broader society and to community members. As such, a commitment by community-based researchers to advocate, stand against tokenism, and be of service beyond traditional research outputs is a form of giving back, especially given the personal and professional costs to the researchers in taking on institutional change.

Lea McChesney and Gwyneira Isaac address the museum context in chapter 3, discussing the Hopi Pottery Oral History Project as a case study in the complex logistics of providing a continuum of accessibility to cultural-heritage resources for contemporary practitioners while regenerating traditional knowledge and practice. Proceeding from a Hopi cultural protocol of "paying back," their project is not so much concerned with the return of objects as it is with establishing practices to accomplish the reconnection of displaced subjects (pottery, in this case) with their home communities.

In chapter 4, Erica D'Elia, Meredith Luze, and Matthew Reeves relate their experiences of trying to give back in the context of public archaeology. They describe their project's engagement with descendants of a slave community at James Madison's Montpelier, and ways in which those encounters changed the shape of the project. They provide the lessons they learned from this type of community engagement.

Part 2, "Repatriating Knowledge," presents three examples of repatriation in practice. In chapter 5, Chie Sakakibara discusses her experience in the repatriation of historic audio recordings to Iñupiat communities of Alaska's North Slope. Rather than simply hand over valuable cultural heritage materials and their associated intellectual property rights, she and her colleague are working with the community to recover detailed contextual information about the materials, develop community-wide consensus on the proper disposition and future uses of these materials and related rights, and support and enable contemporary and innovative uses of these materials by Iñupiaq artists, educators, cultural activists, and by the community more generally.

Similarly, but in an Australian context, Richie Howitt and colleagues, in chapter 6, consider the challenges in bringing current community-centered research ethics and methods to the question of the return of archival materials collected under very different protocols in the past. They identify themes and reference points that might guide the journeys that the development of community archives and community-engaged research tackling longer time frames might consider.

In chapter 7, drawing on her experiences in the Tawahka territory in eastern Honduras, Kendra McSweeney reflects on the importance of "return research" through repeated visits. She found that while familiarity with place, language, and local institutions can expedite the research process, and closeness to informants can be personally fulfilling, these same benefits can also complicate research by raising local peoples' expectations about the potential for assistance, and by demanding a higher level of researcher engagement and responsibility.

Part 3, "Telling Their Stories," shares three case studies in which the scholars took on the responsibility to pass on the stories of the communities with which they worked. This is in part a matter of giving back, and in part a matter of *giving on*. Maria Fadiman, in chapter 8, describes how her work with *curanderos* in the Ecuadorian Amazon led to her producing ethnobotanical booklets for the community, and how this in turn led her to seek other means of community inclusion. But she also points to the problems of returning local, oral knowledge in a Western, printed form.

In chapter 9, I describe my work in documenting place-based community knowledge, both for the communities themselves and for the general public, in my Pacific Worlds project. With protocols in place to protect knowledge that should not go public, this project puts community knowledge on the web. I raise the question of whether or not the project constitutes "giving back," and provide ideas for how it might be done better to encourage more community engagement and, therefore, more benefits.

Roxanne Ornelas, in chapter 10, similarly tells of the admonition she received from an elder at the Fort Berthold Indian Reservation in North Dakota—"Tell them about us"—to keep teaching others the oft-silenced histories of native peoples. She presents how academic research becomes a way to establish an ongoing relationship of reciprocity, in giving back to these nations through scholarship and pedagogy—to inform and to empower. Inasmuch as there are challenges to being the non-Native voice telling the story, it is nonetheless a commitment that many of us take on, often unknowingly.

Part 4, "Advocacy and Beyond," furthers the discussion of what we as scholars can and perhaps should do to further decolonize scholarship and assist Indigenous communities. In chapter 11, Wendy S. Shaw describes her activities while living in the urban Aboriginal community of Redfern in Sydney, Australia. Within the context of the community's struggle to sustain their neighborhood in a gentrifying city, she tells her stories of engagement as both scholar and resident, and how the forging of relationships and responsibilities has continued over time.

Drawing from experiences in northern Indigenous Canada, Uganda, and Vietnam, in chapter 12, Catrina MacKenzie, Julia Christensen, and Sarah Turner identify six key reasons for returning relevant research results in-person to participants: showing basic respect to those who gave of their valuable time to support the study, responding to questions about the findings and research, member-checking the findings, strengthening relationships with communities where we research, responding to what some see as an ethical imperative to return results, and, most significantly, helping to advocate for change.

Finally, in chapter 13, John R. Welch posits that "sovereignty" best sums up what Indigenous peoples desire from researchers, and presents a general framework offering guidance to researchers and others interested in creating benefits that are meaningful and beneficial in specific contexts. Understanding the constituents of sovereignty in local contexts, he asserts, provides researchers with concrete guidance for efforts to assist the people who are assisting them.

The chapters presented herein are just a small part of the conversation that needs to be explored. In all of these cases, obstacles are encountered, lessons learned, and new questions raised. A great many worthy topics are not considered. Much work is being done, for example, on benefit-sharing through participatory methods. That subject is large enough to merit its own volume, so it is not included here. This collection is not a guide to "giving back." It does not (nor could it) lay out hard-and-fast rules about what, how much, and to whom we should give. How can you know if your research benefits the needs of the "community," when in fact communities have multiple and often conflicting needs, interests, and desires regarding research outcomes?

Instead, this volume lays out a series of examples and considerations, offering a first of many forays, one hopes, into this topic and, at the very least, marking out reciprocity in research as an important and distinct area of discussion in the growing field of research ethics and decolonized methodologies.

I have argued elsewhere (Herman 2015) that the Western academic episteme in which our efforts are embedded is governed by a false principle of "rationality" that is atomistic in its view of humans, with its focus on the individual (and thereby, on private property, including intellectual property). It is also mechanistic in its view of the world. Thus efforts to shift the paradigm toward one of greater reciprocity encounter cultural barriers that manifest as institutional barriers—from one's university and its ethics board (IRB or other), from advisers, from funders, and from government agencies. What is clear throughout this volume is that giving back involves negotiating the existing institutional structures in which research is embedded. "Giving back" to Indigenous communities too often requires "pushing back" against established practices and expectations—for that matter, against the entire colonial episteme that subjugated Indigenous peoples and produced and justified exploitative research.

In that sense, this book offers examples and pathways not just of "giving back," but of "pushing back."

Introduction References

Herman, RDK. 2015. "Traditional Knowledge in a Time of Crisis: Climate Change, Culture and Communication." *Sustainability Science* 11 (1): 163–176.

Sharp, Joanne, and Lorraine Dowler. 2011. "Framing the Field." In *A Companion to Social Geography*, edited by Vincent J. Del Casino Jr., Mary E. Thomas, Paul Cloke, and Ruth Panelli, 146–160. Malden, MA: Blackwell.

Notes to Introduction

1. A special issue of the *Journal of Research Practice* (vol. 10, no. 2, 2014) is titled "Giving Back in Field Research." Unlike this volume, it consists of many very small essays (twenty-six) by scholars relating their field experiences.
2. Personal communication, February 23, 2017.

PART 1

Considerations on Research and Reciprocity

1

Doing the Good Work?

The Trajectory of Research Ethics and Reciprocity

RDK HERMAN

I N 2011, SOME COLLEAGUES FROM the Smithsonian and I approached one of the tribal colleges with an idea for a project. The scope of the project was enormous and would require additional expertise from other institutions in the area. When we named a certain major university that was interested in participating, the tribal college people were mum at first, and eventually, under pressure, said simply "No. We will not work with them." We later found out that a research team from that university had, just a few years before, worked with the tribe and gathered a number of oral histories. Afterward, when the tribe asked for copies or transcripts of those recordings, the scholars refused, stating that the materials belonged to the university and that the tribe had no claim to them. They would not, in other words, *give back*. And so that tribe would not work with anyone from that major state university any more.

Rundstrom and Deur remind us that "ethical research does not simply involve an isolated individual seeking to 'do good' or to 'do the right thing.' . . . Reliance upon isolated reflection in developing ethical relations is a peculiarly non-Indian concept" (1999, 238). Rather, doing good research in Indigenous settings requires immersion in a very different approach to research from the outset, and an intimate relationship with the community.

No doubt Native peoples starting voicing their concerns and dis-
pleasures regarding scholarly research in and on their communities as
soon as they were able to grasp what was going on. The earliest discourse
on the subject that I've come across is Vine Deloria Jr.'s famous piece,
"Anthropologists and Other Friends," first published in 1969. Deloria
speaks long and humorously about the problem of anthropological study
of Native peoples. Toward the end of this piece, he tells of an anthropologist
who, over a period of some twenty years, spent close to ten million dollars
studying a tribe of fewer than a thousand people. Deloria says, "Imagine
what that amount of money would have meant to that group of people
had it been invested in buildings and businesses. There would have been
no problems to study!" (Deloria 1988, 23). He concludes by stating that
"it would be wise for anthropologists to get down from their thrones of
authority and PURE research and begin helping Indian tribes instead of
preying on them. For the wheel of Karma grinds slowly but it does grind
finely. And it makes a complete circle" (Deloria 1988, 100).

Without reviewing all that has been said recently about scholarship
as a form of colonialism,[3] it is important to frame scholarship within
the broader history of extractive industries, market economy, and private
property. For it is within this milieu that issues and dilemmas of "giving
back" gain their salience. Indigenous peoples as political entities exist on
the periphery of a world system that over the past five centuries has, to
varying degrees, appropriated their lands and resources; taken away their
sovereignty; decimated them with diseases; disregarded their knowledges
and lifeways as backward, primitive, and heathen; imposed new religions,
customs, and lifestyles; and tried very hard to force them into the global
capitalist system. It is an enormous and all-encompassing legacy of taking.

Research among Indigenous peoples has largely—and usually blindly—
followed suit. Scholars are caught up in a subeconomy of capitalism and
the post-Enlightenment attitudes toward Native peoples: knowledge produced by academic research is positioned not merely as objective and
superior, but as a currency within a larger economy of generated knowledge. It is the intellectual property of the scholars who produce it and
protected against plagiarism by copyright, the accumulation of which
increases their professional capital. *By our publications—or innovations—
we are measured.* For academic (noncommercial) scholars, our ideas
enter the public domain of knowledge where they can be used and cited
by others. There is access to them in the marketplace of knowledge and
ideas. If they do not enter this marketplace, they accrue no value. And as

MacKenzie, Christensen, and Turner elaborate (chapter 12, this volume), the realm of academic publishing is often unsuitable and ineffective as a means of communication to Indigenous communities themselves.

Research among Indigenous peoples has generally involved taking—or what has sometimes been called "data mining": as with the extractive mining industry and its colonial legacy, the scholar goes into the community, digs out the information—usually for free in the name of research—and leaves with it, perhaps never to return and, in most cases, giving nothing back to the community at all. Especially as intellectual property rights have emerged as a new venue for the struggle over who owns knowledge, tribes and Native scholars have been taking a stand against this data-mining approach and putting mechanisms in place to mitigate against such exploitation. But these protective steps are still in fairly early days, and particularly for smaller communities in more remote areas of the world where traditional values still dominate, the potential for exploitation remains strong.

But it is not just intellectual property rights that have Native peoples upset. Rather, it is the entire approach to research as an extractive industry and the way researchers have conducted themselves from start to finish of their studies in tribal communities. This is demonstrated in Deloria's piece on anthropologists, mentioned earlier, as well as in postcolonial critiques such as Mary Louis Pratt's *Imperial Eyes: Travel Writing and Transculturation* (1992), which examines ethnography as a colonizing methodology; and on to Linda Tuhiwai Smith's *Decolonizing Methodologies* (1999); Margaret Kovach's *Indigenous Methodologies* (2009); and Bagele Chilisa's *Indigenous Research Methodologies* (2011). As Kwakwaka'wakw scholar Sarah Hunt has written, "Knowledge production within dominant institutions and disciplinary conferences . . . involve[s] epistemic violence—the work of discourse in creating and sustaining boundaries around what is considered real and, by extension, what is unable to be seen as real (or to be seen at all)" (2014). And it has been the Indigenous perspectives—and voices—that have been rendered unreal.

As a lead-in to this volume's discussions of giving back, this chapter reviews the history of policies and protocols governing research that evoke the need for this volume. This history not only serves as the background for the present discussion, but also tells us a great deal about how research has been understood and framed in the dominant culture. It is both the policies and the socio-legal context that have informed them that give the discussion of "giving back" its potency. Since World War II, various mechanisms have served to codify types of research, on the one hand aiming to minimize certain types of exploitation, on the other hand ensuring that other types of exploitation can continue. These legacies regulate our research today, and have come primarily from three areas: biomedical research, bioprospecting and biopiracy, and intellectual property rights. For some readers, this history is well known, but as the chair of the Institutional Review Board (IRB) for human subjects research at the Smithsonian Institution for three years, I can attest that many scholars are completely unfamiliar with this history, including many who work with Indigenous peoples and/or are Indigenous scholars themselves.

Biomedical Research

Policy regarding inappropriate biomedical research began with the Nuremberg trials of Nazi war crimes for medical experimentation on living subjects. Twenty-three Nazi doctors were found guilty of "crimes against humanity" for experiments that tortured, mutilated, or killed concentration camp prisoners. In the 1947 verdict, the judges included a section that became known as the Nuremberg Code of 1947, called "Permissible Medical Experiments." Outlining a set of ten conditions to be met before research could be deemed ethically possible, the Nuremberg Code became the first international standard of human experimentation ethics (Božnjak 2001, 180).

Following the Nuremberg Code, in 1964 the World Medical Association established recommendations guiding doctors performing biomedical research with human participants. The resulting Declaration of Helsinki, titled "Ethical Principles for Medical Research Involving Human Subjects," was revised in 1975 and several times since. Despite changes and controversy, it remains the cornerstone of medical research ethics—in principle, if not in fact.

Then in 1972, accounts surfaced regarding what is now known as the Tuskegee Syphilis Experiment scandal. From 1932 to 1972, doctors and public officials in the state of Alabama observed four hundred African American men with syphilis but gave them no treatment. The subjects were never told they were participating in an "experiment," and treatment that could have cured them was deliberately withheld. Many of them died painfully, while others suffered permanent blindness or insanity. The children of several were born with congenital syphilis (Brandt 1978).

As a consequence of public outcry over this, the 1974 US National Research Act (Public Law 93-348) established the National Commission for the Protection of Human Subjects of Biomedical and Behavioral Research, adding "behavioral" for the first time. This commission published the 1978 document "Ethical Principles and Guidelines for the Protection of Human Subjects of Research," now known as the Belmont Report. As the Belmont Report states, the commission was directed to consider

- the role of assessment of risk-benefit criteria in the determination of the appropriateness of research involving human subjects,
- appropriate guidelines for the selection of human subjects for participation in such research and
- the nature and definition of informed consent in various research settings.

The US Department of Health and Human Services (HHS), using the Belmont Report and other work of the national commission, codified a set of regulations as Title 45 CFR part 46. This code was adopted in 1991 by fourteen other US federal departments and agencies, creating the Federal Policy for the Protection of Human Subjects, otherwise known as the Common Rule (US Department of Health and Human Services 2011a, 2011b). Together, the Belmont Report and the Declaration of Helsinki led to the establishment of institutional review boards (IRBs) to oversee ethical practices in biomedical and behavioral research. The Common Rule became the code governing IRBs in the United States in 1981. Canada followed a similar trajectory, developing guidelines for research involving human subjects in the 1970s and revising them into the Tri-Council Policy Statement that continues to evolve today, reflecting international standards (Government of Canada 2015). In Australia, the Medical Research Council, established in 1936, issued the 1966 Statement on Human Experimentation that expressly drew on the Declaration of Helsinki; the Medical Research Ethics Committee was established there in 1982. A National Statement on Ethical Conduct in Research involving Humans was promulgated in 1999 in Australia and has been updated to the present. (More about the Australian context is discussed in chapter 6.)

The principles of the Belmont Report and the ethics guidelines for the United States, Canada, and Australia are

- Respect for persons: protecting the autonomy of all people and treating them with courtesy and respect and allowing for informed consent.
- Beneficence: enacting the philosophy of "Do no harm" while *maximizing benefits for the research project* (emphasis added) and minimizing risks to the research subjects (in the Canadian version, this is called "Concern for Welfare"); and
- Justice: ensuring reasonable, non-exploitative, and well-considered procedures are administered fairly.[4]

These principles are a nice start, but the focus remains on mitigation against abuses of research, rather than distributing the benefits thereof. They do not, in other words, call for "giving back."

The problem with the Common Rule and these related guidelines, for geographers and other social scientists, is the legacy of focus on biomedical research. Social science research poses a different and more nuanced set of circumstances that don't fit easily into this rubric. The Common Rule, for example, defines "research" as "a systematic investigation, including research development, testing and evaluation, *designed to develop or contribute to generalizable knowledge*" (emphasis added). This means that qualitative investigation, including oral histories, interviews, and so on, do not qualify as "research" unless you are going to draw generalizable conclusions from it. Yet we know that these activities can pose risks for vulnerable populations such as Indigenous communities.

It is important to note both the principles involved in the Common Rule approach and the practices toward which they are directed. First, risk-benefit analysis points out that the benefits of experiments (to the researcher, and to the body of knowledge as a whole) should clearly outweigh the risks to the subjects. This is easier to assess in biomedical cases than in social and cultural cases, where often researchers do not realize the risks their work poses to members of the community, or the community as a whole, and may assume that the "benefits" of their research (that is, beyond the benefits to their resumes and careers) will somehow serve the community by adding to the published knowledge about them.

Second is crafting appropriate guidelines for the selection of human subjects. Race, gender, age, and other factors come into play here, as they did in the Tuskegee experiment. Who is chosen for the research, and why?

Third, there is the matter of informed consent: ensuring that the subjects of the research know what they are getting into, what it will involve, and why the research is being done. In Indigenous settings, and especially in more traditional societies, the people involved may be trying to absorb and digest so much information about the proposed research project that what the scholar considers "informed" consent is not really very well understood at all by community members. Traditional societies may also adhere to practices of responsibility and reciprocity in their dealings with others that are neither understood nor accepted by the scholars involved.

Biomedical research can still be exploitative and harmful because of the perceived notion of "data as property," as exemplified by the recent Havasupai case. Members of the tribe had given DNA samples to Arizona State University researchers to help find genetic clues to the tribe's devastating diabetes rate. They later learned that their blood samples had been used to study mental illness and theories of the tribe's geographical origins as well. Researcher Therese Markow argued she had adequate permission to do this. The tribe issued a "banishment order" to keep Arizona State University employees from setting foot on the reservation and eventually won a settlement (Harmon 2010). This recent case merely highlights that conflicting notions of research, rights, and restitution still continue.

Bioprospecting and Biopiracy

The second major area that has provoked critical response is bioprospecting and biopiracy. "Bioprospecting" is the subject of many definitions, which have been summarized by Bluemel as "the search for biodiverse genetic or biochemical information *in the wild* for the purpose of commercial exploitation" (Bluemel 2005/2006, 118, emphasis added). Since "the wild" is generally areas traditionally used or occupied by Indigenous peoples, this activity affects the use of resources in their territories. Researchers also frequently utilize traditional knowledge held by Indigenous peoples to find useful plants. Biopiracy, on the other hand, is "the unauthorized or uncompensated removal or use of genetic resources *or traditional knowledge*" (Bluemel 2005/2006, 128; emphasis added).

Extraction is a fundamental principle of the colonial endeavor: colonies are sources of raw materials and markets for finished products. Exploitation of the environment is a fundamental component of the process. And the areas of greatest biodiversity coincide with areas occupied by Indigenous peoples who are the least engaged in the global economy. In the postwar era, ethno-pharmaceutical research and product development has been presented as an improvement over more invasive modes of environmental exploitation, since it depends on conserving environments and mobilizing Indigenous intellectual labor (Roopnaraine 1998, 16). But during the 1960s and 1970s, developing countries started to complain that the industrial North was exploiting their natural resources, often without even mention of compensation. This coincided with the growing realization of the value and importance of germplasm and DNA resources for breeding improved varieties—and, later, for genetically modified organisms or GMOs (Powledge 2001, 274).

So, the question of who owns the modified plant, or even the "newly discovered" strain, has led to conflicts over patenting. As Fecteau (2001, 70) points out, US patent law does not recognize prior *foreign* use of an "invention" as a bar to obtaining a patent, unless such foreign use has been *published* and is available for all to find. For oral-tradition-based peoples in the third world, this effectively declares open season for bioprospecting.

One of the prominent early cases on this was Loren Miller's 1986 patent on a strain of the ayahuasca vine, a native of the Amazon rain forest, that has been used by healers and religious leaders throughout the Amazon for generations. Miller claimed to have built a school for the tribe's people in return for their assistance. Miller's patent was protested by the Coordinating Body of Indigenous Organizations of the Amazon Basin (COICA); he ultimately let the patent lapse, but couldn't see what all the fuss was about (Fecteau 2001, 85). And herein lies the epistemological gap about notions of property. Other—more ill-intentioned—cases have proliferated, from patenting uses of neem to varieties of basmati rice, to quinoa, and more (see Shiva 2001).

The ayahuasca case also points out an ironic side effect of patent law: for Indigenous peoples to patent their plants, the "invention" must not be "patented or described in a printed publication." As DeGeer (2002, 185) points out, cultural anthropologists, ethnobotanists, and other scholars have built careers out of publishing Indigenous botanical knowledge, thereby eliminating the possibility that those communities can patent the plants. At the same time, however, those publications ensure that corporations also cannot patent these resources. And that is what ultimately won the ayahuasca case: Indigenous use had been published.

The patenting of genetic resources is fostered by the Agreement on Trade-Related Aspects of Intellectual Property Rights (TRIPS), a 1994 international agreement administered by the World Trade Organization.

It was a fairly blatant move by developed countries of the North to impose their intellectual property regimes on the South. Bratspies, who compares TRIPS with the old Doctrine of Discovery, asserts that TRIPS was fashioned by the interests and voices of the United States, Europe, and Japan, creating a one-size-fits-all approach to property protection developed largely to serve the needs of a capitalist market economy (2006/2007, 331). Bratspies goes on to say,

> The way TRIPS is structured, it is difficult, if not impossible, for indigenous groups to claim any intellectual property rights over the unmediated products of their traditional knowledge. As a result, indigenous and traditional knowledge is consigned to the global commons . . . with no recognition or reward or protection for the contributions of indigenous innovators. . . .
>
> The TRIPS Agreement's insistence that patent rights be recognized, with the prerequisites of novelty and individual authorship, excludes indigenous peoples from the intellectual property rights system much like the way those same groups were systematically denied property rights to their land during the periods of discovery and colonialism. (326)

TRIPS Article 27.3 requires that states include plants and animals within the "inventions" eligible for patenting (or develop a sui generis plan for protecting these inventions), thus protecting the rights of individual inventors.

TRIPS follows on the heels of the Convention on Biological Diversity (1993), unveiled at the 1992 Earth Summit in Rio. The convention recognizes "the close and traditional dependence of many indigenous and local communities embodying traditional lifestyles on biological resources, and the desirability of sharing equitably benefits arising from the use of traditional knowledge, innovations and practices relevant to the conservation of biological diversity and the sustainable use of its components."

But the convention doesn't offer much toward protecting traditional knowledge and, being a state-level instrument, does not empower Native communities through real engagement. Rather, it invests ownership of biological resources in the state, effectively giving states ownership and control over Indigenous knowledge.

Article 8(j) of the convention states,

Subject to its national legislation, respect, preserve and maintain knowledge, innovations and practices of indigenous and local communities embodying traditional lifestyles relevant for the conservation and sustainable use of biological diversity and pro- mote their wider application with the approval and involvement of the holders of such knowledge, innovations and practices and encourage the equitable sharing of the benefits arising from the utilization of such knowledge, innovations and practices. (1993)

But as Mugabe (1999) points out, some parties to the convention may actually invoke this language so as to not undertake any measures that protect Indigenous peoples' knowledge, innovations, and other rights. He asserts that expressions such as "subject to national legislation" and "as far as possible and as appropriate" were promoted during the convention negotiations "by governments that did not want to commit themselves to protection of indigenous peoples and their rights." Ongoing discussions reflect that, on the whole, these efforts are being made as a result of the recognition that the convention "does not contain adequate legal obliga- tions to protect any property rights of indigenous and local peoples in their traditional knowledge" (Mugabe 1999, 23–25).

With control of access to biodiversity resources in the hands of the state instead of local communities, the government can strike a "pros- pecting" agreement with foreign researchers that overrides Indigenous stakeholders. It may be the local political-economic elites, and not vora- cious multinational corporations, that see the profits to be made from exploiting local resources (Coombe 1998, 95). And as Daes points out, even when the state tries to enact policy to define and protect Indigenous rights and responsibilities regarding their own heritage, this runs contrary to the principle of Indigenous self-determination (2001, 146).

In short, the attempts to enact policy over control of Native biological resources and traditional knowledge are largely about *taking*, not about giving back. And this spills over into the discussion of intellectual property per se.

Scholarship and Intellectual Property

The notion of intellectual property rights is that "new" ideas and innova- tions can be patented, thereby exclusively rendering the profits therefrom to one individual or corporation. This is an extension of the privatization of material property rights and patents into the arena of knowledge and ideas. Intellectual property rights have been granted in Europe since at least the fourteenth century, and as Adkisson notes, they are intended to correct the market failure caused by the public-good characteristics of many innovations. But in correcting one market failure, IPRs creates another market failure in the form of monopoly power over innovations (Adkisson 2004, 460). Intellectual property rights as a whole are a market mechanism intended to spur economic growth. In the US Constitution, the reason for granting intellectual property rights is stated as being to "promote the Progress of Science and the useful Arts." TRIPS in particular is seen by many as "a major element in the trend towards the patenting of practically everything" (Powledge 2001, 275).

The underlying issue here is two very different perspectives on property and commodification, both of which are "commonsense knowledge" to the peoples involved. One is the market economy that dominates the global culture. In this system, most things are or should be private property and marketable. Competition for the accumulation of wealth is what makes that particular world go around. In traditional economies, conversely, very few things are private property, and certainly not nations of beings, DNA, or traditional knowledge (Gudeman 1996, 106–107).

As stated at the outset of this chapter, Western-style research takes place within a market system, and has publications as its own subeconomy therein. It is not surprising then that researchers see the fruits of their labors as private property, even when the data was mined from Indigenous sources ("in the wild"). The only way for Indigenous peoples to protect themselves within this framework is to accept the construct of intellectual property rights. Thus, as Bratspies states, Indigenous groups face "an unpalatable choice: either remake their traditional knowledge in the image of the rights claimed and recognized within the dominant society and break down the essence of their traditional culture into distinct sticks of property, or deny themselves access to existing intellectual property protections" (2006/2007, 333).

The World Intellectual Property Organization states that their work "addresses the role that intellectual property principles and systems can play in protecting TK [traditional knowledge] and TCE [traditional cultural expressions] from misappropriation, and in generating and equitably sharing benefits from their commercialization and the role of IPs [Indigenous peoples] in access to and benefit-sharing in genetic resources." But at this writing, they have only draft ideas.

Among Indigenous peoples themselves, there appears to be a division of opinion regarding intellectual property rights. As Coombe pointed out a while back, the Indigenous peoples in the North (Canada, the United States, New Zealand, Australia, and the Pacific Islands) are more fully recognized in national and international law as Indigenous nations and are engaging intellectual property rights in their assertions of sovereignty and self-determination. In the South, however, Asian, African, and Latin American groups "face more protracted struggles to have their indigenous status recognized, both in the States in which they reside and in the international arena. Legal recognition of their sovereign rights to control territory and resources appears far more remote; consequentially, they have taken a more pragmatic view of the potential short-term benefits of IPRs in alleviating poverty" (Coombe 1998,108) . Either way, Indigenous peoples and their knowledges are fractured and commodified.

One might hope that the United Nations Declaration on the Rights of Indigenous Peoples offers some solution. But my reading of this document shows that, while it gives lip service to protecting Indigenous peoples' lands, territories, resources and traditional practices, it still does so within the framework of state management and international laws, and does not pose a counter-hegemonic system of property.

Emerging Academic Approaches

In academia and beyond, trends away from the "data mining" approach toward research have emerged over the past several decades, particularly in the 1990s: participatory action research, feminist methodology, and postcolonial studies, for example. Much could be said about each of these, but here are some basics.

The first area is called participatory action research, or PAR. "Action research" aims at dealing with real-life problems. Researchers engage with communities to produce active outcomes and strategies for pressing issues through an ongoing process of reflection and action (Smith 2001; Kemmis and McTaggart 2007). Participants themselves collect and analyze data to determine what action they should follow. The line is blurred between researcher and researched, as community members becomes partners in the research process. PAR also does not remove the data and information from their contexts. The data collected is used in situ to make decisions directly (Baum, MacDougall, and Smith 2006, 854).

But as the research project can be designed from the start without consultation, it does not necessarily give the community what it wants or needs. Heikkinen, Kakkori, and Huttunen (2001, 9–10) describe what they call one of the "grand narratives" of successful action research, the case in which certain American Indians on reservations were successfully engaged in becoming better farmers and farm managers. They point out that this could also be read as a story of effective colonization and oppression, in which the Indians were more effectively assimilated. Carter, Pearce, and Jacobson (chapter 2, this volume) point out that while participatory forms of research can be a legitimate means of engagement and effect beyond the academy, participatory research partnerships can either "give back" or reinforce power. It is the ethics underpinning the researchers' conduct, rather than the form of research itself, that needs critique.

The second area in which scholarship has moved toward greater engagement with the research subjects has been feminist methodology. As Fitzgerald explains, aspects of the feminist paradigm include, first, that is not about "the search for the truth, authority or objectivity; its goal is to challenge, contest and resist the production and control of knowledge by the powerful" (Fitzgerald 2004, 236). Feminist research advocates for the primacy of the voices and position of the participants, and the need to advocate for changes to the status quo. The interests and agenda of the researcher(s) are a secondary consideration. Thus the power of the participants can emerge via their participation, thereby inverting the traditional balance of power in the research context. This is very much a part of Indigenous research methodology.

As in PAR, reflexivity is a key element of feminist research. Researchers must understand themselves as active agents in the construction of knowledge and reflect on their positions (in terms of class, race, gender, nationality, age, familial circumstance, and life experiences) as well as those of their research subjects. Fonow and Cook (2005, 2220) point out that feminist researchers may also engage in PAR, pointing out the overlap between the underlying approaches and the methodologies of these two. Both of these are important precursors to Indigenous studies.

The third emergent trend is postcolonial studies. With the cultural turn that took place in the humanities and social sciences in the early 1990s (though beginning at least as far back as Said's 1978 work on Orientalism), scholars working on Indigenous peoples and peoples of the Global South recognized the power relations inherent in the writing of scholarship: that scholarship had largely reinforced the colonizer/colonized relationships of the nineteenth century and had not broken free of them. This resulted in both critical literary and discourse analysis studies that deconstruct the power relations found in texts, but also an engagement with Others in earnest, including giving voice to the community members and looking for ways to balance out the power relations inherent in research. As Shaw, Herman, and Dobbs (2006, 271) state, "One of the aims of postcolonial work is to decentre 'Western' authority over knowledge, requiring 'Western' theory and scholarship not only to listen to 'the other,' but acknowledge and fully incorporate differences to the broader body of intellectual theory."

But since postcolonial theory has emerged largely from the European experience of losing colonies in the wake of World War II, much of it has focused at the state level rather than at the "fourth world" or Indigenous level, where the term "postcolonial" does not really apply. In the early 1990s, as postcolonialism came into vogue, my Hawaiian and Pacific Islander colleagues were saying "*Post*-colonial? You mean they left?" Robert Warrior (2009) later elaborated this point in detail, arguing that the aversion of Native scholars to postcolonial studies is "grounded in the reality that Native Americans remain colonised peoples rather than people facing post-independence realities and challenges. Thus the post in postcolonialism creates a stumbling block to engagement." He echoes Jace Weaver's (2001) notion that "the main thrust and de facto focus of postcolonial studies remain post-independence texts and contexts." This I have found particularly true of the postcolonial work coming out of the United Kingdom, much of which focused on exorcising British guilt over the colonization of South Asia.

Nonetheless, postcolonialism played an important role in awakening Western scholars to the power relations inherent in their work, and in the works of scholars who preceded them. The question remains, where do we go from here? The wave of postcolonialism has largely passed for those to whom it meant a confrontation with a colonial past, but for scholars working with Indigenous peoples—who by most definitions remain colonized—an ongoing negotiation of relationships is required. What benefit does the community accrue from the research? How can research be done in such a way that it operates within Indigenous systems of values and protocols, and ideally, serves Indigenous interests as well?

Indigenous Methodologies

Indigenous scholars have powerfully taken on research methodologies in the past two decades, offering a radical revision of how scholarship should be done in Indigenous communities. As Maori scholar Linda Tuhiwai Smith is often quoted as saying, "The term 'research' is inextricably linked to European imperialism and colonialism. The word itself, 'research,' is probably one of the dirtiest words in the indigenous world's vocabulary" (Smith 1999, 1). Devon Mihesuah has written, "Many writings about Indians . . . seem to be useful to the authors only" (Mihesuah 1998, 8). Her volume addresses topics of oral history, feminist methodology, and ethics and responsibility through a series of case studies. Smith goes further, critiquing the entire Western concept of research and pointing to its devastating effects on Native peoples. She articulates a new Indigenous research agenda that has Indigenous self-determination as its core and healing, transformation, mobilization and decolonization as its directions. These notions have been elaborated by subsequent scholars. Battiste emphasizes the importance of getting away from the Eurocentric biases that have influenced research on Indigenous peoples, arguing that "at the core of this quest is the issue of how to create ethical behavior in a knowledge system contaminated by colonialism and racism" (2008, 501). The answer is to embrace the Indigenous worldview as central, not peripheral, to research that serves the needs of the communities and is done in full partnership with them at all levels.

Along with Smith, Wilson (2008) and Kovach (2009) have provided in-depth considerations and proposed methodologies for conducting research in culturally appropriate ways among Indigenous communities. The emerging approach emphasizes relationships over knowledge, participation over expertise, and holism over specialized understandings. Research, they argue, is inseparable from other aspects of living— as Wilson puts it, "research is ceremony." The methodologies involved reflect the principles elaborated in feminist theory and PAR, but take those much further. When research is conducted according to the principles outlined, "giving back" becomes a nonissue, because the community is fully engaged in and benefiting from the research already.

Indigenous scholars also stress that the appropriate conduct of research in Indigenous settings requires not just a different approach to and understanding of research, but an updated institutional setting that supports this approach. In Champagne and Strauss's (2002) examination of the formation of American Indian/Native American studies in twelve mainstream university settings, successful programs are said to include a highly committed core of Indian and non-Indian faculty and students who support the intellectual and nation-building agenda of Native studies, and an integrated community combining students, faculty, tribal members, and elders. Mihesuah's work (2004) similarly aims at a broad transformation of academic approaches and practices, toward better understanding and serving Native community priorities.

Some Basic Principles

Following this wave of push-back against traditional extractive scholarship, a number of disciplinary organizations and Native and government agencies around the world have promulgated guidelines for conducting research with Indigenous peoples. A growing number of Indigenous communities around the world are setting up their own review boards for research projects and, in some cases, imposing stringent standards on researchers. These approaches share many similarities and collectively reinforce each other. Out of these I have distilled nine consistent principles (table 1.1). Three of these pertain directly to "giving back": benefit, partnership, and reciprocity. But in fact all nine principles collectively promote a research methodology that is more aligned with what Native scholars themselves have called for. A full discussion of these principles can be found in my chapter in McHugh, Bazile, and Gentelet's *Toolbox of Principles for Research in Indigenous Contexts* (Herman 2015).

Conclusion: Parting Thoughts

The recent proliferation of scholarship, guidelines, and policies aimed at protecting Native communities from unwanted or exploitative research is emerging within the context of the various forces discussed in this chapter (see Harding et al. 2012). "Open season" for data mining is coming to an end. But it is all still a struggle, and it is up to us scholars to inveigh against the forces of neoliberalism and the push to privatize everything from harvested DNA to cultural traditions. It is also incumbent on us non-Native scholars to heed, understand, and engage in the principles Native peoples are telling us. It is up to us to further the decolonization of research.

I titled this chapter, "Doing the Good Work?" Most of us who are in the business of research with Indigenous peoples, whether we ourselves are Indigenous or not, are doing so because we have some aim to improve things, and not merely to rack up publications. If you are not actively trying to bring benefit to the community you work with, then you need to ask yourself, what is it you are doing exactly, and who does it serve? Who benefits?

Table 1.1: Compiled Guidelines for Research with Indigenous Peoples

VALUES
Conduct research within the value frameworks of Indigenous peoples, including such values as respect, honesty, kindness, caring, and sharing.

BENEFIT
Ensure that benefit flows to Indigenous peoples from research, and that any potential negative impacts are minimized.

OPENNESS
All aspects of the research project, its aims, methodology, and sponsors, should be openly discussed and negotiated in advance with the community or its representatives.

PARTNERSHIP
Enter into research partnerships with Indigenous individuals, communities, or organizations to the extent that they desire.

RESPECT
Observe cultural protocols and traditions appropriate to the community, the local area, or the research participants

CONSENT
Obtain full and informed consent from those participating in the research or those affected by it. Depending on the context, such consent may be individual or collective, or both.

CONFIDENTIALITY
Confidentiality, anonymity, and public recognition of participants are delicate if not dangerous matters for many Indigenous peoples, and must be clearly and carefully negotiated before any project materials are made public.

PROTECTION
Protect Indigenous knowledge and the intellectual property of traditional knowledge holders and nations.

RECIPROCITY
Research participants and community leaders should have the opportunity to review and revise drafts of the study and should receive copies of the final study. They should receive acknowledgement, fair return, and royalties where appropriate.

Let me return to my story about that tribal college and their refusal to work ever again with a certain university; or the Havasupai and their ban on Arizona State: if nothing else, *not* doing the good work can have very negative consequences for you and your institution. At best, however, it can and should be a transformative experience.

Chapter 1 References and Recommended Readings

Adkisson, Richard V. 2004. "Ceremonialism, Intellectual Property Rights, and Innovative Activity." *Journal of Economic Issues* 38 (2): 459–466.

Battiste, Marie. 2008. "Research Ethics for Protecting Indigenous Knowledge and Heritage." In *Handbook of Critical and Indigenous Methodologies*, edited by Norman K. Denzin and Yvonna S. Lincoln, 497–510. Los Angeles: SAGE.

Baum, Fran, Colin MacDougall, and Danielle Smith. 2006. "Participatory Action Research." *Journal of Epidemiology and Community Health* 60:854–857.

Bluemel, Erik B. 2005/2006. "Separating Instrumental from Intrinsic Rights: Toward an Understanding of Indigenous Participation in International Rule-Making." *American Indian Law Review* 30 (1): 55–132.

Božnjak, Snežana. 2001. "The Declaration of Helsinki: The Cornerstone of Research Ethics." *Archive of Oncology* 9 (3): 179–184.

Brandt, Allan M. 1978. "Racism and Research: The Case of the Tuskegee Syphilis Study." *Hastings Center Report* 8 (6): 21–29.

Bratspies, Rebecca M. 2006/2007. "The New Discovery Doctrine: Some Thoughts on Property Rights and Traditional Knowledge." *American Indian Law Review* 31 (2): 315–340.

Champagne, Duane, and Jay Strauss, eds. 2002. *Native American Studies in Higher Education: Models for Collaboration between Universities and Indigenous Nations*. Berkeley, CA: AltaMira Press.

Chilisa, Bagele. 2011. *Indigenous Research Methodologies*. Thousand Oaks, CA: SAGE.

Convention on Biological Diversity. 1993. http://www.cbd.int/convention/text/default.shtml.

Coombe, Rosemary J. 1998. "Intellectual Property, Human Rights and Sovereignty: New Dilemmas in International Law Posed by the Recognition of Indigenous Knowledge." *Indiana Journal of Global Legal Studies* 6 (1): 59–115.

Daes, Erica-Irene. 2001. "Intellectual Property and Indigenous Peoples." *Proceedings of the Annual Meeting (American Society of International Law)* 95:143–150.

DeGeer, Marcia E. 2002. "Biopiracy: Twentieth Century Imperialism." *New England Journal of International and Comparative Law* 13:179–208.

Deloria Jr., Vine. 1988. "Anthropologists and Other Friends." In *Custer Died for Your Sins: An Indian Manifesto.* 2nd ed. Norman: University of Oklahoma Press.

Fecteau, Leanne M. 2001. "The Ayahuasca Patent Revocation: Raising Questions about Current U.S. Patent Policy." *Boston College Third World Law Journal* 21 (1): 69–104.

Fitzgerald, Tanya. 2004. "Powerful Voices and Powerful Stories: Reflections on the Challenges and Dynamics of Intercultural Research." *Journal of Intercultural Studies* 25 (3): 233–245.

Fonow, Mary Margaret, and Judith A. Cook. 2005. "Feminist Methodology: New Applications in the Academy and Public Policy." *Signs* 30 (4): 2211–2236.

Government of Canada Panel on Research Ethics. 2015. "Introductory Tutorial for the Tri-Council Policy Statement: Ethical Conduct for Research Involving Humans (TCPS)." http://www.pre.ethics.gc.ca/english/tutorial/00_intro_overview_context.cfm.

Gudeman, Stephen. 1996. "Sketches, Qualms, and Other Thoughts on Intellectual Property Rights." In *Valuing Local Knowledge: Indigenous People and Intellectual Property Rights,* edited by Stephen B. Brush and Doreen Stabinsky, 102–121. Washington, DC: Island Press.

Harding, Anna, Barbara Harper, Dave Stone, Catherine O'Neill, Patricia Berger, Stuart Harris, and Jamie Donatuto. 2012. "Conducting Research with Tribal Communities: Sovereignty, Ethics, and Data-Sharing Issues." *Environmental Health Perspectives* 120 (1): 6–10.

Harmon, Amy. 2010. "Indian Tribe Wins Fight to Limit Research of Its DNA." *New York Times,* April 21. http://www.nytimes.com/2010/04/22/us/22dna.html?ref=us&_r=0.

Herman, RDK. 2015. "Guidelines for Conducting Research in Indigenous Settings: Ethical, Appropriate and Successful Methodologies." In *Toolbox of Principles for Research in Indigenous Contexts: Ethics, Respect, Equity, Reciprocity and Cooperation,* edited by Nancy Gros-Louis McHugh, Suzy Basile, and Karine Gentelet. Quebec: First Nations of Québec and Labrador Health and Social Services Commission.

Heikkinen, Hannu L. T., Leena Kakkori, and Rauno Huttunen. 2001. "This Is My Truth, Tell Me Yours: Some Aspects of Action Research Quality in the Light of Truth Theories." *Educational Action Research* 9 (1): 9–24.

Hunt, Sarah. 2014. "Ontologies of Indigeneity: The Politics of Embodying a Concept." *Cultural Geographies* 21 (1): 1–6.

IPSG. 2009–10. "AAG Indigenous Peoples Specialty Group's Declaration of Key Questions about Research Ethics with Indigenous Communities." http://www.indigenousgeography.net/IPSG/pdf/IPSGResearchEthicsFinal.pdf.

Kovach, Margaret. 2009. *Indigenous Methodologies: Characteristics, Conversations, and Contexts.* Toronto: University of Toronto Press.

Kemmis, Stephen, and Robin McTaggart. 2007. "Participatory Action Research: Communicative Action and the Public Sphere." In *Strategies of Qualitative Inquiry*, 3rd ed., edited by Norman K. Denzin and Yvonna S. Lincoln, 271–330. Thousand Oaks, CA: SAGE.

McHugh, Nancy Gros-Louis, Suzy Basile, and Karine Gentelet. 2015. *Toolbox of Principles for Research in Indigenous Contexts: Ethics, Respect, Equity, Reciprocity and Cooperation.* Quebec: First Nations of Québec and Labrador Health and Social Services Commission.

Mihesuah, Devon A. 1993. "Suggested Guidelines for Institutions with Scholars Who Conduct Research on American Indians." *American Indian Culture and Research Journal* 17 (3): 131–139.

———. 1998. *Natives and Academics: Research and Writing about American Indians.* Lincoln: University of Nebraska Press.

———. 2004. *Indigenizing the Academy: Transforming Scholarship and Empowering Communities.* Lincoln: Bison Books.

Mugabe, John. 1999. *Intellectual Property Protection and Traditional Knowledge: An Exploration in International Policy Discourse.* Nairobi, Kenya: ACTS Press, African Centre for Technology Studies.

NCAI Policy Research Center and MSU Center for Native Health Partnerships. 2012. *"Walk Softly and Listen Carefully": Building Research Relationships with Tribal Communities.* Washington, DC/Bozeman, MT: NCAI Policy Research Center/MSU Center for Native Health Partnerships.

Powledge, Fred. 2001. "Patenting, Piracy, and the Global Commons." *BioScience* 51 (4): 273–277.

Pratt, Mary Louise. 1992. *Imperial Eyes: Travel Writing and Transculturation.* London: Routledge.

Roopnaraine, Terry. 1998. "Indigenous Knowledge, Biodiversity and Rights." *Anthropology Today* 14 (3): 16.

Rundstrom, Robert, and Douglas Deur. 1999. "Reciprocal Appropriation: Toward an Ethics of Cross-Cultural Research." In *Geography and Ethics: Journeys in a Moral Terrain*, edited by James D. Proctor and David Marshall Smith, 237–250. London: Routledge.

Shaw, Wendy, RDK Herman, and G. R. Dobbs. 2006. "Encountering Indigeneity: Re-imagining and Decolonizing Geography." *Geografiska Annaler* 88B (3): 267–276.

Shiva, Vandana. 2001. "Special Report: Golden Rice and Neem: Biopatents and the Appropriation of Women's Environmental Knowledge." *Women's Studies Quarterly* 29 (1/2): 12–23.

Smith, M. K. 2001. "Kurt Lewin, Groups, Experiential Learning and Action Research." The Encyclopedia of Informal Education. http://www.infed.org/thinkers/et-lewin.htm.

Smith, Linda Tuhiwai. 1999. *Decolonizing Methodologies: Research and Indigenous Peoples.* London: Zed Books.

US Department of Health and Human Services. 2011a. "45 CFR 46 – FAQs." http://answers.hhs.gov/ohrp/categories/1562.

———. 2011b. "45 CFR 46.116 "Informed Consent Checklist." http://www.hhs.gov/ohrp/policy/consentckls.html.

Warrior, Robert. 2009. "Native American Scholarship and the Transnational Turn." *Cultural Studies Review* 9 (2): 119–130.

Weaver, Jace. 2001. *Other Words: American Indian Literature, Law, and Culture.* Norman: University of Oklahoma Press.

Wilson, Shaun. 2008. *Research Is Ceremony: Indigenous Research Methods.* Winnipeg, Manitoba: Fernwood.

Notes to Chapter 1

1. See Deloria 1988, Smith 1999, Kovach 2009, Chilisa 2011, and Hunt 2014 for some examples.
2. The Australian version includes a category of "merit and integrity," focusing largely on doing the research correctly and that the project is beneficial.

2

Working the Academy

A Form of Giving Back?

JENNIFER CARTER, TRISTAN PEARCE, AND CHRIS JACOBSON

R ECIPROCITY AND "GIVING BACK" have long been associated with community-based and participatory forms of research as a way of working for the people encountered and as a moral imperative. The original agenda of these approaches was to unsettle academic privilege and intellectualism in research to work for and with people encountered "in the field" (Arnstein 1969; Bunge 1969). This agenda continues to some extent today, but too often is exploited by academic, government, private, and other stakeholders as a validation of research, policy, and program implementation, or even to the detriment of community groups, rather than genuinely working for social change (mrs c kinpainsby-hill 2011). Recognizing the colonialism inherent in institutional structures that act as "formulas of domination" that can co-opt and commodify the knowledge of Indigenous peoples, Indigenous scholars, communities, and postcolonial academics challenge the academy to cooperate in ways of working, thinking, relating, questioning, being, and changing our worlds (Smith 2012; Briggs 2013). Thus, those of us within the academy must be cognizant of the trajectories our engagement may perpetuate and recognize the benefits that can come from holding Indigenous systems and the academy in tension.

Fieldwork in particular, as the "heart of geography," brings particular commitments and responsibilities, because what we obtain in the field is "not free for the asking" (Stevens 2001, 66, 70). Among the commitments of fieldwork with people are ensuring no harm to co-researchers/research partners, carefully and honestly reproducing their needs, and providing a benefit other than an academic output. Reciprocity between researchers and community members often includes the exchange of material forms of giving, but a less tangible aspect of reciprocity concerns the obligation of the researcher beyond the community, one that results from the relationships formed and knowledge gained during field research. In many instances, community members place the onus on researchers to "change their worlds" through the people they know and institutions they work in. Matching the reciprocity in fieldwork to the structures of the academy, however, is a challenge because institutional pressures work against achieving equity in research partnerships (Valentine 2005; de Leeuw, Cameron, and Greenwood 2012).

This chapter presents case studies from Australia (Carter), Canada (Pearce), and New Zealand (Jacobson), drawing on semi-structured interviews, observations, and experiences of researchers to depict the ways in which universities need to be changed to allow ways of giving back that should be inherent in research with Indigenous peoples. The first case, Aboriginal Australia, shows how ethics processes can be detrimental to Indigenous communities but can also be overcome by working to change systemic procedures. It details the weaknesses in universities caused by research grant and publication metrics, when dealing with research in Indigenous contexts, but also illustrates opportunities for reenvisioning a culturally competent academy that works to change itself. The second case study, from Arctic Canada, further details the importance of changing research metrics to value community inputs and publications, and the role of researchers as advocates. The third case study, from Aotearoa-New Zealand, further exemplifies the cumbersome nature of rigid ethics procedures and suggests alternative Indigenous structures be used. Together these fundamental challenges of research management require reworking to more effectively give back to Indigenous peoples.

Aboriginal Australia

Many Aboriginal communities in Australia are located in remote areas that contain natural resources and offer commercial development opportunities. The initial case studies are drawn from the principal researcher's experiences with community members wishing to participate. These cases detail reflections from participatory fisheries (trepang) mapping and modelling in the Northern Territory, where community members hoped to obtain a fishing license, and from participatory sustainable development of plants for pharmaceutical purposes and timber products in Cape York, Queensland, both of which are remote parts of Australia. The subsequent case study is based on research with Aboriginal people in southeast Queensland, a more urbanized locale, where Aboriginal people simply want to be involved in publicly funded natural resource management. Finally, the section presents the opportunities brought about by the cultural competence policy agenda enacted within universities.

The principles that guide ethical research with Indigenous communities in many Australian universities are often shrouded in rigid bureaucratic processes that don't account for localisms and the interpersonal nature of researcher-community relationships. At the commencement of participatory research in the Northern Territory of Australia on trepang—a valuable marine resource that traditional owners wished to commercialize—the Northern Territory University (now Charles Darwin University) ethics committee required signatures from Indigenous peoples to approve the research (Carter 2001). The nominated community representative explained the effect of colonialism on his community: "We want you working with us, we won't sign a form. The last time we signed a form our land was taken away." The researcher explained to university officials the loss of power and personal trauma caused to Indigenous peoples by colonization, and how such rigid, systemic requirements for their written consent repeated such trauma, and eventually the university research managers permitted verbal approval, provided the details of consent were recorded. As explained later by Indigenous co-researchers, "We wouldn't be working with you if we didn't want to." This parallels Stevens's (2001, 70) summation, from his many years of experience, that community members will participate in research if they feel the research is of benefit or interest to them and "its success comes to matter to them." Nevertheless, as found by Valentine (2005), each time personnel changes on ethics committees, the new staff need to be educated about the legacies of colonialism and how it applies to research protocols in the field.

During that same research, the final report to the donor contained a university-written confidentiality provision to not disseminate the report, which contained the whereabouts of the trepang resource, without the consent of Indigenous landowners. Government officials ignored that provision, and the report was circulated to commercial fishing interests. The Indigenous community couldn't fund a legal challenge or prevent the data's appropriation, meaning that the ethics committee's angst about the researcher-community relationships was less critical than protecting the rights of Indigenous people to publish or withhold publication about the research. Ultimately the research provided more benefit to others than to the community, partly because of these tokenistic attempts to work for the benefit of Indigenous peoples.

On the basis of this tokenism in protecting knowledge and confidentiality, subsequent research in Cape York, Queensland, was conducted within a more robust partnership that formalized the involvement of the regional representative land council bodies in partnership with the University of Queensland, where the researcher was then located. These bodies have appropriate resources (including lawyers) and are formally recognized by government as having the authority to protect Indigenous communities' legal rights. The work was conducted with two communities; the first was the Kaanju people, who hoped to develop their plant resources for pharmaceutical purposes and income (Carter, Claudie, and Smith 2006). The influence of the land councils in the partnership helped convince university management and the funding body to restrict the publication of geographic information system data—which again contained locations of valuable medicinal plant resources—and retain it within the community. That funding body sought more detailed reports containing the data, but they yielded when confronted with the explicit protective provisions in the original funding contract negotiated by the representative land council body, and received only summary reporting. These contracts are unusual under university intellectual property provisions, in which intellectual property is normally conferred on the institution, and they can meet with institutional resistance that requires insistence on the part of the researcher to protect community knowledge and confidentiality.

Another community in Cape York, the Wik and Wik-Way people (and their constituent language groups), wished to develop timber products from the trees on their lands (Carter et al. 2004). This research was part of a lengthy native-title negotiation, during which Indigenous community representatives requested land use planning research to develop strategies to assert their use rights in timber that was to be clear-felled by a mining company. Advocacy to the University of Queensland research managers on the part of the researcher resulted in the national body who funded the work accepting the concept of "background and foreground" knowledge within a research agreement (that stood outside the standard ethics committee protocols), where background knowledge is that knowledge held by each party at the start of the project and remains their intellectual property; foreground knowledge is the knowledge that arises from joint research endeavors. To this day, that national funding body's contracts with universities and communities internationally retain this principle to avoid data mining and to favor a partnership approach wherein partners together brings their knowledge, skills, and capacities to the research but each retains their equity in the work.

It can also be difficult to convince committees and risk-averse managers, who may depict Aboriginal people as unable to understand or make decisions about research participation, about Indigenous people's agency. As part of surveying the timber resource during this research, Wik and Wik-Way landowners requested that their knowledge of the vegetation and fauna be documented. They required the researcher to commit to learning Indigenous names of fauna and flora, investing substantial time instructing the researcher to "write that down" and performing traditional songs and stories for documentation that had not been requested as part of the research by the community's elected representatives. The researcher was at first hesitant to record their knowledge (to avoid being seen as extractive) but was expected to demonstrate competency at understanding "the knowledge"—including details of stories and a progressive ability to use local language and understand their significance—prior to more in-depth knowledge being imparted. Availability of a younger-generation community member with technological skills in computing and video recording enabled the researcher to lobby the university to alter the budget so that more funds could be allocated for community members to themselves record important knowledge. After this "initiation," both on Indigenous people's country and in their own presence, researchers were expected to advocate for traditional owners to all manner of institutions and actors (including other universities) for their rights to land, governance, and employment in the timber resources development, and for employment on all subsequent research projects. This advocacy role was performed on-country, in our supporting organizations 1,200 km away, in our sponsoring university 3,000 km away, with international partners in Africa, and with constant instructions by Indigenous community members to "speak up"—meaning to work for them and in recognition that their own advocacy would not have the same impact without inside knowledge of universities and their goals being held by the researcher. These instructions to advocate for community needs operate on a hard-won trust between community members and researchers. Community members, secure in their culture and land tenure, recognized and accepted differences in knowledge bases, capacities, and practices that align with differing roles in a research enterprise. But the academy often reinterprets these relationships in mechanistic and non-trusting ways. For example, both Indigenous people and their non-Indigenous allies with no connection to the research community take on gatekeeping and adversarial roles legitimized through ethics procedures and internal politics. Dale's (1993) thesis in particular notes the importance of Indigenous people "farming the bureaucracy," in that Aboriginal clans take the turn of adopting a researcher and instructing them as to their behaviors, language, and needs in order that each researcher be a resource for different clans and advocate for them to the researchers' institutions. However, institutions frequently make the mistake of talking to Aboriginal people from other communities who have not been instructed to speak for that particular community, thereby denying the authority and agency of that community to choose their representative (whether Indigenous or not) and presenting an increasing challenge to hybrid scholar-advocates, who must negotiate identity politics within their institutions. Universalizing ethics procedures and research partnerships ignores the diversity and localism within and between communities and violates their agency in building relationships with specific researchers to work with them or advocate for them or in withholding that honor. Clearly more education and cultural competence within institutions is needed.

Another challenge involves university management expectations on staff that they achieve outputs such as peer-reviewed publications by which their university is measured against others, rather than advocating for communities and their needs. The principal researcher was part of a team who conducted research in the rural town of Eidsvold, with Wakka Wakka people, far closer to her new home institution of the University of the Sunshine Coast (Carter and Hollinsworth 2009). Eidsvold is closer to major regional centers and considered far less remote, with no land tenure security for Indigenous people because of European settlement. The local government land management body funded travel and participants' time and required the research team to produce protocols for engagement with this community and others in southeast Queensland. Some 80 percent of the Aboriginal population of Australia lives in settled urban and regional areas, but these communities are neglected, because they are either small or dispersed among non-Indigenous areas, erasing the presence of Indigenous peoples in urbanized areas. Indigenous peoples are also seen by some non-Indigenous peoples as having "lost culture," or as lacking in social or cultural characteristics that distinguish them from non-Indigenous co-residents. The research was well received by Indigenous residents because "no one ever comes to see us," and the presence of the research team was seen to validate their "authenticity" as Indigenous people, their connection to their lands, and their worth as people with stories. However, the researcher strongly believed that there was a specific obligation to engage with traditional owners within the university's geographic footprint in southeast Queensland. The research grant was not ranked highly in research metrics because it was not a national competitive grant, and many of the outputs, such as the detailed protocols for engagement and community feedback documents, were not valued by the university because they didn't contribute to reportable products or attract additional government funding as a consequence of such reporting. Our institution therefore considered our accomplishment of this work with this community to be of low significance. There remains a constant struggle to educate university managers about the breadth of tangible and intangible benefits of research with marginalized communities, including Indigenous people, and to uphold the university mission as being a public-good institution.

We were also tasked by Wakka Wakka Eidsvold community members to use our position as "experts" to persuade the governance structures of the local land management funding body to widen Aboriginal representation on their board, to invest in ongoing community consultation and on-country activities, and to raise the salience of potential Aboriginal involvement in technical programs in various portfolios of forestry, revegetation, and endangered species (work that previously had no Aboriginal input at all). We were also able to facilitate visits by state cultural heritage officials to brief community members on legislation and their rights, and to prepare a comprehensive review of legislation, protocols, examples of contracts and benefit-sharing, and negotiations for use by Aboriginal organizations and corporations. The clear preference of community members was for us to be "carrier pigeons," delivering a message crafted by specific informants, rather than that their interests be represented by others, even when Indigenous, who did not visit the community and who had not accepted the specific role of delivering their message. The obligation of researchers to advocate frequently to institutions and others comes at the expense of research metrics and institutional accolade and frequently results in the academic staff being told "you are not a researcher."

Advancing cultural competence within our universities presents one fundamental way to educate and rework institutions, and thus for researchers to give back. The Australian sector-wide policy framework for embedding Aboriginal and Torres Strait Islander knowledges and perspectives in curriculum, which is part of a general process of Indigenous cultural competence, includes research, staffing, and governance and increased engagement or participation of Indigenous students and community (Universities Australia 2011). One element advanced by the researcher from within this framework has been the provision of specific Indigenous studies courses and of components integrated into other courses and programs. In recent years, our university has expanded from one to thirteen stand-alone Indigenous studies courses, and 54 percent of undergraduate and postgraduate programs contain at least some Indigenous content thanks to the lobbying of several staff, including the principal researcher. While the incorporation of Indigenous content is critical for the learning and graduate outcomes of all graduates, such work has particular impact on the Indigenous students, who can more effectively integrate their lives and learnings within the classroom. Every one of these new courses and additional curriculum initiatives has required considerable time and effort from academic staff in an increasingly overcrowded and regulated higher education sector. Attempts to lobby for cultural competence in the institution often encounter explicit or covert resistance, sometimes because of a failure to value Indigenous knowledge and peoples, sometimes just because of the considerable demands placed on all academic staff, and sometimes because of a "fear of getting it wrong" and appearing racist. In particular, outside of health, education, and social sciences, many staff are yet to be persuaded of the relevance of Indigenous content in their curricula. Other specific initiatives in support of either Indigenous studies or Indigenous students have included persuading the university to sponsor "elders" days, engaging regularly with community leaders, providing Indigenous-specific scholarships for honors and higher-degree students to encourage their research, and creating the Indigenous Studies Research group, another element in the cultural competence framework that was welcomed by senior management—although this structure has been denied the recognition and resources available to other formal research assemblages that show more direct and overt commercial potential.

Poverty and disadvantage among Indigenous Australians is intergenerational and underpinned by massive structural and historical factors.

Academics have limited capacity to transform this oppression but have been able, within the academy, to take a stand against tokenism; lobby for more effective protection of Indigenous peoples' knowledge and interests; promote the diversity of local communities and their agency in building relationships with researchers; advocate for, and facilitate, a greater number of university and other institutional staff to work for the benefit of our partner communities; and see more than double the number of Indigenous students enrolled, graduating, and becoming staff in our institution through advocating for cultural-competence policy. In this way we have given back in recognition of the profound generosity and tolerance shown to us and other researchers by Indigenous communities and have honored their injunction that we speak on their behalf and intercede, on "our" country (home institutions), when and as we can.

Arctic Canada

The Canadian Arctic is recognized as a global hot spot for climate change (IPCC 2013). Temperatures in the Arctic have been increasing at twice the global average, recent years have witnessed an unprecedented reduction in summer sea ice cover, permafrost is melting in some regions, and extreme weather conditions have been described as being more unpredictable and frequent (IPCC 2013). Inuit—the Indigenous peoples of the Arctic—are highly sensitive to these changes because of their profound interdependence with the natural environment (e.g., subsistence hunting and fishing), and many Inuit are already experiencing challenges to their lives and livelihoods from climate change (Pearce et al. 2010).

Several projects have recorded local and traditional knowledge of the environment and changing conditions, also referred to as traditional ecological knowledge (TEK) or Inuit Qaujimajatuqangit (IQ) (Pearce et al. 2010). Others have identified opportunities to support Inuit adaptation or enhance resilience to current and expected future climate change (Ford et al. 2010; Pearce et al. 2015). This involves working with Inuit in communities to document conditions that are relevant and important to them beyond those selected a priori by researchers and to identify adaptations are relevant, feasible, and desirable (Pearce et al. 2010). The outcomes of this research are highly detailed case studies of localized experiences dealing with climate change. Dissemination of these outcomes present opportunities for researchers to "work the academy" and give back to the communities in which they work by (1) contributing the community's voice to climate change decision-making forums and (2) lobbying research donors to fund communities to implement adaptation initiatives of their choosing and independent from external university, government, or private groups.

The main international responses to climate change concerns have been to seek reductions in greenhouse gas emissions to mitigate climate changes and to support communities to adapt to the inevitable effects of climate change, most often in developing countries. Small and often remote populations, including those in developed countries, like Inuit in the Canadian Arctic, who are highly sensitive to climate change impacts, are often missing from international climate change negotiations. Decisions are made by those with limited, if any, knowledge of the plight of the people most affected by their decisions. Researchers working with communities to document how they are experiencing and responding to climate change have an obligation to disseminate research findings. For the purposes of the Intergovernmental Panel on Climate Change (IPCC) reports and Conference of the Parties (COP) negotiations, this means publishing research findings in peer-reviewed journals. The IPCC synthesizes existing peer-reviewed literature related to climate change mitigation and adaptation, which then informs the COP, the supreme decision-making body of the United Nations Framework Convention on Climate Change (UNFCCC). By publishing the knowledge and experiences of communities dealing with climate change, researchers are giving back by ensuring that the community's voice is included in IPCC reports and COP negotiations. Researchers, together with regional partners (territorial governments and Inuit organizations) have also disseminated findings at COP conferences through side events and information booths, which have included opportunities for community members to share firsthand experiences and answer questions. Knowledge dissemination is a continuing and iterative process that involves researchers and community members collaborating to ensure that research findings are published and disseminated to reach the decision makers.

Despite Canada's past negligence at cutting greenhouse gas emissions to mitigate climate change, governments have contributed funds to support community-scale adaptation research. Most of this funding has been for research focused on assessing community vulnerability to climate change and identifying what people and what resources are vulnerable; and to what stresses, in what way; and asking questions such as "What is the capacity of the system to adapt?" (Pearce et al. 2012). Less funding has been available for implementing adaptation strategies. Research has identified the position of non-climatic factors in influencing how Inuit experience and respond to climate change, including the role of Inuit TEK or IQ in enhancing adaptive capacity or resilience to climate risks affecting subsistence hunting (Ford et al. 2010). Inuit leaders remain concerned that some elements of TEK important for subsistence and adaptation are not being transmitted to younger-generation Inuit, resulting in many younger and inexperienced hunters being less equipped to participate in subsistence, especially under changing climatic conditions (Ford, Smit, and Wandel 2006; Pearce et al. 2010; Pearce et al. 2011). It is argued that supporting efforts like the generation and transmission of TEK among generations, while not directed at climate change per se, inadvertently enhance the capacity of individuals and communities to deal with current and expected future climate change risks (Pearce et al. 2010; Pearce et al. 2015); however, federal funding guidelines for climate change adaptation in arctic communities have excluded projects focused on the implementation of adaptation initiatives. Successive funding calls focused on risk assessments, or assessments of vulnerability, are essentially repeating completed research. This disconnect between research funding priorities and community priorities has exhausted communities who are tired of being asked the same questions without seeing support for action.

Representatives of government funding agencies argued that they first needed to know how communities are vulnerable to climate change before funding the implementation of adaptation initiatives. Clearly the years of research that documented how Inuit are experiencing and responding to climate change, much of which was funded by the same government agencies, had not reached decision makers. There was a need to make explicit the connection between initiatives like supporting TEK generation and transmission and adaptation to climate change with empirical evidence. Researchers together with community partners responded by publishing new peer-reviewed papers that did just this, and complemented them with summary reports written for government (Pearce et al. 2011; Pearce et al. 2015).

In an act of giving back to the community, researchers partnered with community members to submit a funding proposal to Health Canada's Climate Change Adaptation Program for Northern First Nations and Inuit Communities. The proposal lobbied for funding to support the transmission of TEK based on Inuit modes of learning and guiding principles, as a means for enhancing capacity to deal with current and expected climate change risks affecting subsistence hunting. The proposal was successful and the project was funded. In an unprecedented move, Health Canada allocated the full project budget to be administered by the community partner organization (>$130,000 CDN/one year). In this case, the community elected to hire university researchers to support the project goals rather than using the dominant research paradigm of researchers administering project budgets and hiring local assistants and interpreters. This shifted the balance of power to the community and empowered community members to administer the project according to Inuit values and priorities. The project, Nunamin Illihakvia: learning from the land, was touted by community members and Health Canada as a success that supported the transmission of TEK among generations and empowered community members to take action to address climate change. A subsequent proposal the following year, Tumivut: tracks of our ancestors, again focused on TEK transmission but on different aspects of the environment: traveling on the sea ice and hunting caribou. The project was funded and the budget was again transferred to the community organization to administer (>$130,000 CDN/one year).

The Nunamin Illihakvia and Tumivut projects set a new precedent for how community-based research funding can be administered and represent some of the first federal government–funded projects focused on implementing community-identified adaptation strategies that are indirectly linked with climate change. This new balance of power generated considerable support for the projects within the community and created momentum for action that has surpassed the duration of the projects. For researchers, the projects were successful in terms of practical outcomes and new peer-reviewed papers. In the eyes of the university, however, the projects were less successful. The researcher's host university tracks research income, which influences the university's share in federal transfer payments and the researcher's performance evaluation. Since project funds were transferred to the community, it appeared on the university's financial books that the researchers were unsuccessful in obtaining funding, when, in fact, they were very successful in obtaining funding and in shattering outdated notions that universities are better equipped than communities to administer project funds for community-based research. Continued efforts are being made by the researchers to instill change in how the university calculates research income to include, and celebrate, the success of community-led and administered research projects.

Aotearoa-New Zealand

In Aotearoa-New Zealand, Te Tiriti o Waitangi (the Treaty of Waitangi) dominates political and public discourse around relationships between Māori and *pākehā* (non-Māori). Clauses about acting in accordance with the principles of the treaty are common in organizational charters, including those of universities. Treaty "principles" are not specifically stated in the treaty but have emerged from court cases, Waitangi Tribunal reports, and a (nonbinding) government statement (Hayward 1997). This public discourse acts alongside a private discourse around ethnicity. Attachment to place in a predominantly bicultural society brings unique obligations. For *pākehā*, this can stem from a multi-positional duty of respect for Tangata Whenua as first people through community connections, through family bonds, through schooling, and through a sense of place-making (see Stephenson, Ruru, and Abbott 2011, for examples). Indigenous concepts become imbued in our lives in a way that focuses a different lens on the "public" discourse of what it means to be Indigenous or non-Indigenous. Acting in accordance with treaty principles, and in accordance with our own positionality and the ways that structures such as universities affect it, becomes part of the fabric of giving back.

One of the ways that universities attempt to manage researcher-community interactions is through human ethics processes. These usually involve a written description of participant groups, research methods, risks, and risk management strategies, by the researcher(s). A decision about whether the participation, research methods, risks, and risk management strategies are appropriate is then made by an external "expert" group, in the form of a human ethics committee; communities are not often required to provide evidence of support for research, unless a permit is required, yet researchers are usually unable to publish unless research is approved by such a committee. Human ethics processes are important in that they ensure a degree of safety for universities and for communities and an external check on the quality and perceived impact of research on communities; however, they inherently treat participants as subjects in the research process, and act to reinforce power by providing "permission" for research with communities, independent of the communities themselves. This can blur the intent of the process and act to reinforce colonial sentiment rather than giving effect to treaty principles or supporting researchers to act ethically in accordance with their own positionality—or even to address real ethical dilemmas they encounter, thus affecting their ability to "give back."

For example, during a multi-country research project in New Zealand, the principal researcher was interested in exploring the experiences of all parties in co-management through a participatory process. This interest developed from her engagement in bicultural processes and listening to the experiences of her community. The multiple nationalities in the project meant that ethics approval was required in three countries. This should have required a process of review in New Zealand, and then expedited review in the other two countries; however, the reality required full approval in all three. The process in New Zealand required both a commitment to human ethics and Indigenous committee approval (independent of the university), with post-funding requests to team changes. The process in the second country required changes to detail the exact method (which is difficult for participatory methods), changes to the use of Indigenous terms and procedures (because of the lack of knowledge of the committee and despite approval from the New Zealand Indigenous committee), and changes to the risk disclosure component of the information sheet, resulting in a lengthy two-page information sheet and one-page agreement form devoid of context. In the third country, information was to be stored in a second location, contrary to the requests of the second committee and the permitting process for the Indigenous group involved. Although approvals were gained, they failed to address some of the ethical issues faced.

Ethics and positionality of researchers with Indigenous communities is a constant challenge. First, the timing of when ethics approval is sought and the common waiting periods between submission and acceptance of proposals are of concern. Indigenous peoples are often considered a high-risk group, and methods need to be well advanced before approval can be gained; this requires considerable time before approval, and any background fieldwork is nominally unusable under ethics procedures. The result is a slow and cumbersome process for all parties, and even then, communities can be reticent to sign consent sheets given the implied positionality of authority in consent procedures. In this example, a total of nine months was spent on ethical reviews for a three-year project. Processes such as Indigenous committee approvals should expedite this process and provide assurance to university ethics committees, but in reality, ethics committees often duplicate the process, demoting the originals to an exercise in consultation. The first Indigenous committee review and their support gained no currency with the second country committee, and the third (rightly) required supporting documentation from cases particular to that country.

Second, ethical issues such as equitable payment for input, payment methods, coauthorship, intellectual property rights, academic independence, and Indigenous oversight are rarely sufficiently addressed in such approvals, especially when a committee homogenizes Indigenous groups as one type of community, without a specific understanding of each group's individual perspectives and needs. Separate contracts or letters of agreement with Indigenous (and non-Indigenous) groups are a means to address this, but their position is often considered secondary to ethical approval, and/or too complex to manage in conjunction with ethics.

Third, a range of ethical issues can arise with partners affiliated with an Indigenous representative organization rather than with the people with authority to speak on an issue in a particular local area. In part, this is an artifact of postcolonial settlement with Indigenous peoples, wherein partner organizations are a more recent (but nonetheless necessary and important) embodiment of Indigenous agency imbued with its own perspectives, rather than grassroots participants. The researcher must navigate issues of agency, representation, and academic rigor, as well as their own relationships and experiences that complicate their positionality and that the current ethical approval process is poorly equipped to comprehend, let alone manage, given the once-off nature of approvals and the end-of-project report that is signed by someone without contextual knowledge.

In summary, Indigenous research is inherently political, and significant ethical concerns arise, particularly given researcher commitment to giving back. It is evident that the current system is cumbersome for both Indigenous peoples and researchers. The development of Indigenous research approval committees is a step toward addressing these issues, as would be appropriately experienced Indigenous advisers. Experience presented here suggests that alternatives that empower rather than disempower communities are urgently needed.

Conclusion: Moving toward a Relational Connection

The case studies exemplify the desires of Indigenous peoples for academic and related institutions to be culturally inclusive and competent, and the key roles played by non-Indigenous or nonlocal Indigenous researchers in this challenge. Coombes (2012) laments that most research is initiated by the researcher and that there is little evidence of researchers exiting the community when the community is in control of their own knowledge, or evidence of whether the work is used politically and for the well-being of nonacademic participants.

One way that researchers give back includes fighting rigid structures and processes that protect the academy and reinforce structural power. Ethics committees, for example, reinforce power by bestowing "permission" or may reduce Indigenous partnership to "consultation," as shown in New Zealand. They are unable to deal with the individual, place-based relationships of trust in which researchers are expected to understand the colonial hegemony involved in asking people to sign a form and other processes, as shown in both New Zealand and Australia. Further, discourses and processes that homogenize Indigenous peoples and communities ignore local difference and agency. Further, they often embody permission from a representative agency instead of from the community, as shown in Australia and New Zealand, which can undermine the authority of the community itself to choose its researcher. It is important that the relationality of researchers and reciprocity be understood in more complex ways than reproducing binaries of "Indigenous" and "non-Indigenous" people, so that a beneficial and reciprocal relationship, authorized by partner communities, takes precedence over rigid structures and processes that re-entrench colonial power (Jacobson and Stephens 2009). Such "reciprocal" relationships must be cognizant of the potential "false dawn" (Briggs 2013), wherein research co-opts or forces knowledge hybridity by means of structural domination of institutions (e.g., by processes of grant provision, procedural jurisprudence, and the like.). Instead, they must be seen as spaces of negotiation about how research can be designed, conducted, and shared in ways that challenge such structures (Smith 2012) as well delivering research outcomes.

Researchers in Australia and Canada have lobbied donors for funding to be provided directly to communities to control research—in particular, the Canadian researchers worked to realign research priorities set by national agencies with community priorities, using their publications as evidence and based on their knowledge of community needs. The Canadian example, where funds went directly to community for implementation, eventually allowed the community to hire their chosen researcher, redressing the power imbalance in funding allocation, decision making, and deference to authority—and at the expense of the researcher during his performance review with managers, as warned by Louis (2012).

Power, knowledge, and representation have been problematized in participatory forms of research as they can replicate existing hierarchies and binaries, as shown by the Australian and New Zealand challenges around who can represent communities. The politics of representation and identity politics has led some to question the right of non-Indigenous researchers to work with and for Indigenous communities (Hodge and Lester 2006); however, these phenomena are complex and multifaceted, often changing with time, familiarity, personality, relationship, practices, and experiences. For example, relationships are both distant and close, the researcher is not always in a powerful position and may be victimized by other stakeholders, and the gap between researcher and researched may be so negligible that the researcher is considered an insider (Sharp and Dowler 2011). These cases show that researchers act on expectations from their partner community and that they advocate for their needs, including in their home universities and other institutions, which may not recognize the right of the community to authorize who speaks for them.

Researchers' education, networks, or social status are frequently called on to advise people on a wide array of matters, to volunteer or lobby for community needs, and to publicize partner community needs in NGO forums and the media or to advise Indigenous delegations to international meetings, which are all intangible ways of giving back to the community. Disseminating research articles and information in Canada ultimately helped give Indigenous communities a voice in international decision-making forums. Contemporary research for and with Indigenous communities requires agendas of inclusivity and cooperation beyond the academy, and also moral questioning, particularly around the dominant structural forces of global economic restructuring that threaten both community and institutional forms to seek commercial imperatives (Bunge 1969; Valentine 2005). Indigenous peoples have their own agency and reasons for engaging, which may differ from those of the institution.

In Australia, researchers have changed the way funding bodies protect the data of Indigenous peoples and recognize the intellectual property of all. In part, this overcomes de Leeuw, Cameron, and Greenwood's (2012) warning that participatory research may cause Indigenous people to feel less able to be critical, thereby reinforcing the power relations they purport to overcome, and that even coproduction of knowledge suggests there is difference, and othering, prior to stating that this division has been overcome. Partnerships within participatory research can either give back or reinforce power, and it is the ethics underpinning conduct rather than the form of research itself that needs critique. Ethical researchers show their "insiderness" and understanding of community needs and aspirations and act in ways that give back.

Research has also prioritized distant "authentic" or "discrete" Indigenous community groups rather than the contemporary intercultural relationships and Indigenous realities under colonialism (Kobayashi 2001; Gilmartin and Berg 2007). Giving back therefore requires persuading our colleagues to incorporate Indigenous content in their curricula, particularly from Indigenous peoples from the local area (including urban areas); to engage respectfully with Indigenous communities; and to encourage Indigenous peoples' participation in academia through structures such as research groups and through support such as providing scholarships. This agenda of cultural competence within universities will in part help to re-work the academy.

Universities are yet to recognize the personal and professional demands of giving back, including the time and lack of recognition involved. Through the epistemology of participatory research and its moral enactment, the researcher is more of a hybrid of scholar-activist (de Leeuw, Cameron, and Greenwood 2012). While all research, and the researcher's positionality, is power-laden, participatory forms of research can be a legitimate means of engagement and effect beyond the academy (de Leeuw, Cameron, and Greenwood 2012). There are institutional structures, processes, and cultures that must be decolonized through cultural competence and ethical researchers committed to reworking the academy to bring about better research outcomes for Indigenous peoples. Mrs c kinpainsby-hill writes of a participatory praxis that is "close to home," one that helps transform the academy as well as the practices of staff in teaching, research, activism, and professional structures and relations, and "disrupts the unhelpful boundaries between researcher and researched and between community and university"(2011, 221).

The goal is research that is not simply production or even coproduction of knowledge, but a relational connection between people, in which the usual complexities of people and injustices among peoples become part and parcel of reciprocal research. Reworking the academy requires professional and personal commitment to advocate, stand against tokenism, and be of service beyond traditional research outputs, as a form of giving back, despite the personal and professional costs to the researcher in taking on institutional change. In requiring researchers to commit to reciprocity with communities, the academy—which often touts community-researcher relationships in its promotions and achievements—must also recognize its commitment to supporting meaningful community-researcher relationships and support researchers to do so. As such, we argue that researchers need to work the academy to work for community.

Chapter 2 References

Arnstein, S. 1969. "A Ladder of Citizen Participation." *Journal of the American Institute of Planners* 35:216–224.

Briggs, J. 2013. "Indigenous Knowledge: A False Dawn for Development Theory and Practice?" *Progress in Development Studies* 13 (3): 231–243.

Bunge, W. 1969. *The First Years of the Detroit Geographical Expedition: A Personal Report Published by Detroit, Society for Human Exploration.* Detroit, MI: Society for Human Exploration. LCCN: 72180053. Dewey: 910/7/11LC:G74.

Carter, Jennifer. 2001. *Collaborative Ecological Research with Indigenous Australians: The Trepang Project.* PhD diss., Northern Territory University, Australia.

Carter, Jennifer, Phillip Norman, Robin Thwaites, and Peter Frost. 2004. "Lessons for Community-Based Resource Use Planning in Zimbabwe and Northern Australia." In *Community-Based Resource Planning: Studies from Zimbabwe and Northern Australia,* edited by R. Thwaites, J. Carter, and P. Norman, 83–97. Canberra: Australian Centre for International Agricultural Research.

Carter, Jennifer, David Claudie, and Nicholas Smith. 2006. "An Indigenous Role in Partnerships for Sustainable Homelands Occupation in Australia." *Sustainable Development* 14:162–176.

Carter, Jennifer, and David Hollinsworth. 2009. "Institutionalised Views of Aboriginal Rurality." *Journal of Rural Studies* 25:414–424.

Coombes, Brad. 2012. "Collaboration: Inter-Subjectivity or Radical Pedagogy?" *Canadian Geographer / Le Géographe canadien* 56 (2): 290–291.

Dale, Allan Patrick. 1993. *Farming the Bureaucracy: An Assessment of Planning for Rural Developments for Aboriginal Communities in Eastern Australia.* PhD diss., Griffith University, Brisbane.

De Leeuw, Sarah, Emilie S. Cameron, and Margo L. Greenwood. 2012. "Participatory and Community-Based Research, Indigenous Geographies, and the Spaces of Friendship: A Critical Engagement." *Canadian Geographer / Le Géographe canadien* 56 (2): 180–194.

Ford, J. D., B. Smit, and J. Wandel. 2006. "Vulnerability to Climate Change in the Arctic: A Case Study from Arctic Bay, Canada." *Global Environmental Change-Human and Policy Dimensions* 16 (2): 145–160.

Ford, J., T. Pearce, F. Duerden, C. Furgal, and B. Smit. 2010. "Climate Change Policy Responses for Canada's Inuit Population: The Importance of and Opportunities for Adaptation." *Global Environmental Change* 20 (1): 177–191.

Gilmartin, Mary M., and Lawrence D. Berg. 2007. "Locating Postcolonialism." *Area* 39 (10): 120–124.

Hayward, J. 1997. "Appendix: The Principles of the Treaty." In *National Overview*, vol. i, edited by Alan Ward. Waitangi Tribunal Rangahaua Whanui Series. Wellington, NZ: GP Publications. http://www.justice. govt.nz/tribunals/waitangi-tribunal/treaty-of-waitangi/tribunals/ waitangi-tribunal/documents/public/treaty-principles-appendix-99.

Hodge, Paul, and John Lester. 2006. "Indigenous Research: Whose Priority? Journeys and Possibilities of Cross-Cultural Research in Geography." *Geographical Research* 44 (1): 41–51.

IPCC (Intergovernmental Panel on Climate Change). 2013. *Climate Change 2013: The Physical Science Basis. Contribution of Working Group I to the Fifth Assessment Report of the Intergovernmental Panel on Climate Change.* Edited by T. F. Stocker, D. Qin, G.-K. Plattner, M. Tignor, S. K. Allen, J. Boschung, A. Nauels, Y. Xia, V. Bex, and P. M. Midgley. Cambridge, UK: Cambridge University Press.

Jacobson, C., and A. Stephens. 2009. "Cross Cultural Approaches to Environmental Research and Management: A Response to the Dualisms Inherent in Western Science?" *Journal of the Royal Society of New Zealand* 39 (4): 159–162.

Kobayashi, A. 2001. "Negotiating the Personal and the Political in Critical Qualitative Research." In *Qualitative Methodologies for Geographers: Issues and Debates*, edited by M. Limb and D. Dwyer, 55–70. London: Arnold/Hodder Headline.

Louis, Renee Pualani. 2012. "Timely, Tasteful, Rigorous, and Relevant." *Canadian Geographer / Le Géographe canadien* 56 (2): 288–289.

mrs c kinpainsby-hill. 2011. "Participatory Praxis and Social Justice." In *A Companion to Social Geography*, edited by V. Del Casino, M. Thomas, P. Cloke, and R. Panelli, 214–234. Blackwell Companions to Geography. Oxford, UK: Wiley-Blackwell.

Pearce, T., B. Smit, F. Duerden, J. D. Ford, A. Goose, and F. Kataoyak. 2010. "Inuit Vulnerability and Adaptive Capacity to Climate Change in Ulukhaktok, Northwest Territories, Canada." *Polar Record* 46 (237): 157–177.

Pearce, T., H. Wright, R. Notaina, A. Kudlak, B. Smit, J. D. Ford, and C. Furgal. 2011. "Transmission of Environmental Knowledge and Land Skills among Inuit Men in Ulukhaktok, Northwest Territories, Canada." *Human Ecology* 39:271–288.

Pearce, T., J. D. Ford, A. Caron, and B. P. Kudlak. 2012. "Climate Change Adaptation Planning in Remote Resource-Dependent Communities: An Arctic Example." *Regional Environmental Change* 12:825–837.

Pearce T., J. Ford J., A. Cunsolo Willox, and B. Smit. 2015. "Inuit Traditional Ecological Knowledge (TEK), Subsistence Hunting and Adaptation to Climate Change in the Canadian Arctic." *Arctic* 68 (2): 233–245.

Sharp, J., and L. Dowler. 2011. "Framing the Field." In *A Companion to Social Geography*, edited by V. Del Casino, M. Thomas, P. Cloke, and R. Panelli, 140–160. Blackwell Companions to Geography. Oxford, UK: Wiley-Blackwell.

Smith, Linda Tuhiwai. 2012. *Decolonising Methodologies: Research and Indigenous Peoples.* Dunedin, NZ: Otago University Press.

Stephenson J., J. Ruru, and M. Abbott. 2011. *Marking Place: Exploring Land-Use Tensions in Aotearoa New Zealand.* Dunedin, NZ: Otago University Press.

Stevens, Stan. 2001. "Fieldwork as Commitment." *Geographical Review* 91 (1/2): 66–73.

UA (Universities Australia). 2011. *National Best Practice Framework for Indigenous Cultural Competency in Australian Universities.* Canberra, ACT: Australian Government Department of Education, Employment and Workplace Relations (DEEWR).

Valentine, Gill. 2005. "Geography and Ethics: Moral Geographies? Ethical Commitment in Research and Teaching." *Progress in Human Geography* 29 (4): 483–487.

3

Paying Back

The Hopi Pottery Oral History Project

Lea S. McChesney and Gwyneira Isaac

T HE VAST COLLECTIONS OF Native American objects housed in several prominent institutions in the eastern United States hold significant amounts of pottery from the US Southwest. These collections materialize the nationalist and extractive enterprises of the late nineteenth-century museum-collecting epoch. In this chapter, we examine the shared but problematic legacies of these historic museum collections, as well as questions raised by our collaborative research group—the Hopi Pottery Oral History Project (HPOHP)—as a means to both rearticulate and retheorize the pottery according to Hopi values that have, until now, been largely overlooked in the way that many of these large national collections are represented (figure 3.1).

The HPOHP brings together Karen Charley and Valerie Kahe (Hopi potters from the First Mesa community of northeastern Arizona), Lea McChesney (curator of ethnology from the Maxwell Museum of Anthropology, University of New Mexico), Gwyneira Isaac (curator of North American ethnology from the Smithsonian's National Museum of Natural History, NMNH), and Leigh Kuwanwisiwma and Stewart Koyiyumtewa (director and tribal archivist, respectively, from the Hopi Cultural Preservation Office, HCPO).[1] The aims of the HPOHP align with the post-NAGPRA field of contemporary practices mandated by federal legislation, but we have formulated the project not in reaction to that, but in response to Hopi cultural protocol and customary law emphasizing "paying back"—that is, the giving-back process integral to relationships of reciprocity and responsibility. Through this concept of "paying back," we explore current methods used to disrupt colonial regimes of value maintained by museums and their collections, as well as examine how we might implement them, considering ways to dismantle what has become known as "the salvage ethnology" paradigm (Gruber, 1970), which is rooted in postindustrial perceptions of cultural loss that is embedded in Anglo-American concepts of authenticity.[2]

We acknowledge that it is not only individual collection-related histories that need redressing, but also the intellectual paradigms and institutional processes that have shaped and that continue to structure how collections are maintained (i.e., classification, documentation, dissemination). These practices have far-reaching implications that require broader, multidimensional ideological shifts necessitating a high degree of accordance from a diverse range of individuals and groups with varying perspectives, motivations, and interests: Hopi potters, dedicated community members, and offices that shape cultural heritage and education within the Hopi community, as well as museum-based collections managers, curators, administrators, and museum directors.[3] Finding a framework that brings greater understanding of the ongoing and responsive dynamics at play throughout these widely distributed and diverse cultural contexts is at the heart of our endeavor.

By introducing the concept of "paying back"—a term frequently used in Hopi social interactions involving pottery within kinship exchanges—we attempt to recognize a wider network of interdependent participants. We employ it as a concept to subvert the problematic linear dynamics that are at the foundation of the "salvage enthology" paradigm. In the "paying back" model, a cyclical framework grounded in Hopi values is introduced. As explored here, this model contributes to understanding how different elements and realms are interconnected, forming a cycle of creation, growth, deterioration, reclamation, and renewal through time and between multiple generations—with nurturance and sustenance as key values in this context.

The Material and Intellectual Appropriation of Hopi Pottery

After the Civil War, following government land surveys and the establishment of trading posts and reservations, the Southwest Indian artifact-collecting frenzy became part of federal efforts to incorporate the region into the new nation-state. During this time period, precontact

FIG. 3.1—Southwest Native American pottery at the United States National Museum (USNM). Smithsonian Institution Archives. Image # MNH-4321.

(before Spanish colonization in 1540), historic (c. 1600–1800), and the then-contemporary (i.e., nineteenth-century) or "modern" Puebloan pots were imagined as relics of a way of life presumed to be rapidly disappearing under "the onslaught of civilization" (Ahlstrom and Parezo 1987, 267). Advanced by newly built railways that expanded across the North American continent, facilitating the movement of people and goods, the systematic and ostensibly industrial mode of collecting eventually resulted in the extractive "mining" of Puebloan material culture—especially from the Hopi mesas—in an effort by museums and anthropologists to try to stem the loss of these objects from the forces of European colonization and American assimilation. This large-scale dislocation of objects from their communities was rationalized according to what later became known as the "salvage ethnography" paradigm (Gruber 1970) and the trope of the "vanishing Indian" (Warren 1999; O'Brien 2010). It is worth noting that in the twenty-five-year period between 1879 and 1904, the Smithsonian alone removed more than forty thousand Puebloan objects—the majority of them pottery (Berlo 1992, 3; Parezo 1987, 10–11; Wade and McChesney 1980).

At the same time, Lewis Henry Morgan's taxonomy of cultural evolution was implemented as a classificatory framework at the Smithsonian's Bureau of American Ethnology (BAE), which also informed the collection and documentation of early Peabody Museum collections. This approach relegated Puebloan people to a stage of "barbarism," determined by the degree of technological development evident in their material culture, including decorated pottery traditions. This typology permeated Alexander Stephen's unpublished catalogue of the Peabody Museum's Thomas V. Keam Collection from the 1880s, a copy of which also exists in the National Anthropological Archives (NAA) (Wade and McChesney 1980; McChesney 2003).[4]

Jesse Walter Fewkes's 1895 archaeological excavations for the BAE at the ancestral Hopi site of Sikyatki and subsequent publications established the "Hopi complex . . . as a source by which [American] antiquity could be interpreted" because of its lack of European influence (Hough 1932, 264; see Fewkes 1973 [1898, 1919]). By characterizing Puebloan peoples through their material remains, Fewkes defined a culturally specific pottery type and created a generalizing term for past Puebloan cultural achievements that, according to McChesney, resulted in nomenclature to represent a "classical" period in American antiquity. In so doing, Fewkes fashioned a canonical inscription akin to the Renaissance practices that emphasized the role of archaeology in reviving ancient Greek and Roman cultural forms. As with Stephen before him (see note 4), Fewkes participated in Western modes of cultural reproduction through these authoritative institutional and nascent professional narratives. Consequently, the precontact pottery of Sikyatki, with its golden body color and elaborate polychrome designs, was represented as the apogee of "primitive" technology. In its institutional reception and promotion to American audiences, Sikyatki Polychrome became inextricably intertwined with evolutionary and aesthetic concerns of the time. Together, these values also grounded Hopi pottery in nineteenth- and twentieth-century representations of Native American objects as "classical" art.

The intellectual paradigms and classificatory conventions of Fewkes's era endure into the twenty-first century, further detaching these objects from Hopis' ongoing cultural systems and heritage through a form of typological marginalization (Phillips 2011; McChesney 2012, 2014). These conventions objectify the Hopi past through Western frameworks, thereby erasing Hopis as authors of their own history (cf. Dilworth 1996, 8). In effect, Hopis have been geographically and intellectually dispossessed of their cultural heritage, especially in relation to the institutional practices that position museum collections as scientific, art historical, and chronologically informative resources critical to inscribing the history of the nation-state (figure 3.2).

What is the ongoing legacy of these now museum-based resources to their source communities? How do we redress these physical and semiotic extractive paradigms in a post-NAGPRA era of museum practice? Based on prior fieldwork and a collaborative research group, we set out to explore how museum collections of Hopi pottery materialize not only Anglo-American institutional and professional narratives, but also, and more importantly, ongoing social relationships with members of their home communities, activating Indigenous ontologies when community members are reconnected with these resources. We also seek to make explicit our own positionality in this process and the way in which our professional practice is intertwined with community concerns.

The Hopi Pottery Oral History Project

The HPOHP emerged from Lea McChesney's 1990s fieldwork with Hopi potters from First Mesa, following her earlier curatorial work with the Peabody Museum's Thomas V. Keam Collection. During her

FIG. 3.2—USNM display cases, "Tribes of the Lower Colorado Valley, in exhibit hall, late 19th century." Smithsonian Institution Archives. Image # MNH-3697.

twenty-five-year commitment to this work, Lea's collaborative work with Hopi potter Karen Charley, and their mutual concern with the social role of pottery gradually took a prominent role. McChesney and Charley (2011, 2015) shared a growing recognition for the need to inscribe Hopi meanings into the representations of this tradition. As their interests increasingly focused on the significance of intimacy in potters' relationships to their work, and the social networks in which it is implicated (McChesney 2007), their collaboration recognized the need for first-person engagement of potters with these cultural heritage resources.

Subsequent conversations between Isaac and McChesney explored expanding Hopi potters' access to include pottery collected by John Wesley Powell and James and Matilda Coxe Stevenson in the NMNH collections. Isaac's interest in intergenerational perspectives introduced Valerie Kahe, a young Hopi potter from First Mesa and niece of Karen Charley, to the emergent team. McChesney, Charley, Kahe, and Isaac then began to work together on the NMNH Hopi pottery collections. Following a weeklong research visit to NMNH, the team identified a fundamental outcome of the work as the production of hands-on experiential knowledge about the pottery. This goal spoke directly to the inadequacy of the widely used printed and digital images of pottery that are the current means by which Hopi potters receive information about museum collections. In order to privilege hands-on knowledge within research and engagement programming, the group set out to build a project that brought together potters and museum collections (figure 3.3).

By 2013, discussions with the director of the Hopi Cultural Preservation Office (HCPO), Leigh Kuwanwisiwma, and the tribal archivist, Stewart Koyiyumptewa, had helped to develop plans for the dissemination of this traditional knowledge of pottery to younger generations of Hopis and to research the Hopi social values embodied by it. An especially vital component for the project became interviews that would record Hopi potters' perspectives on the pottery. Charley and Kahe suggested they could conduct interviews, each focusing on their own respective peer groups, a research phase that is currently ongoing. This particular focus and methodology led the group to title the project the Hopi Pottery Oral History Project—or the HPOHP (figure 3.4).

Kuwanwisiwma and Koyiyumptewa helped to structure the project as a means to support ongoing efforts to establish Hopi cultural affiliation for formal repatriation requests in compliance with NAGPRA. The HCPO also found an urgency to interview the older generation of potters, both on the mesas and in interacting with museum collections, in order to demonstrate the continuity of pottery as a Hopi tradition throughout historical eras. Access to and work with these collections by community members will provide data for testing theories about Hopi migrations while enriching potters and subsequent generations of the long history of Hopi pottery with new interpretations of its design motifs.

Our conversations developed a scaffolding of intercultural and interinstitutional dialogue and programming for the project. Meetings with staff of the Museum of Northern Arizona (MNA) and Northern Arizona University (NAU) faculty enlarged our institutional nexus. These institutions' long-standing relationship with Hopi communities includes programs to document and enhance Hopi cultural heritage. MNA's new environmentally and culturally sensitive collections storage facility (opened in 2009) was identified as a potential interim location for loans of NMNH pots, offering improved community access to these collections. The museum's campus also encompasses potential housing for potters'

FIG. 3.3— Lea McChesney, Gwyn Isaac, Valerie Kahe, and Karen Kahe Charley (left to right) in NMNH Hopi pottery collections at the Museum Support Center, Suitland, Maryland, May 2012. Photograph courtesy Recovering Voices Program, Smithsonian Institution.

visits. In exploring new contexts for the ongoing pottery tradition in Hopi communities, the HPOHP hoped to incorporate concepts reflecting Indigenous concerns, such as sovereignty, process, authority, the internal community, history and family, linkages between family and foodways, and social relations.

During this second phase of the project, we are identifying funding for collective potters' visits to museums, as well as for bringing select pieces to other institutions, such as Flagstaff's MNA, with opportunities for community members to work with the pots. Our conversations are directed toward strengthening ties with Hopi communities and contributing to HCPO initiatives, with the hope that this project might assist efforts to develop a Hopi cultural community center where collections could eventually reside. Plans for a Hopi center that would specialize in cultural resources and activities have been in development during the past two decades. Recent conversations with the planners for the center have identified the HPOHP as a potential pilot project toward that effort. Short-term outcomes for the HPOHP include peer-created perspectives on pottery that are made available to the community through (1) convening an intergenerational festival at Hopi in April 2017 and July 2018 to discuss the pottery tradition among potters at different stages of their

FIG. 3.4—First meeting at the Hopi Tribe's Cultural Preservation Office, Kyakotsmovi, Arizona, October 2012. Left to right: Stewart Koyiyumptewa, Lea McChesney, Leigh Kuwanwisiwma, Karen Charley, Gwyn Isaac. Photograph courtesy HCPO staff.

careers; (2) producing publications and educational materials about Hopi pottery for the community with information and images selected by potters; and (3) holding workshops to bring together different generations of potters and community members to exchange knowledge about pottery traditions, including building forums for less recognized and noncommercial potters.[5] Our long-term project goals include (1) archiving interviews and transcripts with the HCPO in sustainable formats to increase the accessibility of the information to Hopi community members; (2) developing collaborations between museums in the eastern United States and the HCPO and Hopi Tribe for the relocation of pottery to the MNA and/or a Hopi community.

"Paying Back": Hopi Customary Law and Collaborative Protocols

For Hopis, any effort undertaken on someone's behalf for another is acknowledged through a material repayment, either as a return gift or as service, a practice known as "paying back." Examples of a typical "payback" include pottery bowls mounded with ground cornmeal given from the bride's to the groom's matrilineal members for their contribution toward her woven wedding attire; foodstuffs distributed to guests at a wedding—including Christian ones—to recognize their attendance; foodstuffs provided to guests at a naming ceremony to acknowledge even the modest gift of a bib for the infant; and food "paying back" those who provision the deceased for the afterlife. A form of customary law, this pervasive practice of reciprocation, both embedded in and constitutive of social relations, implicates non-Hopis as well as Hopis.

In one sense, "paying back" refers to the settling of a debt—*haayiwta*. It is a specific step in a process that may take several years (no time limit is specified) to convey ownership. One example from McChesney's research was the payback for wedding robes that was undertaken by the bride's mother with other members of her lineage. Once paid back with the requisite baked goods, the daughter was privileged to use her garments as she preferred during her lifetime, including in the future for her burial. The acknowledgment and balancing out of such a debt is undertaken even if the original partners to the wedding no longer reside together. While some no longer practice orthodox forms of paying back, Hopis still consider the exchange necessary for ownership or conveyance of a right or privilege.

As these exchanges can play out over generations, the paying-back process simultaneously recognizes the initial contribution and allows for a continuing interaction. Rather than ending the debt and cutting off social relations established by the gift, the return gesture (re)generates them, providing the groundwork for continued exchanges that strengthen social relations. Analogous to Mauss's concept of the gift as part of "total prestations" (Mauss 1990), Hopi reciprocity forms a cycle of obligation underlying the mechanics of society as a whole. In Hopi, the completion of the paying back of something, even over many years, materializes social relationships and establishes mutuality between parties in ways that extend these through time. Nonparticipants are open to social criticism, being sanctioned as *qahopi*—"stingy" and asocial. Paying back is thus a dynamic that provides a central foundation for Hopi social life (Whiteley 2004a, 2004b). More than merely an economic transaction, paying back is a dynamic of cultural reproduction (Weiner 1980), which is the sense in which we recognize it here as integral to our methodology.

Hopi pottery is central to payback exchanges and integral to building a vibrant social world extending beyond the primary focus on identity and interaction, lineage and clan. For matrilineal Hopis, this process begins within the first month of life through the naming ritual and, ideally, continues throughout a lifetime. Supplemented by preparations in the weeks from the time of birth, the culminating ceremony occurs in the child's natal home but is sponsored at the discretion of senior women of the father's matrilineage, whose home and clan identity are elsewhere. When its head is washed—immersed in a pottery bowl originating in a home independent of the child's own that becomes a treasured gift—the infant's sensory organs of sight and smell develop tangible perceptions of the "sweetness" of clay at the outset of life. "Sweetness" is a significant aesthetic dimension of Hopi pottery relating to the appealing smell of wet clay, likened to the smell of rain in the desert—a highly desirable and propitious experience evoking the potential fertility of the earth. By virtue of those who participate, the ritual also generates "interrelatedness" in new social relationships that, over the course of a lifetime, grow into a wide social network valued for its thriving nature (McChesney 2007).

The imperative to pay back extends to the national museums of our affiliations, which are historically implicated in the extractive research paradigms of the past. In Hopi thought and practice, the materializing of social obligation is critical to developing and maintaining relationships on any scale, whether dyadic, institutional, or societal. An imperative for respecting Hopi protocols, paying back is a responsibility for all who engage in social interactions with Hopis. The HPOHP raises responsibility for paying back to the level of obligation, solidifying previously fragmented individual actions on McChesney's part, including her gifts of prior publications to potters with whom she worked, and her depositing her dissertation (McChesney 2003) with the HCPO. Through the project we hope to establish a nexus of relations among communities and museums that is grounded in this protocol as a formal principle rather than as an undertaking of ad hoc exchanges. As the naming ritual illustrates and as we recognize, pottery is integral to this foundational dynamic of social life that implicates us through our research and professional engagement with potters and their communities.

With the insertion of Hopi authority and the protocol of paying back as a formative structure for the project dynamics, the HPOHP aims to promote new ways of thinking about and formally representing the meaning of the Hopi pottery tradition, as a cultural practice, that are more adept at understanding the dynamics between Hopi and Anglo-American conventions. Unlike other reciprocal exchanges between museums and Native communities undertaken in the "NAGPRA era" that are derived from compliance with the federal mandate (Killion 2007; Moore 2010; Nash and Colwell-Chanthaphonh 2010), this project proceeds from the Hopi customary law that encourages, but does not compel, a return effort.

A Reciprocal Theory of Research

Although developed outside the formal protocols mandated by NAGPRA, the HPOHP project engages with several directions toward which museum-community relations have grown in post-NAGPRA soil. The impact of repatriation has been not only to foster collaborative relationships between Native communities and the institutions housing their cultural heritage, but also to begin to reconfigure how we conceptualize tangible and intangible heritage, thereby promoting the opening of disciplinary paradigms and practices to new ways of understanding the past, while implementing "decolonizing methodologies" using "dual frameworks" that combine Indigenous knowledge and European epistemologies (Isaac 2007; Killion 2007; Peers and Brown 2003, 13; Smith 1999). Repatriation and its successor practices are specific instances of the larger effort to decolonize museums and disciplinary practices through critiquing Eurocentric models and establishing more inclusive engagements through Indigenous agency and research methodologies based in their cultural protocols (Kreps 2003; Rappaport 2005; Field 2008; Bruchac, Hart, and Wobst 2010; Smith 1999, 15).

This larger field of revisionist museum practices includes efforts to re-narrate and reclaim tribal histories, often through the use of collections, including photographic archives (e.g., Denetdale 2007). In this context, it is understood that "restorative methodologies" recover dislocated collections and advocate partnerships that transform museums into new spaces for negotiation and the re-curation of objects (e.g., Bruchac 2010; see also Rosoff 2003). Likewise, long-term collaborative approaches that result in reciprocal partnerships increase the likelihood of bridging and sharing different systems of authority, thereby providing the means to address the inequities between museums and communities (Swan and Jordan 2015).

Revisionist approaches activated through this nexus of museums and communities draw on frameworks based on the dynamics of redoing or looking back on something, but now with self-awareness or the acknowledgment of past culpabilities. Aaron Glass argues, in regard to processes involving the re-visioning of the social role of objects, that "there is a huge diversity of terms used in the discourse of object returns, all of which address the undoing of some past deed through use of the common prefix "re": repatriation, restitution, reparation, restoration, recover, reinstatement . . . revitalization" (Glass 2004, 118), to which we add "regeneration," which recognizes Hopi intentionality (McChesney 2014). This theme was explored further in "After the Return," a workshop organized by Kimberly Christen, Mark Turin, and Joshua A. Bell at the NMNH in 2012, which looked at how digital technology was being used to circulate and/or return collections-related knowledge between museums and communities. The organizers noted they had learned through their work and fieldwork experiences that "giving and receiving are rarely mono-directional or linear, and have to be thought of as reciprocal and cyclical ongoing processes" (Bell, Christen, and Turin 2013, 2). The current literature on museum/community relationships also illustrates an underlying anthropological interest in "highlighting the ways in which objects are embedded in a nexus of social relations, the meanings of which are contextual as well as temporally bound" (ibid. 2013, 3).

The concepts of repatriation, return, revitalization, and now regeneration, however, must also be viewed in concert with the ethical responsibilities that triggered this rerouting of objects, knowledge, and power in the first place. Often projects designed to return collections-based information to communities are grounded in Anglo-American values that privilege the increased circulation of knowledge. This outcome, however, is not always the desired end result for communities that are looking to reestablish their control over or ownership of these objects, and to limit the scope of their circulation. In his critique of digital surrogates being sent by museums to communities as a means to build relationships, director Jim Enote of the Zuni A:shiwi A:wan Museum and Heritage Center points out that if the digital versions are so useful, why don't the museums return the originals to communities and keep the copies? Circulating images, especially digital surrogates, is not the same as the obligations linked to give-and-take relationships. He addresses this aspect by directly questioning the different values ascribed to giving: "I think also we should think about the power of giving. That there is responsibility in giving and moving information like this" (Enote, cited by Bell, Christen, and Turin 2013, 8).

In light of these different approaches to the distribution and acknowledgment of responsibilities toward cultural heritage, any project such as the HPOHP benefits from an exploration of the different cultural values ascribed to the process of reciprocity, as well as how these play out between museums and communities. This reorientation requires a close understanding of the difference between collaboration and co-curation—a field in which the prefix "co" implies that different parties operate together. The methods for collaboration often work toward exchanging and sharing ideas and different approaches to knowledge. In anthropological contexts and in museum/community-based partnerships, these collaborations rarely approach issues about co-ownership, unless it is of the intellectual products of the union, such as publication.

The concept of co-curation of collections with shared responsibilities between communities and museums may be a more fitting model for honoring the cycle of giving and receiving. Being equally invested in co-curation would require the exchange and reciprocation not only of intellectual approaches, but also of financial, management, programming, physical, and educational responsibilities. Sharing or redistributing power and authority on this level may be why some museums look to intellectual collaboration or the return of objects, rather than seeking out a relationship that creates the ongoing reciprocation of services and obligations, such as those stemming from a co-curation approach. As McMullen (2008) astutely observes, need and committed relationships are not always coterminous and may well be problematic from either perspective.[6]

One particular social value recognized by HPOHP is the critical role that pottery plays in establishing and sustaining matrilineal and interlineage relationships in Hopi society. Knowledge of the value of the pottery to create and maintain family and clan relationships, and the ties formed between lineages of women and their sites for collecting clay, as well as the specific technical skills in making and firing pottery that are reproduced through intergenerational interactions, are often disregarded by collectors or museums who place a higher value on the iconographic elements of pottery than its role as a social being that characterizes and embodies Hopi society. As Charley and McChesney (2007) point out, the "blush" found on Hopi pots that emerges through the potter's relations with the clay, her technical skill in forming and firing the pot (a process she does not control), is likened by Hopi potters to the warmth felt during an emotionally meaningful interaction between people. From a potter's perspective, the appreciation of this key aesthetic component of the pot should not be limited to Hopis but should be shared by all. After firing, a glowing pot is seen as an embodiment of the artist's gratification that comes from the successful realization of her work. In effect, Hopi pots materialize and make both accessible and durable a fleeting, highly valued human experience: the warm sensation of happiness in mutually satisfying intimate social relations.

Pots also present the potential for stimulating affection among those with whom one is not related—in the hope of relating. With the capacity to bring social relations into being, pottery personifies concepts of what it means to be Hopi, as well as how this membership or citizenship is perceived outside of the community. In HPOHP discussions held at the Museum of Northern Arizona (MNA) in 2012, NAU professor and Hopi participant Lomayumtewa Ishii introduced the idea of this project serving to honor the sovereignty of Hopi pottery. The values in this context bring pottery to bear upon conceptualizations of Hopi citizenship and the rights of individual Hopis as part of a recognized and self-governing tribe.

These meanings, however, are misunderstood by non-Hopis who purchase pottery represented by non-Hopis as part of a set of values shaped by externally driven art markets. While color variation is valued by Hopis for its embodiment of emotional warmth, it is often seen by collectors as a flaw in the firing, resulting in some potters using electric kilns that provide a more evenly controlled heat and, therefore, uniform finish to the pot's surface. Thus, promoting these socially centered Hopi values among other Hopis and with younger generations has become a core goal for the HPOHP, as is the education of the general public about the values that exemplify Hopi society embodied in their pots.

Alongside the concept of repatriation, which has returned sacred objects to the religious societies and largely male domains of Hopi, the HPOHP project could instead be likened to the "rematriation" of Hopi pottery—physically, geographically, and intellectually—reconnecting it to the women who have kept this practice and related social networks flourishing within their communities across centuries. Through the reproduction of these social and aesthetic values, Hopi pottery has the capacity to regenerate Hopi society in and through time. With the reorientation to rematriation and implementation of protocols that acknowledge paying back, we recognize that our actions are implicated in ensuring that this capacity both extends into other non-Hopi social arenas and can be fostered within Hopi communities. Throughout this project, we have returned to this idea of reciprocity and the rethinking of how social networks involve specific obligations—in this case set by Hopi ideals. We want to emphasize that through it we are not engaging Hopis as a constituency, audience, or interest group within museums, as would be the case with a standard stakeholder approach (see, for instance, Vergeront 2012), but instead repositioning the authority that determines the basis by which this work proceeds (cf. Clifford 2004, quoted in Field 2008, 170). Employing the concept of paying back in the context of this project requires the HPOHP research group to consider the network of obligation from a personal, institutional, and broader social perspective—to recognize that, as scholars and museum professionals, we authors also are involved in Hopi social networks grounded by their concepts of cultural reproduction (figure 3.5).

By foregrounding the often unspoken expectations that accompany the structuring of responsibilities within collaborative partnerships, as well as highlighting the specific dynamics and values stemming from Hopi culture—such as specific obligations toward reproduction (of pottery, society, and knowledge)—we determined that the concept of reciprocity more closely evoked Hopi concepts of responsibility and obligation, as well as cycles of exchange over time. We find a correlation with the dynamics involved in the revisiting and reapplication of ethnographic methodological approaches, their resulting modifications over time, and the bridging of formerly disjunctive bodies of anthropological and Hopi knowledge through new kinds of research with museum collections. Combining this perspective with ideas about reciprocity proved an effective means to critically reflect on our current methodological tool kit, as well as to encompass Hopi approaches to the project. By conceptualizing these values through a reciprocal framework, we could both identify the economies and expectations linked to reciprocity and explore the longitudinal and cyclical impacts that these cross-cultural, interdisciplinary intersections and patterns of behavior have, both on communities and on the larger theoretical field of anthropology.

Challenges and Structures

In developing this project, the HPOHP team has had to face a number of problems that ultimately have shaped its purpose, scope, and audience. While the concept of paying back and the potential expectations about circular dynamics may seem tidy and evoke ideas about "coming full-circle" or "completing the circle," obligation-based social networks at Hopi and the NMNH museum in particular introduced numerous challenges and unexpected routes. On the one hand, kinship and other social responsibilities at Hopi are time-consuming to maintain and involve a wide range of activities and commitments. On the other, university and museum-based research frameworks privilege controlled time frames, such as two-to-three-year projects with expectations of research results published soon after. This kind of timeline is determined largely by grants with reporting deadlines, as well as expectations from institutions about how the production rate of research reflects on their reputations as centers for perpetually generating original scientific discoveries. Our concern was that these dynamics could result in a scenario in which researchers and community members have diametrically opposing needs and expectations, caused by different perceptions of and values assigned to peoples' time, as well as their views of time.[7] In addition, many of the collections involved in this project are the result of long-term relationships and, therefore, the HPOHP is informed and attempts to be responsive to these multigenerational, multi-century projects with the need for an ongoing dialogue between Hopis and museums.

Another challenge was presented by the enduring and problematic nature of the salvage-ethnology lens through which contemporary projects are conceived and evaluated. In particular, we were faced with asking, how can we solve the predicament that the HPOHP project might potentially contribute to museums' continued accruing of things, becoming another layer of the extraction of knowledge from communities? In response to this pitfall, our interests largely focused on prioritizing dynamics that enabled transmission between community members. The collections are respected for their Hopi value as "speaking subjects," not dislocated objects. As the salvage paradigm focuses on "loss," we also attempted to disrupt this dynamic by folding the erosive, extractive history back into a cyclical framework where it is Hopi authorship that shapes the ways in which feedback and dialogue are used, within both the community and the museum. As a result, our central emphasis has become the intergenerational transmission of knowledge. This methodology has become a key interest for Indigenous communities working with museum collections across the globe. Examples include the work done by Sven Haakanson at the Alutiq Museum; work by Aaron Crowell and Dawn Biddleson at the Anchorage Museum, where workshops using museum objects are held for younger generations to learn such things as snowshoe construction; as well as parallel projects in European museums by Alison Brown and Laura Peers with the Blackfeet.[8]

Rather than enabling the museum to be the key recipient of knowledge produced by the project, a fundamental need was instead to work with Hopis to find out how they wanted to transmit this knowledge and to whom. From this emphasis, we developed visits to include a mix of generations, and designed programming in the community that acknowledged this method as central to the dissemination of knowledge there. Our methodology for museum visits included videotaping their entirety as a means to record conversations and the collective and cumulative body of knowledge developed through these hands-on/speaking dialogues between generations and the pottery. These videos are duplicated and shared among participants, with the plan to circulate this knowledge within the community.

Looking at the broader landscape that is now shaped by decolonizing ideologies, such as the move to dismantle the "salvage" paradigm, a number of important dynamics and boundaries become visible. First, discrete grant-funded projects that advocate the privileging of community and Indigenous methodologies do not always have the longevity, authority, or expansive network needed to formalize the necessary changes in museums. Often "soft" money is used to try to solve "hard" institutionalized and deep-rooted social problems. Second, a substantial portion of the terminology and intellectual architecture stemming from these decolonizing methodologies is pioneered in academic publications with limited circulation—most of which takes place among those who already inhabit museums or academia. In short, the diverse networks and infrastructure needed to fully dismantle the salvage paradigm in museums is not incorporated into the structural, governmental, or managerial processes that are necessary to transform institutions such as museums.

This point returns us to our question posed at the beginning of this inquiry—how do we redress the physical and semiotic extractive paradigms in a post-NAGPRA era of museum practices? We are further impelled to consider an additional line of inquiry: How do we dismantle this extractive salvage paradigm in a social structure that, based on encounters in other arenas of our professional practice, does not subscribe to collaborative methodologies? This perception alerts us to the fact that many of the problems that museums, researchers, and communities are trying to address through decolonizing methodologies also exist outside of the museum and are constantly being reinforced through a wider set of social practices. This line of thinking is not to suggest that museums are not able to introduce change, but instead to highlight how community engagement projects throw into relief broader dynamics, histories, and social issues at play (Coombes and Phillips 2015).[9] We would be naïve if we thought museums were the *only* instruments that could dismantle these cultural misperceptions and social inequities. Yet the persistent belief in cultural hierarchies found in current power regimes is a multigenerational and multi-century problem requiring long-term solutions.

We thus see the need to develop the HPOHP as a sustainable community engagement *structure*—rather than as a short-term project. In order to deal with the broader social issues mentioned above, we also hope to create a foundation for reeducating the general public at a national level about Hopi values that are often misinterpreted or misunderstood in public venues, especially in the art market. Consequently, we focus on using practices that honor Hopi values as well as shared frameworks that generate new social connections and forms of engagement.

Conclusion: "Paying Back" as Cultural Heritage Regeneration

Peter Whiteley (2004a, 2004b) documented an offering by Hopi ritual elders to US president Millard Fillmore in 1852 as a means of "opening diplomatic relations" between political entities—a heightened caliber of social relations to be sure. This historically overlooked act is noteworthy on multiple levels. Most importantly, Hopi leaders directly addressed the seat of power of a young America thirty years prior to the establishment of the Hopi Reservation in 1882. The overture occurred more than twenty years before the 1875 establishment of Thomas Keam's trading post in northeastern Arizona that both initiated a commercial market for Hopi pottery and served as the outpost for hosting government expeditions, including the Hayden Expedition (US Geological Survey) that same year (McChesney 1994, 6). Whiteley observes that, with their modest gesture, "the Hopi sought to embrace the president in their own sphere of sociality and mutuality" and "incorporate [him] into the Hopi world" (2004a, 65).

Multiple studies of Hopi communities in subsequent decades have documented and explored Hopis' intentions to engage Anglos and other outsiders in the symbolic construction of their world in particular ways not limited to colonial encounters (Kealiinohomoku 1989; Lomawaima 1989; Sekaquaptewa 1972). No doubt like most representatives of the US settler colonial enterprise, however, in the end Fillmore's response was qahopi: stingy and unable to recognize, let alone participate in, Hopi cultural protocols that undergird all social relations, including political and economic ones.

The effort to engage colonial agents in Indigenous terms is not unique to Hopis. In his classic characterization of the museum as a "contact zone," James Clifford (1999, 439) described the effort of Tlingit elders to engage the Portland Art Museum staff and other "white interlocutors" in

FIG. 3.5—Karen Kahe Charley and Lea McChesney collaborating in Karen's pottery studio, Keams Canyon, Arizona, July 2013. Charley and McChesney have been collaborating since 1994; McChesney has been working in the First Mesa community of the Hopi Reservation, becoming socialized into the "paying back" cultural protocol, since 1991. Photograph by Gwyneira Isaac.

relational terms of mutual engagement and responsibility, acknowledging a "shared history" despite their differences and the imbalance of power between them. These Tlingit elders apparently intended to structure the social relations of the encounter in such a way that museum staff would engage on their terms. Similarly, Howard Morphy (2006, 494) described Aboriginal "sites of persuasion" and ongoing attempts since the eighteenth century of Aboriginal Australian peoples to engage Europeans in a performative (if not linguistic) rhetoric of Aboriginal values "by including them [European colonizers] in ceremonial performances and trying to enter into relations of exchange."

More than a century and a half later, we are hoping to build shared recognition of the fact that it is well past time to heed Hopis' consistent calls for mutual engagement, altering the tenor of our interactions and the structure of our research relationships. Significantly, the rewards of this reorientation are not restricted to Hopis alone. To this time, most non-Hopis have neither known nor acknowledged the principles grounding the social interactions of Hopi pottery's production and circulation. At the same time, non-Hopis do not recognize that pottery is a "metaphorical reiteration of cosmological ideas" (Sekaquaptewa and Washburn 2004, 457). Neither do museums and researchers fully acknowledge historical and contemporaneous actions as enmeshed equally in Hopi concerns and in our own. While collaboration is an "organizing trope" for much contemporary ethnographic research that entails "understanding and working with *difference*," engaging in collaborative interactions is often difficult for sharing control, negotiating, and working through—or with—those differences. The efforts may unfold in unanticipated ways (Campbell and Lassiter 2015, 21, 23; emphasis original). Certainly we have found that physical distances and cultural differences hamper Hopis' access to their cultural heritage housed in institutions they do not control.

Following from her dissertation research, through collaborative ethnography McChesney has worked to translate Hopi potters' aesthetic values and ontology to non-Hopi audiences, seeking to widen the audience of speakers of the embodied language of their pottery (e.g., Charley and McChesney 2007; McChesney and Charley 2011, 2015), as well as to write reflexively of her prior (mis)representations of Hopi pottery (McChesney 2014). Her approach accords not only with post-NAGPRA museum practice but also with broader anthropological practice in collaborative ethnography and ethics as also explored by Isaac (Campbell and Lassiter 2015; Isaac 2015; Lassiter 2005). Modeling this project on other community-oriented efforts (e.g., Bernardini 2005; Denetdale 2007), and in using a Hopi protocol to guide how we structure formal interactions around Hopi pottery among various constituencies and audiences, we hope to communicate across boundaries and between knowledge domains, providing firsthand forms of engagement in newly created socially diverse spaces. By designing an intercultural interstitial space, to paraphrase Myers (2006, 532; Mithlo 2004), we rearrange the relations of Native and non-Native participants while paying back the contributions of generations of Hopi potters to American and global public culture by constructing the formal means to represent pottery as a tradition from Hopi perspectives. To summarize Campbell and Lassiter, ours is a material effort to craft understanding while constructing new, mutually engaged ways of being in our interactions among all parties to the collaboration.

Finally, it is noteworthy that our "re-search" group finds that the project has already brought a return to the NMNH, albeit unintentionally, dispelling a number of assumptions often held by museums and collectors.

First we note that the work of the HPOHP so far has helped to discredit the assumption that photographs and digital surrogates can convey the knowledge needed by community members in order to fully comprehend the objects they want to engage with or study. Rather, it is essential for people to have hands-on relationships with museum objects, which Hopi potters relate to as "speaking subjects." Second, although museums are perceived to be resistant to modern interpretations of nineteenth-century museum objects, believing the primary interpretation to be the most "untainted," new interpretations of the social value of Hopi pottery generated by the project and shared with museum staff and visitors were perceived by this audience to increase the meaning and significance of the museum's collections. These positive reactions came from NMNH board members, and other Native American community members, who until now had contact with only market and consumer-driven interpretations of the pottery.

In consonance with Hopi concepts of the regenerative power of reciprocity, the HPOHP has demonstrated its compelling nature to non-Hopis. Even incipient efforts at this stage reveal that these collections no longer materialize their value from extractive research paradigms alone, but instead inhabit a multidimensional, cyclical value system made from collaborative engagements that simultaneously generate and regenerate cultural heritage in their home communities, even while garnering positive recognition for the institutions partnering in these opportunities. In so doing, we underscore the often unrecognized and undervalued aspect of private and public institutional obligations to communities that operate alongside research agendas. Serving as inspiration for potential future projects at the NMNH, part of our "national museum," we now enter an era of intercultural relations that foreground reciprocal relations—as Hopis have intended all along.

Acknowledgments

Lea McChesney's primary affiliation is with UNM's Maxwell Museum of Anthropology, where she is curator of ethnology; she also serves as director of the Alfonso Ortiz Center for Intercultural Studies in UNM's Department of Anthropology. During the course of this research, McChesney also held a secondary affiliation as an associate of the Peabody Museum of Archaeology and Ethnology, Harvard University, and accessed collections as a researcher according to protocols of the museum. She gratefully acknowledges the support of staff at the Peabody Museum of Archaeology and Ethnology, Harvard University, and the Maxwell Museum of Anthropology, University of New Mexico, in her continued research. She wishes in particular to thank Karen Charley, Valerie Kahe, and the late Wilmer Kavena, Hopis who have encouraged her understanding of the social value of their pottery, and warmly acknowledges the contributions of all parties to this collaboration. This chapter reworks portions of her previous publications, especially McChesney 2014. Isaac recognizes Leigh Kuwanwisiwma and Stewart Koyiyumptewa of the HCPO for their support and ongoing insight and feedback on the project, as well as to Robert Breunig of the Museum of Northern Arizona, Lomayumtewa Ishii, Kelly Hayes Gilpin, and George Gumerman IV of Northern Arizona University, for ongoing discussions about the potential network of institutions and people that will make up the HPOHP. Acknowledgment also goes to the Smithsonian Institution's Consortia for the initial funding for the project under the Grand Challenges grants, and to the NMNH Recovering Voices program for its ongoing support. The authors gratefully acknowledge all participants in and organizers of the 2017 First Intergenerational Hopi Pottery Festival, and especially wish to recognize the First Mesa potters: Loren Ami, Ramona Ami, Karen Kahe Charley, Alice Dashee, Grace Douma, Larson Goldtooth, Darlene James, Valerie Kahe, Adelle Tewayguna, Gloria Mahle, Emmaline Naha, Fawn Navasie, Gwen Setalla, and Grace Tahbo.

Chapter 3 References and Recommended Reading

Ahlstrom, R. V. N., and Nancy Parezo. 1987. "Matilda Coxe Stevenson's 'Dress and Adornment of the Pueblo Indians.'" *The Kiva: Journal of the Arizona Archaeological and Historical Society* 52 (4): 267–274.

Bell, Joshua A., Kimberly Christen, and Mark Turin. 2013. "After the Return: Digital Repatriation and the Circulation of Indigenous Knowledge." *Museum Anthropology Review* 7 (1/2).

Berlo, Janet C. 1992. "Introduction: The Formative Years of Native American Art History." In *The Early Years of Native American Art History: The Politics of Scholarship and Collecting*, edited by Janet C. Berlo, 1–21. Seattle: University of Washington Press.

Bernardini, Wesley. 2005. *Hopi Oral Tradition and the Archaeology of Identity*. Tucson: University of Arizona Press.

Brown, Alison, and Laura Peers. 2013. "The Blackfeet Shirts Project: Our Ancestors Have Come to Visit." In *Museum Transformations*, edited by Annie Coombes and Ruth Phillips. The International Handbook of Museum Studies. Vol. 4. Hoboken, NJ: Wiley.

Bruchac, Margaret M. 2010. "Lost and Found: NAGPRA, Shattered Relics, and Restorative Methodologies. *Museum Anthropology* 33 (2): 137–156.

Bruchac, Margaret M., Siobhan M. Hart, and H. Martin Wobst. 2010. *Indigenous Archaeologies: A Reader on Decolonization.* Walnut Creek, CA: Left Coast Press.

Campbell, Elizabeth, and Luke Eric Lassiter. 2015. *Doing Ethnography Today.* Oxford, UK: Wiley. http://reader.eblib.com.libproxy.unm. edu/%28S%28frc3z1o5jskahubqxdp3tfso%29%29/Reader.aspx?p=17 25831&o=765&u=vO9WgmOLwfLmj81DuQI8FA%3d%3d&t=1449 936649&h=606F49B2AD5CE6E4DBAD149215A4003598769DF9&s =40676540&ut=2382&pg=1&r=img&c=-1&pat=n&cms=-1&sd=2# ebook.

Charley, Karen K., and Lea S. McChesney. 2007. "Form and Meaning in Indigenous Aesthetics: A Hopi Pottery Perspective." *American Indian Art Magazine* 32 (4): 84–91.

Clifford, James. 1987. "Of Other Peoples: Beyond the 'Salvage' Paradigm." In *Discussions in Contemporary Culture*, vol. 1, edited by Hal Foster, 121–130. Seattle: Bay Press.

———. 1999. "Museums as Contact Zones." In *Representing the Nation: A Reader*, edited by David Boswell and Jessica Evans, 435–457. London: Routledge.

———. 2008. "Looking Several Ways: Anthropology and Native Heritage in Alaska." *Current Anthropology* 45 (1): 5–29.

Clouse-Radigan, Abby. 2011. Cross-Collections Guide: Matilda Coxe Stevenson. Manuscript, Collections and Archives Program, Smithsonian Institution.

Coombes, Annie, and Ruth Phillips, eds. 2015. *Museum Transformations.* The International Handbook of Museum Studies. Vol. 4. Hoboken, NJ: Wiley.

Denetdale, Jennifer. 2007. *Reclaiming Dine History: The Legacies of Navajo Chief Manuelito and Juanita.* Tucson: University of Arizona Press.

Dilworth, Leah. 1996. *Imagining Indians in the Southwest: Persistent Visions of a Primitive Past.* Washington, DC: Smithsonian Institution Press.

Erikson, Patricia P. 2005. *Voices of a Thousand People: The Makah Cultural and Research Center.* Lincoln: University of Nebraska Press.

Fewkes, Jesse Walter. 1973 [1898, 1919]. *Designs on Prehistoric Hopi Pottery.* New York: Dover.

Field, Les. 2008. *Abalone Tales: Collaborative Explorations of Sovereignty and Identity in Native California.* Narrating Native Histories. Durham, NC: Duke University Press.

Foster, Hal, ed. 1987. *Discussions in Contemporary Culture.* Vol. 1. Seattle: Bay Press.

Fowler, Don S. 2000. *A Laboratory for Anthropology: Science and Romanticism in the American Southwest, 1846–1930.* Albuquerque: University of New Mexico Press.

Glass, Aaron. 2004. "Return to Sender: On the Politics of Cultural Property and the Proper Address of Art." *Journal of Material Culture* 9 (2): 115–139.

Gruber, Jacob W. 1970. "Ethnographic Salvage and the Shaping of Anthropology." *American Anthropologist* 72 (6): 1289–1299.

Hoerig, Keith A. 2010. "From Third Person to First: A Call for Reciprocity among Non- Native and Native Museums." *Museum Anthropology* 33 (1): 62–74.

Holmes, William H. 1886. "Origin and Development of Form and Ornament in Ceramic Art." In *Fourth Annual Report for the Bureau of American Ethnology.* Washington, DC: US Government Printing Office.

Hough, Walter. 1932. *Biographical Memoir of Jesse Walter Fewkes, 1850–1930.* National Academy of Sciences Biographical Memoirs. Vol. 15. www.nasonline.org/publications/biographical-memoirs/memoir-pdfs/fewkes-jesse.pdf.

Isaac, Gwyneira. 2005. "Re-Observation and the Recognition of Change: The Photographs of Matilda Coxe Stevenson (1879–1915)." *Journal of the Southwest* 47 (3): 411–455.

———. 2007. *Mediating Knowledges: Origins of a Zuni Tribal Museum.* Tucson: University of Arizona Press.

———. 2014. "The Price of Knowledge and the Economies of Heritage in Zuni, New Mexico." In *Museum as Process: Translating Local and Global Knowledges,* edited by Raymond Silverman, 152–168. New York: Routledge.

———. 2015. "Perclusive Alliances: Digital 3D, Museums and the Reconciling of Culturally Diverse Knowledges." *Current Anthropology* 56 (12): S286–S296.

Kealiinohomoku, J. W. 1989. "The Hopi Katsina Dance Event 'Doings.'" In *Seasons of the Kachina*, edited by Hartman Lomawaima, 51–64. Hayward, CA: Ballena Press.

Killion, Thomas W., ed. 2007. *Opening Archaeology: Repatriation's Impact on Contemporary Research and Practice*. Santa Fe: School for Advanced Research Press.

Kreps, Christina F. 2003. *Liberating Culture: Cross-Cultural Perspectives on Museums, Curation, and Heritage Preservation*. London: Routledge.

Kuyawama, Takami. 2003. "'Natives' as Dialogic Partners: Some Thoughts on Native Anthropology. *Anthropology Today* 19 (1): 8–13.

Lassiter, Eric. 2005. *The Chicago Guide to Collaborative Ethnography*. Chicago: University of Chicago Press.

Lomawaima, Hartman. 1989. "Introduction." In *Seasons of the Kachina*, edited by Hartman Lomawaima, xxi–xxiii. Hayward, CA: Ballena Press.

Mauss, Marcel. 1990. *The Gift: The Form and Reason for Exchange in Archaic Societies*. Trans. W. D Halls. London: Routledge.

McChesney, Lea S. 1994. "Producing 'Generations in Clay': Kinship, Markets, and Hopi Pottery." *Expedition* 36 (1): 3–13.

———. 2003. *The American Indian Art World and the (Re-) Production of the Primitive: Hopi Pottery and Potters*. PhD diss., New York University (Ann Arbor, MI: University Microfilms).

———. 2007. "The Power of Pottery: Hopi Women Shaping the World." *Women's Studies Quarterly* (Special Issue: Activisms) 35 (3/4): 230–247.

———. 2012. "(Art)Writing: A New Cultural Frame for Native American Art." In *No Deal: Indigenous Art and the Politics of Possession*, edited by Tressa Berman, 2–31. Santa Fe: School for Advanced Research Press.

———. 2014. "From Entangled Objects to Engaged Subjects: Knowledge Translation and Cultural Heritage Regeneration." In *Museum as Process: Translating Local and Global Knowledges*, edited by Raymond Silverman, 130–151. New York: Routledge.

McChesney, Lea S., and Karen K. Charley. 2011. "Body Talk: New Language for Hopi Pottery through Cultural Heritage Collaboration." *Practicing Anthropology* 33 (2): 21–27.

———. 2015. "From a Potter's Perspective": Hopi Pottery and the World Market." In *Artisans and Advocacy in the Global Market: Walking the Heart Path*, edited by Jeanne Simonelli, Katherine O'Donnell, and June Nash, 43–74. Santa Fe: School for Advanced Research Press.

McMullen, Ann 2008. "The Currency of Consultation and Collaboration." *Museum Anthropology Review* 2 (2): 54–87.

Mithlo, Nancy M. 2004. "'Red Man's Burden': The Politics of Inclusion in Museum Settings. *American Indian Quarterly* 28 (3/4): 743–763.

Moore, Emily. 2010. "Propatriation: Possibilities for Art after NAGPRA." *Museum Anthropology* 33 (2): 125–136.

Morphy, Howard. 2006. "Sites of Persuasion: *Yingapungapu* at the National Museum of Australia." In *Museum Frictions: Public Cultures / Global Transformations*, edited by Ivan Karp et al., 469–499. Durham, NC: Duke University Press.

Myers, Fred R. 2006. "The Complicity of Cultural Production: The Contingencies of Performance in Globalizing Museum Practices." In *Museum Frictions: Public Cultures / Global Transformations*, edited by Ivan Karp et al., 504–536. Durham, NC: Duke University Press.

Nash, Stephen, and Chip Colwell-Chanthaphonh. 2010. "Editorial: NAGPRA after Two Decades." *Museum Anthropology* 33 (2): 99–104.

O'Brien, Jean. 2010. *Firsting and Lasting: Writing Indians Out of Existence in New England*. Minneapolis: University of Minnesota Press.

Parezo, Nancy J. 1987. "The Formation of Ethnographic Collections: The Smithsonian Institution in the American Southwest." In *Advances in Archaeological Method and Theory*, vol. 10, edited by Michael B. Schiffer, 1–47. San Diego: Academic Press.

Patterson, Alex. 1994. *Hopi Pottery Symbols*. Based on work by Alexander M. Stephen. Boulder, CO: Johnson Books.

Peers, Laura, and Alison K. Brown. 2003. "Introduction." In *Museum and Source Communities: A Reader*, edited by Laura Peers and Alison K. Brown, 1–16. London: Routledge.

Phillips, Ruth B. 2011. "How Museums Marginalize: Naming Domains of Inclusion and Exclusion." In *Museum Pieces: Toward the Indigenization of Canadian Museums*, 95–101. Montreal: McGill-Queen's University Press.

Rappaport, Joanne 2005. *Intercultural Utopias: Public Intellectuals, Cultural Experimentation, and Ethnic Pluralism in Columbia*. Durham, NC: Duke University Press.

Rosoff, Nancy B. 2003. "Integrating Native Views into Museum Procedures: Hope and Practice at the National Museum of the American Indian." In *Museum and Source Communities: A Reader*, edited by Laura Peers and Alison K. Brown, 72–79. London: Routledge.

Sekaquaptewa, Emory. 1972. "Preserving the Good Things in Hopi Life." In *Plural Society in the Southwest*, edited by Edward M. Spicer and

Raymond H. Thompson, 239–260. Albuquerque: University of New Mexico Press.

Sekaquaptewa, Emory, and Dorothy Washburn. 2004. "*They Go Along Singing*: Reconstructing the Hopi Past from Ritual Metaphors in Song and Image." *American Antiquity* 69 (3): 457–486.

Smith, Linda Tuhiwai. 1999. *Decolonizing Methodologies: Research and Indigenous Peoples*. London: Zed Books.

Swan, Daniel C., and Michael Paul Jordan. 2015. "Contingent Collaborations: Patterns of Reciprocity in Museum-Community Partnerships." *Journal of Folklore Research* 52 (1): 39–84.

Vergeront, Jeanne. 2012. "Stakeholders and Engagement." *Museum Notes*. March. http://museumnotes.blogspot.com/2012/03/stakeholder-engagement.

Wade, Edwin L., and Lea S. McChesney. 1980. *America's Great Lost Expedition: The Thomas Keam Collection of Hopi Pottery from the Second Hemenway Expedition, 1890–1894*. Phoenix, AZ: Heard Museum.

Warren, Louis S. 1999. "Vanishing Point: Images of Indians and Ideas of American History." Review essay. *Ethnohistory* 46 (2): 361–372.

Weiner, Annette. 1980. "Reproduction: A Replacement of Reciprocity." *American Ethnologist* 12 (2): 210–217.

Whiteley, Peter. 2004a. "Ties that Bind: Hopi Gift Culture and Its First Encounter with the United States." *Natural History* (November): 26–31.

———. 2004b. "Bartering Pahos with the President." *Ethnohistory* 51 (2): 359–414.

Notes to Chapter 3

1. In 2012, the HPOHP became one of the first community-driven projects funded under the Recovering Voices initiative, which was established at the NMNH in 2010 to facilitate Native American communities' efforts to research, disseminate, and transmit Indigenous languages and knowledge to younger generations. Leigh Kuwanwisiwma retired as director of the HCPO at the end of 2017. As subsequently explained, "paying back" in the Hopi conception does not carry negative connotations of revenge, as it does in Anglo-American and Eurocentric concepts.

2. James Clifford, Virginia Dominguez, and Trinh Minh-Ha individually and collectively challenged this paradigm in the section "Of Other Peoples: Beyond the 'Salvage' Paradigm" in Hal Foster's edited volume, published

thirty years ago (Foster 1987, 121–150). Clifford identified a dominant "geopolitical and historical paradigm" denoting a "pervasive ideological complex" that both organized and continued to ground Western collecting practices (Clifford 1987, 121). Even in a post-NAGPRA context we are struggling to break this paradigm and implement structural, institutional changes to shift lines of authority and reconfigure a new social and ideational space of intercultural practice.

3. We thank our colleague Les Field for steering us away from using the common term "stakeholders" that would gloss these multiple and divergent interests, obfuscating the power differentials we recognize, and preclude the incorporation of Hopi protocols or the self-determined emphases articulated by participants that shape our project's focus.

4. Effectively Thomas Keam's field assistant, Alexander MacGregor Stephen prepared a manuscript catalogue of the objects he and Keam collected that ultimately were deposited in the Peabody Museum. That manuscript is in the Peabody Museum archives, and a duplicate can be found at the National Anthropological Archives; see Patterson (1994). In his ceramic typology, Stephen drew specifically on the work of the Smithsonian's William Henry Holmes (1886) (Wade and McChesney 1980, 13). Morgan set the theoretical framework for the Smithsonian and an anthropological research agenda for the Southwest, influencing Keam, Stephen, and the Stevensons (Fowler 2000, 95).

5. The First Intergenerational Hopi Pottery Festival was held on April 29, 2017, on Third Mesa, Hopi Arizona, and was funded by the Smithsonian Institution's Recovering Voices program; the Arizona Commission on the Arts; Mesa Media, Inc.; the Hopi Cultural Preservation Office; and UNM's Alfonso Ortiz Center for Intercultural Studies (see http://recoveringvoices.si.edu/events/HopiPottery.html). At the time of this writing plans are afoot for a second festival in summer 2018, along with continuing activities of the HPOHP.

6. McMullen's (2008) critique of the economies of collaboration between Native American communities and museums demonstrates that ideological frameworks for pluralism and collaboration are well studied, yet there is vast unspoken territory where financial relationships and expectations about reciprocity are worked out.

7. This tension dates to the origins of the Americanist tradition. The first ethnologists working for the BAE commonly fought the prioritization of publication over time spent in the field. They argued for the need to return to the same communities time and time again, a practice that

shaped long-term fieldwork practices and regional expertise that contributed to the Boasian frameworks later used to dismantle the evolutionary schemas of the nineteenth century (Isaac 2005).

8. For Sven Haakanson's work in this area, see the film *Sharing Alutiq Stories*, which was made following a journey in 2011 by Alutiiq weavers to St. Petersburg, Russia, to view ancestral baskets collected by Russian traders. This film outlines the work of Alutiiq weavers and Kodiak organizations to revitalize the art of basket making (produced by the WonderVisions and the Alutiiq Museum). See the website Alaska Native Collections: Sharing Knowledges (http://alaska.si.edu/) for Aaron Crowell and Dawn Biddleson's work with Alaskan communities. For Alison Brown and Laura Peers' project with the Blackfoot community, see "The Blackfoot Shirt Project: Our Ancestors Have Come to Visit" (Brown and Peers, 2013).

9. See Coombes and Phillips' (2015) exploration of museums of sites of transformation, where social histories, institutional agency, and innovation are factors considered to understand the dynamics of social change in relation to museums.

4

Making Footprints Where Our Ancestors Left Theirs

Engaging with the Descendant Community at
James Madison's Montpelier

ERICA D'ELIA, MEREDITH LUZE, AND MATTHEW REEVES

HE ANTHROPOLOGICAL SUBFIELD of archaeology presents a significant challenge to the concept of "giving back" to one's research subjects. Archaeology draws from the material remains of people in the past to gain historical understanding wherein the actual subjects of archaeologists' research are typically long dead. Does this mean that archaeologists are absolved from all responsibility to give back? In years gone by, archaeological work followed the tried-and-true formula of an archaeologist excavating a site and then retreating to the lab or university office to process the data and write up the final report. The results of this effort, though valuable for success in academia, were seldom shared with the public. Over the past several decades, this formula has become an increasingly unacceptable practice.

Archaeological work takes place inside real communities made up of living, breathing people who often have an interest in the outcome of the research. So, even though the research subjects are no longer living, archaeologists do have a responsibility to give back to the subjects' descendants and the communities in which the work is done. The stakes are especially high for sites that relate to the history of slavery because its legacy can still be felt in the sociopolitical issues surrounding race and racism.

Archaeologists must be careful not to reproduce the systematic injustices caused by slavery and segregation, or echo the biases of early anthropologists, which supported a racial hierarchy and served to reinforce existing ideas about the inferiority of African Americans (LaRoche and Blakey 1997; Wilkie 2004). Instead, archaeologists should work to challenge these narratives and to serve and empower descendant communities.

Giving back in archaeology can take many forms, and the unique relationship among archaeologists, their research subjects, and interested communities necessitates a different approach than is seen in the greater anthropological field. Other chapters in this volume describe approaches ranging from giving back photographs of community members (McSweeney) to developing websites of school curricula rooted in community lifeways (Herman) to political advocacy on behalf of communities (MacKenzie, Christensen, and Turner). At James Madison's Montpelier, the archaeology team has made a strong commitment to giving back to communities of descendants by providing opportunities to connect with their history, ceding some control over the research and interpretive goals and ensuring more prominent and accurate representation of their ancestors on the landscape.

The Beginnings of Public Archaeology and Collaboration

Today, much archaeological work is conducted within the realm of public archaeology. This vast and ever-growing arena refers broadly to the many ways in which archaeologists work with the public or for the benefit of the public. Though public outreach is now an increasingly common practice, particularly with the growth of community-based participatory research (CBPR), throughout archaeology's long history it was not typical to involve the public in any stage of the work (Atalay 2012; Nicholas and Hollowell 2007).

The beginnings of public archaeology arose from twentieth-century legislation, particularly the Antiquities Act of 1906 and the National Historic Preservation Act of 1966, which sought to protect historical and cultural resources for the public good. From these legislative efforts, the field of cultural resource management (CRM) developed—federally mandated archaeological work, often in advance of infrastructure and development that would threaten the resources and heritage sites in the area (McDavid and Brock 2015; Nassaney 2012b). When the term "public archaeology" was first used in 1972 by Charles McGimsey, it was defined in relation to the responsibility of archaeologists to preserve the past for the public good (McGimsey 1972; Nassaney 2012b). In essence, archaeologists were stewards of the past. They investigated and protected cultural resources in the interest of the public, which was not clearly defined, but left as an amorphous "other." It is no surprise that under this colonialist approach the public had little input in the archaeological process, and the results of the archaeological work were rarely accessible. This early conception of public archaeology was still mired in older theoretical models that privileged objects over people and situated archaeologists as the sole authorities of the archaeological record and therefore the past—beliefs that preserve rather than challenge the dominant ideology (Zimmerman 1998).

More recently, and largely thanks to the activism of marginalized groups, as well as the rise of postcolonialism and the changing demographic of the discipline, archaeologists have stopped to consider the beneficiaries of their work (Nassaney 2012a). This consideration has prompted widespread changes in the way archaeologists conduct public outreach. Political activism of the 1960s and 1970s drew increased attention to issues concerning the rights of marginalized groups—women, the working class, African Americans, and Native Americans—and partnerships with descendant and local communities have helped extend the benefits to others outside the discipline (see Colwell-Chanthaphonh and Ferguson 2008; Deloria 1969; Derry and Malloy 2003; Little and Shackel 2007; Nassaney and Levine 2009; Silliman 2008).

The 1990s saw two events that marked a turning point in the manner in which archaeology was conducted vis-à-vis descendant groups. The first was the 1990 passage of the Native American Graves Protection and Repatriation Act (NAGPRA). Although not the first law mandating repatriation (it was preceded by the National Museum of the American Indian Act in 1989), NAGPRA gained widespread attention across the archaeological field. This act required archaeologists, as well as other academic and museum professionals receiving federal funds, to consult with federally recognized Native American groups, particularly concerning Native human remains, burials, and associated objects. "The public" was no longer a broad and poorly defined concept, but specific living and breathing people with a vested interest in the work being conducted. An eventual by-product of NAGPRA's passage was that some archaeologists realized they needed to be more responsive to the communities their work affected and to share decision-making power (McDavid and Brock 2015).

The second event was the excavation of the historically known African Burial Ground in lower Manhattan in the early 1990s in advance of a federal building construction project that brought archaeologists into conflict with African American descendant communities. Descendants at the African Burial Ground disagreed with the direction of the research and demanded control of the project to ensure that the spiritual connection to the site of some four hundred burials was preserved. Eventually, they would have input over the project, including decisions about who conducted the research and the subsequent interpretation of the site (LaRoche and Blakey 1997; McDavid and Brock 2015). There is no federal legislation similar to NAGPRA requiring archaeologists to consult with African American descendant communities, but as the African Burial Ground project clearly demonstrates, it is in within archaeologists' best interests, and indeed best practice, to do so.

Beyond the lack of legislated consultation, descendants of enslaved peoples also have no legal means of reclaiming their histories for themselves, nor do they always have objects to repatriate. Although the histories of Indigenous peoples and enslaved peoples are largely ones of forced erasure and assimilation, these took very different forms and had different legacies. Indigenous groups were believed to be dying off and therefore were considered exotic in ways that enslaved peoples were not. Consequently, anthropologists collected extensively from Indigenous groups in "salvage anthropology," creating vast holdings in museums that in some ways preserve Indigenous histories. Conversely, objects representing African American life were deemed to have little value as a consequence of prevailing racist ideologies and were not collected by museums (Singleton 1997). The differing historical treatments of Indigenous and enslaved peoples led to different approaches to these groups in the nineteenth, twentieth, and twenty-first centuries by the white-dominated society. As Deloria (1969, 172) stresses, Euro-Americans "systematically excluded blacks from all programs, policies, social events, and economic schemes. [The white man] could not allow blacks to rise from their position. . . . With the Indian the process was simply reversed . . . [and] Indians were therefore subjected to the most intense pressure to become white." Some African Americans today can trace their lineage back to specific plantations and ancestors, but in many cases the lack of records makes this task difficult or impossible. A large focus for members of African American communities, as shown in the civil rights movement, has been on reclaiming rights rather than identities and on reinserting themselves in the historical record. For Montpelier, this means that archaeologists must reach out to descendant communities in both the lineal and cultural sense.

History and anthropology have long alienated marginalized groups. Since its beginnings archaeology has been conducted in a "top-down" manner, so even when some forms of public outreach emerged, they still served the needs of archaeologists and not the greater community. Truly collaborative work was unable to emerge, in part because archaeologists failed to ask the right questions. By and large, the initial research questions were generated by archaeologists, not the communities, and if the archaeologists did not ask questions of interest to the communities they studied, then those communities were far less likely to be interested in the results (Reeves 2004). When working in the public interest, it is necessary to have public participation from the project's earliest stages. Collaborative research between archaeologists and descendant communities must come from a place where power is shared. The terms of power sharing will always be context-specific, but neither group can have complete control of the project's direction (McDavid and Brock 2015). The work conducted at James Madison's Montpelier since the early 2000s provides an excellent example of how a positive relationship between archaeologists and descendant communities can yield mutually beneficial results.

James Madison's Montpelier

James Madison's Montpelier is the plantation estate of the fourth president of the United States, James Madison, and his wife, Dolley. Today, it sits on over 2,700 acres in Orange County in Virginia's Piedmont region. The site is dedicated to interpreting the lives of the Madisons within the context of the development of the US Constitution and beyond, addressing ideas such as the formation of a nation, slavery, the Civil War, and emancipation. Though the mansion is the most prominent feature on the landscape, it was but one part of the working plantation enmeshed within the larger social and economic framework of the antebellum South. The Madisons, of course, were not the only people who resided at Montpelier. At its peak, as many as one hundred enslaved men, women, and children also lived and labored on the grounds.

James Madison died in 1836 and Dolley sold the Montpelier property in 1844 in a transaction that included many of the remaining slaves. The property changed hands several times before it was purchased in 1901 by the duPont family, who owned it for much of the next century. Marion

duPont Scott died in 1983, and her will expressed a wish that ownership
of the estate be transferred to the National Trust for Historic Preservation
so that it could be opened to the public and restored to its nineteenth-
century appearance. In the roughly 150 years before the National Trust
took ownership of the property, Montpelier's many owners made significant changes to the mansion and landscape. At three times its original size
and covered in pink stucco by the end of the duPont years, it was hardly
recognizable as the former Madison family home.

Since the early 2000s, the estate has been managed by the Montpelier
Foundation, which faced the challenge of determining whether the
Madison home could be restored and which period of its history would
be most appropriate for interpretation. After conducting thorough fea-
sibility studies, the foundation determined that enough of the historic
structure remained to make restoration possible. Thus, the first priority
was to return the mansion to its appearance during James and Dolley's
retirement years (1817–1844). The mansion is now largely restored, with
ongoing research and updates to the interior and the interpretation, but
this tells only part of the story of Montpelier. Without addressing slavery, it is
impossible to understand American history and culture, nor to properly
and fully appreciate the complex realities of the author of the Constitution
and how these issues have shaped the course of race relations into the
present.

The Archaeology of Slavery and Representation on the Landscape

It is impossible to divorce the context of slavery from the history of
plantations in America; indeed, it is impossible to divorce it from the
founding and development of the United States. Yet interpretation at
historic plantations has made it very easy for visitors to come and learn
about the "great white men" who dominate American history without
ever considering those who made their lives and achievements possible.
When the homes and work spaces of the enslaved do not exist on historic
plantations, it is too easy for visitors to ignore the existence of slavery. One
of the ways in which Montpelier is able to give back to the descendant
communities is through the excavation and restoration of spaces associated with the enslaved community. The physicality of the buildings on the
landscape helps remind visitors that the estate was a working farm, not
simply a mansion on a picturesque landscape. More than just giving back,

the archaeological exploration of areas of enslavement, and restoration of these spaces, enables the staff at Montpelier to interpret a more complete and complex history through its public tours. The restoration of slave dwellings is not merely tokenism, but a way for visitors to experience and compare what nineteenth-century life was like for both blacks and whites on a working plantation. The reconstructed buildings occupy as prominent a space on the landscape as they are a part of the visitor experience.

During the early years of the mansion's restoration, Montpelier hosted a descendant gathering designed to bring the enslaved community in focus through engagement with the modern descendant communities. One outcome of this event was the restoration of the Gilmore Farm, the home of a freedman and his family. Around this time, archaeology staff from Montpelier were instrumental in creating the Orange County African American Historical Society (OCAAHS), with whom they cosponsored many events, including a descendant reunion and community-involved excavation of the Gilmore Cabin (Reeves 2004). By partnering with the local African American community, Montpelier hoped to promote a more fluid link to direct descendants of the enslaved community locally and farther afield.

In 2010, Montpelier received a grant from the National Endowment for the Humanities to research the enslaved community with a focus on understanding the complex lives of various enslaved groups through their respective homes and household goods. The grant funded four seasons of archaeological work, which took place in three phases: first, excavation of the Stable Quarter, a home for enslaved artisans and craftsman; second, excavation of the South Yard, a six-building complex for domestic slaves including two duplex quarters, two smokehouses, a detached kitchen, and an additional dwelling within the formal grounds of the mansion; and third, excavation of the Tobacco Barn Quarter and Field Slave Quarter (Reeves 2015b). The Tobacco Barn Quarter served as the site of a tobacco barn and later agricultural wheat threshing complex, but the recovery of domestic artifacts indicates that it was also used as a short-term habitation for enslaved people, possibly concurrently with its use as a tobacco barn. The Field Slave Quarter was a complex of at least three separate home-sites, two defined by the presence of subfloor pits and the third defined by artifact distribution patterns.

The results of this work highlighted differences in home structure, spatial organization and privacy, and access to material goods among these groups (Greer 2014). In the most tangible sense, the research

allowed the home and work sites of the enslaved people to be reconstructed on the landscape so that visitors are forced to confront the issue
of slavery and freedom during their tour. Based on the results of previous and ongoing research, as well as generous philanthropic donations,
Montpelier has been able to begin reconstructing the South Yard, first
with timber-framed "ghost" structures of the six buildings and later
through complete reconstruction.

In a continued effort to place more buildings associated with the
enslaved community back on the landscape and to involve the public in
the process, the log cabin reconstruction workshop was born. In 2010,
archaeologists were able to define the exact size and location of a log
cabin structure believed to be associated with the enslaved community. The structure lies just outside the formal grounds, along a modern
path between the visitor center and the mansion. It probably served as
a home for some of the skilled artisans and craftsmen who labored on
the Montpelier plantation, including Granny Milly, a matriarch of the
enslaved community who lived to be over one hundred years old. Enough
evidence exists to say that the home was an at-grade structure consisting
of two rooms and two stick-and-mud chimneys. The structure is currently
called the Stable Quarter, but its potential association with Granny Milly
and other enslaved workers is discussed on the interpretive signage. The
archaeology staff generally refers to the structure as Granny Milly's cabin,
in part to pay homage to her. It is also far more meaningful to the African
American community and to the totality of the visitor experience if the
name of an enslaved individual can be associated with a particular place
(Wilkie 2004). The formal designation of the building, for now, remains
the Stable Quarter.

The ambitious goal for the log cabin workshop was to reconstruct, over
the course of the week, a historically accurate (but still "ghost") cabin to
be placed at the site of Granny Milly's former home. Over a dozen people
participated, and they spent the week learning historical techniques for
log cabin building, such as how to hew and notch logs. Though some
winter weather complicated the workshop plans, by the end of the week
all of the logs had been hewn and were ready to be assembled at a future
date. Within weeks, the construction team was able to use the logs to
build a ghosted cabin. Though physically located very close to the South
Yard, Granny Milly's cabin bears little resemblance to the timber-framed
duplexes. While Granny Milly's cabin was built in the style of most homes
of the time for both enslaved and free people (log structures with a clay

floor and stick-and-mud chimneys), the duplexes in the South Yard had a more refined appearance thanks to the use of processed materials (milled timbers, masonry chimneys, and sashed windows).

The main reason for the difference lay in location: while Granny Milly's cabin was outside the view of the main house, the structures in the South Yard were meant to be seen by Madison's guests—and as such Madison controlled their aesthetics (Reeves and Greer 2012). The differences between the quarters in the South Yard and Granny Milly's cabin are discernible even to casual visitors. Many people comment on the differences between the two building styles, even occasionally remarking that the timber-framed structures are "too nice" to be homes for enslaved people, opening opportunities for archaeologists and tour guides to discuss the complexities of the enslaved community and plantation social dynamics. The plantation was a complex space, and reconstruction of the plantation as a whole allows visitors to consider how

> plantations are landscapes of embedded meaning. While these landscapes were initially intended to convey and reinforce the power and economic structures of the plantation, they were also landscapes that could have long, multigenerational histories that entwined family and individual histories to places. These embedded meanings could supersede and negate the intentional texts of the built environment. Through collective experiences slaves could come to control and appropriate the spaces of the plantations. (Wilkie 2004, 111)

Prominently replacing these buildings on the landscape hopefully encourages visitors to think about how they would feel occupying them. What kind of privacy, or lack thereof, might they have felt as they went about their personal lives with their homes in the shadow of the big house?

In addition to the mansion tour, Montpelier also offers both self- and interpreter-led tours of the plantation and several "in-depth" tours concerning specific topics. One of these tours, "Slavery at Montpelier," offers visitors a look at the paradox of slavery in America and challenges typical portrayals of slavery. As McDavid (1997, 117) observes, "Traditional public interpretations of plantation life, which have tended to focus almost exclusively on the lives of the planter class, have the effect of reinforcing the idea that planter class values and ideologies were natural and inevitable. Expanding the focus to include the lives of all the people who lived on a plantation is one way of deconstructing the dominant planter ideologies" (cf. Singleton 1995,127–128).

The "Slavery at Montpelier" tour explores issues such as how to reconcile a nation where "all men are created equal" with the reality that some men (and all women) were not considered equal at all. The tour also highlights some of the lives of particular enslaved persons as well as James Madison's conflicting personal and political views on the institution of slavery itself. Representation of the enslaved community on the landscape and thorough interpretation is an important goal in and of itself because it brings issues of race, racism, and segregation to the forefront of the minds of visitors and allows them to draw connections between these historical events and the current sociopolitical climate. This is not to say that interpreting slavery at Montpelier is not fraught with complexities; many visitors come only to learn the "great white men" history of the place, while others argue that slavery is not discussed enough. Balancing the interests of diverse publics challenges the archaeologists and other staff to deeply consider how to effectively discuss the history and legacy of slavery. Beyond simply inserting the enslaved community into the interpretation, Montpelier has continued to seek ways to involve descendant communities in meaningful ways.

Collaboration with Descendants

Montpelier is in a position to interpret not just the period of plantation slavery, but also how the lives of African Americans changed after emancipation as they transitioned to a new status as freedmen. Some of the former slaves, like George Gilmore, remained local after emancipation. Gilmore and his wife Polly established their own farm on land then owned by Dr. James A. Madison, the former president's nephew. Gilmore was able to purchase the land in 1901, and it was passed down to his son after his death. Members of the Gilmore family may have been living at the Gilmore Cabin as late as 1930, and descendants of the family remain in the area today (Reeves 2004; Schneider and Reeves 2010). Archaeological work and restoration of the Gilmore home took place in 2001 with the involvement of descendants of the family.

The 2001 OCAAHS descendant reunion was an important event that shaped future work by the Montpelier Archaeology Department. It was then that Archaeology Director Matthew Reeves connected with one of the descendants of George and Polly Gilmore, and through this and subsequent meetings Reeves arranged to have five descendants of the Gilmore family participate in excavations at their ancestral home. This inspired Montpelier to host an "excavation expedition" specifically for descendants in October 2001 with members of the Gilmore family.

The participants remained engaged and enthusiastic for the entire week, connecting to their family's history through the material remains of their past that they were uncovering. The artifacts and stories that participants touched and shared enabled them to feel a strong connection to their ancestors, like the Gilmore descendant who located a human molar at the site and diagnosed the abscess on the tooth through his training as a dental technician. Holding the abscessed tooth and realizing the pain his ancestor must have experienced was a profound moment for this descendant and deepened his connection to the archaeological work through the connection to this ancestor. Moments like these, which occur frequently throughout expeditions, testify to how the relationship descendants have with archaeology can change after they participate in the archaeological process.

Beyond just participating in the archaeological work, the descendants were invited to help design an interpretive plan for the cabin. Descendants were given a voice equal to the archaeologists and historians working at the site and helped determine which period in the site's history would be interpreted. They also stressed the need to emphasize the role of the Gilmore farm within the local community (Reeves 2004).

This process of involving descendants, the local community, and the general public in the ongoing excavations has become the cornerstone of Montpelier's public archaeology LEARN expedition programs. The programs are grounded in the belief that it is vital for the public to understand how the work of archaeology is conducted and how archaeological research can lead to complex, multi-voiced interpretations of the past. The process of collaboration necessitates that archaeologists give up some of the power they have over both the research design and the ultimate goals of the work in order to meet the needs of both specific and general publics.

Montpelier's Archaeology Department has actively worked to involve the public in the ongoing archaeology for over twenty years through week-long expedition programs. These programs offer an immersive hands-on experience wherein participants stay on the property for the duration of the week and work side by side with archaeologists in the field. The setup of the expedition programs enables participants not only to see the results of archaeological work in reconstructions and interpretations, but also to be a part of unearthing it. Participants are not required to have any archaeological experience and frequently have not been exposed to an active excavation before arriving at Montpelier. Over the course of the week, participants learn how to properly use a trowel, recognize and document stratigraphic changes, identify artifacts, and prepare samples in the laboratory for processing, cataloging, and research. Lectures, discussions, and archaeological tours build on this hands-on experience by exploring how archaeologists use the information to better understand the past. The goal is to bring together all steps of the process and allow participants to see how each step ultimately benefits the final interpretation.

Montpelier first experimented with immersive programs in 1991 with a weeklong workshop run through the National Trust for Historic Preservation. This program, held annually at the end of September, attracted a significant number of interested participants. Many have returned over the past twenty-five years as a core set of participants who continue to take part in expeditions to this day. Inspired by the success of this program, Montpelier partnered with Earthwatch in 2006 to expand its programming and began offering three annual weeklong excavation programs, again attracting numerous returning volunteers.

In 2009, Montpelier launched its own expedition program with complementary lectures and tours on archaeology. The excavation expeditions remained popular, but offered a glimpse into only one segment of the archaeological process. Consequently, in 2013 Montpelier began its LEARN program to offer expeditions for all four phases of excavation and restoration: Locating sites through metal detecting, Excavating sites, Analyzing artifacts in the laboratory, and Reconstructing the original log cabin and timber-frame structures; the final component aims to develop a Network of advocates for archaeological heritage and the Montpelier Foundation, and to engage with stakeholders, archaeologists, and other members of the public through social media and special alumni programs. The Archaeology Department hosts over ten expeditions per year under the LEARN program, which introduces participants to the history of Montpelier as well as past and current archaeological projects. Participants tour the Madisons' home as well as other sites, such as the Gilmore Cabin and the Civil War camps, which are integral to understanding how Montpelier changed and developed throughout the country's history. These tours also illustrate features and architectural elements excavated by the archaeology department and allow participants to connect their work during the expedition to the overall research process.

Although the various iterations of the expedition program have attracted nearly six hundred participants since 1990, the expeditions' use for strengthening bonds with, and meeting the interests of, descendant communities has only recently begun to be explored. Despite the success of the initial Gilmore descendant expedition, Montpelier had difficulty attracting descendants to its programs in the ensuing years. In the winter of 2014–2015, Montpelier finally gained traction on a possible descendant expedition with the help of a descendant who had previously been involved with excavations and events at Montpelier and has a large network of contacts within the larger descendant communities. She was able to connect with another family who had recently discovered each other through DNA testing and encouraged them to contact Montpelier about participating in an expedition. This family is composed of descendants from another contemporaneous plantation located in Orange County. Through this contact, Montpelier's Archaeology Department was able to put together a descendant expedition program held in April 2015.

Montpelier also reached out to its network of local and national descendant groups to offer the program to descendants of enslaved people across the United States. By the start of the expedition a total of thirteen people had registered, eleven of whom were descendants of enslaved people, plantation owners, or both. Unlike many community-oriented projects, and much traditional anthropological research, with locally rooted stakeholders, this expedition wound up bringing in nonlocal descendants, many of whom had never been to Montpelier, for a descendant project. Instead of capitalizing on a preexisting attachment and investment to a place, this expedition attempted to create that attachment through archaeology. The descendant expedition featured special lectures by staff members who had conducted research on sites at Montpelier where enslaved people had lived and worked as well as a tour of the 1910 Montpelier Train Depot exhibit on segregation. These additional lectures and tour aimed to provide the descendants with a clearer idea of the research being undertaken on the enslaved community at Montpelier and to drive discussions on the way slavery and its aftermath are currently interpreted.

As soon as the descendants arrived in the field, the Montpelier archaeologists noticed a different dynamic both within the expedition group and between the expedition members and archaeology staff than in traditional non-descendant expeditions. Like most participants, the descendants brought with them a preexisting interest in history and archaeology; however, they also possessed a strong personal connection to, and investment in, the history at Montpelier. Most of the descendants were less interested in the particular methodologies of digging than in the stories of the artifacts they were finding and how the results are used to interpret the past. Lunch breaks frequently went long while participants used the opportunity of being together with relatives to share their knowledge of their families' genealogy. From these conversations it was abundantly clear that the participants had their own sets of research questions that they wanted to investigate, and their questions might not align with the questions archaeologists were asking.

For descendants, the experience of doing the archaeology—working in the same ground and touching the same objects their ancestors had held nearly two hundred years ago—had a powerful effect. One expedition member commented, "Doing this is more real to me than what you hear about and what you talk about." Some participants mentioned the doubts that family members had expressed about their participation, asking why they wanted to go back and work again in the fields in which their ancestors had been forced to work. For the participants who faced these questions, working in the same soil as their enslaved ancestors intensified their experience, making it an act of love. This connection that descendants made through literally touching their ancestor's belongings made this a spiritual, as well as learning, experience. Despite this, participants occasionally joked about the staff "cracking the whip" when it was time to resume work, which discomfited members of the all-white staff (one of Montpelier's continuing struggles is the lack of African American staff in archaeology and other departments). Comments such as this, albeit joking, drew attention to the continuing parallels of white dominance at the site. White archaeologists primarily controlled the discussion of enslaved African American history, a continued control over, and colonization of, African American (as well as Indigenous) history that has been an increasing critique of the discipline (see McSweeney, this volume; cf. Atalay 2006; Deloria 1969; LaRoche and Blakey 1997; Nicholas and Hollowell 2007). History is still largely in white hands, although African American scholars, like their Native American counterparts, are becoming increasingly more prominent in the field. The staff members involved in the expedition were conscious of this power imbalance and strove to maximize the opportunity to rectify it by better understanding how the descendants viewed and experienced the site and carrying that perspective forward in the site's interpretation.

Communing with the ancestors and connecting their stories to the work the descendants were doing at the site became a central component of the expedition. As another descendant observed, "It's been exciting to see that we're all involved in making certain that we have our own footprint in the same place [that] our ancestors had their footprint." Not only are the descendants helping to uncover the history of their ancestors, they are also becoming part of that history through the process of uncovering it. Making their own footprints alongside those of their ancestors also included reclaiming the history that they learned about in the tours, lectures, and fieldwork. One of the most memorable examples of this reclamation features the story of Granny Milly. Very shortly after learning about Granny Milly, several descendants began affectionately addressing the eldest expedition member, an eighty-two-year-old woman, as Granny Milly. Incorporating Granny Milly's story into their experience at Montpelier accentuated the ancestral connection many of the descendants felt and also formed deeper bonds between them. Finding artifacts and working closely with other descendants encouraged the participants to share memories, stories, and other pieces of history they knew about their enslaved ancestors.

On the final day of the expedition, all participants took part in a roundtable with the entire archaeology staff and representatives from the curatorial and interpretation departments. The discussion questions ranged from how Montpelier can encourage more African American involvement in its archaeology programs to what additional research topics archaeologists should pursue to what stories and interpretation methods Montpelier should use in the reconstructed South Yard buildings. Another large component of the discussion addressed how Montpelier can draw more African American visitors and become a better partner with African American communities. Although the archaeology staff hoped to focus attention specifically on archaeology to see how their methodologies and results were perceived, the discussions quickly homed in on interpretation and outreach more broadly. Many of the descendants were concerned with contextualizing slavery at Montpelier, humanizing the enslaved community, and generally expanding the museum's approach to interpreting areas where enslaved people lived and worked by incorporating new interpretive techniques.

The roundtable proved to be a valuable opportunity to discuss the direction of interpretation at Montpelier and to build on the feedback previously offered by descendants. Overall, the descendants had very ambitious ideas for South Yard's interpretation, and several participants who live locally have since joined the advisory committee for the new exhibits, bringing their knowledge of archaeology and experience on the property to the interpretive conversations. As John W. Franklin, the senior manager of the Smithsonian National Museum of African American History and Culture (NMAAHC), observed, "African Americans have avoided these institutions because our story was absent. It's very important to engage the communities who were enslaved in the process" of archaeology and exhibit development (James Madison's Montpelier 2015). In discussing the possibilities for increased outreach to African Americans, the expedition members stressed that in order to be interested in visiting, African Americans need to be able to see themselves as historically vital members of the plantation. Slavery and sites of enslavement are uncomfortable and painful topics for many African Americans, so these sites must strive to challenge the demeaning portrayals of their ancestors and instead replace them with authentic portrayals of enslaved people as members of a vibrant, skilled, and intellectual community. Another important change participants suggested was having people of color be more visible at Montpelier to make the museum a more inclusive and welcoming environment for the African American community both locally and nationally.

The day after the official conclusion of the descendant expedition, Montpelier hosted a groundbreaking ceremony for the South Yard reconstruction project. Nearly all of the expedition members attended the ceremony, in addition to hundreds of members of the public, both casual visitors and interested members of the descendant communities. The groundbreaking ceremony featured hymns by the River Bank Choir of nearby Culpeper, Virginia; speeches by Montpelier descendant and board director Margaret H. Jordan and NMAAHC's John W. Franklin; and a libation ceremony by Reverend Youtha Hardman-Cromwell, who had previously conducted a libation ceremony at Montpelier's Slave Cemetery in 2007. The libation ceremony had been requested by the OCAAHS as a traditional ritual African offering and blessing for the South Yard and struck a spiritual chord in the community. Both before and after the official ceremony, archaeologists were stationed around the open excavation areas to explain the ongoing archaeological work and answer questions about the project. Following the groundbreaking, visitors adjourned to the visitor center for a reception.

Five months after the April expedition, two of the participants returned with another descendant, who had been previously involved in interpretation and events at the museum, for another ceremony to place a symbolic quartz crystal in the foundation of the first reconstructed duplex in the South Yard. The original crystal had been found during the duplex's excavation in 2011 among the rubble of the collapsed northwest pier of the building. The crystal had likely been placed in the pier during the building's construction to ward off bad omens and spirits, a practice common in many African American spiritual traditions (Reeves 2014). Ritual actions and objects, such as this crystal, had been frequently discussed during the descendant expedition, and participants recalled learning certain habitual behaviors as children, such as throwing salt into the corners of their homes, which might have evolved from similar practices.

Both the descendants and archaeologists felt strongly that a crystal should be placed in the same area of the foundation in the reconstruction, so the Archaeology Department located a crystal of approximately the same size, shape, color, and clarity to place in the reconstruction. The original was then kept for possible display in the duplex. Although on a much smaller scale than the South Yard groundbreaking, the ceremony to place the quartz crystal in the foundation of the first reconstructed duplex in the South Yard was also advertised to the public, especially local African American communities and former expedition members. For those who were interested in the ceremony but could not attend, the event was streamed live. During the ceremony, Dr. Reeves made a brief speech about how the original crystal was found and what it represents before the three descendants together held the symbolic crystal and placed it into a specially designed pocket in the reconstructed pier. The involvement of descendants in these ceremonies has helped enhance their connection to their ancestors as well as honor the memory and beliefs of the enslaved individuals. The partnerships that Montpelier has formed with the descendant community have emerged as a powerful way to give back.

Conclusion: Making More Footprints

Giving back to the community means much more than just including descendants and other stakeholders in excavations or having them visit an archaeological site. Giving back means making the descendant community part of the larger whole—the research questions, the research process, the interpretation of results, and the final dissemination (whether publication, interpretation, or reconstruction of a site). Just as we as archaeologists want to be accurate and authentic to the people and groups we study, we need to be genuine to the public constituents we try to engage in our research. This also means recognizing the multi-vocality of these constituents; there is no one descendant community—as the expedition participants were quick to point out, there are many communities. We are, after all, studying human beings who have lineal and cultural descendants, community members, and larger constituencies who are interested in engaging with their past. The process of giving back means being collaborative with these constituent groups in three main areas: connecting with people, engaging them in the process of discovery, and incorporating them into the final outcomes.

As discussed, Montpelier has made strides (in some areas baby steps and in others stronger strides) in including the voices of descendants. One of the most effective ways we have found to help foster connections with descendants was through a lead contact person. Having this person rally individuals to come out for our programs was instrumental in making them happen. We have consistently found that trying to make contacts with individuals to come out for a week of excavations, even if we know the individual, is difficult at best. Such longer commitments of time often need a group of individuals to come out together, especially when they have no idea what an archaeological excavation is all about. In many cases, having one individual who might have a preexisting interest in archaeology visit the site and then relate his or her testimony to other individuals is a means to attract others to participate.

Sites of enslavement are undoubtedly of historical importance, but as has been noted elsewhere (see Singleton 1997) some communities would prefer a focus on more recent events and accomplishments. We faced a silent resistance to participation with just the idea of digging in the soil. Many participants recounted with humor that their first response to our invitation to come to a former plantation to dig was, "Didn't our ancestors already do this?" While it was presented in a light-hearted manner, the underlying message was that we needed to work a little harder to convince some of the saliency of our project. Once they arrived, the participants continually recounted the spiritual connection they felt with finding artifacts and connecting with the soil and space of their ancestors. As such, the spiritual discovery was just as much a part of the experience as handling the artifacts in the ground.

While working with descendants on site we noticed they were often highly engaged in the research discussions. Participants brought up ways they viewed the objects in ways the staff and many other archaeologists researching enslaved communities had never considered, such as seeing tools and other large equipment as weapons of resistance. Moments like these pointed out the very different ways people in the communities being studied saw the same objects, and how actually including them in the discussion can improve how archeologists view the archaeological record. We formalized this research engagement by explicitly presenting these discussions as a desired outcome and by scheduling dedicated times for them to occur. Many conversations still took place spontaneously through the course of the weeklong expedition, but specifying this as a project goal at the beginning of the week encouraged many conversations leading up to and following the scheduled times, with rich discussions during the designated meetings.

Follow-up after the event was one area where we found momentum was hard to maintain. We sent surveys for participants to fill out and had no success in response. Where we did have success was inviting participants to particular events after the April program. Everyone we invited to the crystal placement ceremony was invested enough to come back and participate. Later that same year, we invited several participants to take part in a review of a new exhibit design, and they were very glad to spend an entire day reviewing the information and themes we aimed to present in the cellar spaces and South Yard at Montpelier. The following year, the Archaeology Department attempted to capitalize on the success of the 2015 expedition and began contacting individuals about a second descendant expedition. Plans never got off the ground, however, partly because of difficulties in gathering enough interested participants, and the idea was sidelined. In lieu of the expedition, we were able to organize a well-attended weekend descendant reunion, and some attendees did stay for excavations. This suggested that descendant programs with excavation at their core may not be the most effective way to involve the descendant communities, despite their continued interest in archaeology at the museum. As with other Indigenous and descendant groups around the world, it is important to recognize the demands that African American communities are facing and to understand that archaeology may not be a priority in the face of all of the other issues with which their communities are grappling.

In the end, continued involvement and giving back to the community needs careful planning and definition of outcomes. Turning a successful

one-off event into a sustained movement takes considerable effort, especially to keep that one event, however successful or well-intentioned,
from appearing too much like tokenism. Projects cannot plan for success
simply by inviting participants to take part in the archaeological process;
there need to be carefully defined outcomes and strategies used in gaining
the trust of the community. This is particularly relevant when it comes to
disenfranchised groups and exploring sites of their oppression. By having
successful engagement, we can ask questions of how we can begin to heal
from painful events in the past and demonstrate how archaeology can
be cathartic. By asking meaningful questions of the community directly,
we have a chance to successfully give back rather than continue to take
from the community constituents. By giving back we gain trust, heal past
wrongs, and make the past something that all can claim.

Chapter 4 References and Recommended Reading

Atalay, Sonya. 2006. "Indigenous Archaeology as Decolonizing Practice."
    American Indian Quarterly 30 (3/4): 280–310.
Atalay, Sonya. 2012. *Community Based Archaeology: Research with, by,
    and for Indigenous and Local Communities.* Berkeley: University of
    California Press.
Colwell-Chanthaphonh, Chip, and T. J. Ferguson, eds. 2008. *Collaboration in
    Archaeological Practice: Engaging Descendant Communities.* Lanham,
    MD: AltaMira Press.
Deloria Jr., Vine. 1988 [1969]. *Custer Died for Your Sins: An Indian Manifesto.*
    Rev. ed. Norman: University of Oklahoma Press.
Derry, Linda, and Maureen Malloy, eds. 2003. *Archaeologists and Local
    Communities: Partners in Exploring the Past.* Washington DC: Society
    for American Archaeology.
Farnsworth, Paul. 1993. "'What Is the Use of Plantation Archaeology?' No
    Use at All, If No One Else Is Listening!" *Historical Archaeology* 27 (1):
    114–116.
Greer, Matthew C. 2014. Did Money Matter? Interpreting the Effect of
    Displayed Wealth on Social Relations within an Enslaved Community.
    Master's thesis, University of Southern Mississippi, Hattiesburg.
James Madison's Montpelier. 2015. "James Madison's Montpelier Breaks
    Ground in South Yard Enslaved Community Site." YouTube
    video, 03:14. Posted June 2015. https://www.youtube.com/
    watch?v=ysde9mccZVw.

La Roche, Cheryl, and Michael L. Blakey. 1997. "Seizing Intellectual Power: The Dialogue at the New York African Burial Ground." *Historical Archaeology* 31 (3): 84–106.

Little, Barbara J., and Paul A. Shackel, eds. 2007. *Archaeology as a Tool of Civic Engagement.* Lanham, MD: AltaMira Press.

Mack, Mark E., and Michael L. Blakey. 2004. "The New York African Burial Ground Project: Past Biases, Current Dilemmas, and Future Research Opportunities." *Historical Archaeology* 38 (1): 10–17.

McDavid, Carol. 1997. "Descendants, Decisions, and Power: The Public Interpretation of the Archaeology of the Levi Jordan Plantation." *Historical Archaeology* 31 (3): 114–131.

McDavid, Carol, and Terry P. Brock. 2015. "The Differing Forms of Public Archaeology: Where We Have Been, Where We Are Now, and Thoughts for the Future." In *Ethics and Archaeological Praxis*, edited by Cristóbal Gnecco and Dorothy Lippert. New York: Springer.

McGimsey III, Charles R. 1972. *Public Archaeology.* New York: Seminar Press.

Nassaney, Michael S. 2012a. "Decolonizing Archaeological Theory at Fort St. Joseph, an Eighteenth-Century Multi-Ethnic Community in the Western Great Lakes Region." *Mid-Continental Journal of Archaeology* 37 (1): 5–23.

Nassaney, Michael S. 2012b. "Enhancing Public Archaeology through Community Service Learning." In *The Oxford Handbook of Public Archaeology*, edited by Robin Skeates, Carol McDavid, and John Carman, 414–442. New York: Oxford University Press.

Nassaney, Michael S., and Mary Ann Levine, eds. 2009. *Archaeology and Community Service Learning.* Gainesville: University Press of Florida.

Nicholas, George, and Julie Hollowell. 2007. "Ethical Challenges to a Postcolonial Archaeology: The Legacy of Scientific Colonialism." In *Archaeology and Capitalism: From Ethics to Politics*, edited by Yannis Hamilakis and Philip Duke, 59–82. Walnut Creek, CA: Left Coast Press.

Potter, Parker. B. 1991. "What Is the Use of Plantation Archaeology?" *Historical Archaeology* 25 (3): 94–107.

Reeves, Matthew B. 2004. "Asking the 'Right' Questions: Archaeologists and Descendant Communities." In *Places in Mind: Public Archaeology as Applied Anthropology*, edited by Paul A. Shackel and Erve J. Chambers. New York: Routledge.

———. 2014. "Mundane or Spiritual? The Interpretation of Glass Bottle Containers found on Two Sites of the African Diaspora." In *Materialities of Ritual in the Black Atlantic,* edited by Akinwumi Ogundiran and Paula Sanders, 176–197. Bloomington: Indiana University Press.

———. 2015a. "Sleeping with the 'Enemy': Metal Detecting Hobbyists and Archaeologists." *Advances in Archaeological Practice* 3 (3): 263–274.

———. 2015b. "Scalar Analysis of Early Nineteenth-Century Household Assemblages: Focus on Communities of the African Atlantic." In *Beyond the Walls,* edited by Kevin R. Fogle, James A. Nyman, and Mary C. Beaudry. Gainesville: University Press of Florida.

Reeves, Matthew B., and Matthew Greer. 2012. "Within View of the Mansion: Comparing and Contrasting Two Early Nineteenth-Century Slave Households at James Madison's Montpelier." *Journal of Middle Atlantic Archaeology* 28:1–13.

Silliman, Stephen W., ed. 2008. *Collaborating at the Trowel's Edge: Teaching and Learning in Indigenous Archaeology.* Tucson: University of Arizona Press.

Singleton, Theresa. A. 1995. "The Archaeology of Slavery in North America." *Annual Review of Anthropology* 24:119–140.

———. 1997. "Facing the Challenges of a Public African-American Archaeology." *Historical Archaeology* 31 (3): 146–152.

Stahlgren, Lori C. 2010. "Negotiating History, Slavery, and the Present: Archaeology at Farmington Plantation." In *Archaeologists as Activists: Can Archaeologists Change the World?* edited by Jay M. Stottman. Tuscaloosa: University of Alabama Press.

Schneider, Stacy, and Matthew Reeves. 2010. "The Gilmore Story—Family History." In *Historical, Archaeological and Architectural Research at the Gilmore Cabin,* edited by Matthew Reeves. Technical Report. Montpelier Station, VA: The Montpelier Foundation.

Wilkie, Laurie A. 2004. "Considering the Future of African American Archaeology." *Historical Archaeology* 38 (1): 109–123.

Zimmerman, Larry J. 1998. "When Data Become People: Archaeological Ethics, Reburial, and the Past as Public Heritage." *International Journal of Cultural Property* 7 (1): 69–86.

PART 2

Repatriating Knowledge

5

Collaborative Reciprocity Revisited

Giving Back through the Community-Partnered Iñupiaq
Music Heritage Repatriation Project

CHIE SAKAKIBARA

"PROMISE US THAT YOU are not going to disappear." Sitting down across the small wooden kitchen table from me, Martha Aiken, then in her late seventies, said so. It was in late November of 2004, on my very first day in the Arctic. I was a third-year doctoral student in geography at the University of Oklahoma. The long darkness of the arctic winter had already set in, and the temperature was well below zero Fahrenheit outside. That afternoon I had flown into Barrow, Alaska, the northernmost town of the United States, in order to introduce myself and my fieldwork proposal to the Iñupiaq community. When I landed on the snow-covered tundra, Lollie Hopson (a former community liaison for the Barrow Arctic Science Consortium, who had just retired) kindly gave me a ride to Martha's house near the small village airport. I later learned that Martha was revered by the community within and beyond Barrow as one of the wisest elders on the Arctic Slope, thus I needed her blessing to start working in the community. As she conversed with Lollie in Iñupiaq, Martha glanced at me a few times. Following Lollie's departure, she nudged me to sit down. As a young graduate student, I did not hesitate to introduce myself and my research agenda with vim and vigor. "So, you want to interview us," responded Martha calmly, sipping tea. "Yes, I would love to." My eager statement was followed by a long silence. I was getting nervous, as it started feeling like I had said something that was completely inappropriate, which may have automatically failed my qualification to be there. Then Martha made her statement: "Promise us that you are not going to disappear." In a calm voice, followed by a pause, she then explained that she had seen many *tanik* (white) scholars coming to Barrow from the lower forty-eight, soliciting help from the villagers without any form of compensation and never returning to the community to report back or to reciprocate the villagers' hospitality. "Wherever them *tanik* went . . . we never see them again. We are so tired of these people. We had too many of them."

As RDK Herman articulates this problem in chapter 1, academic scholarship has a historical and lingering association with the act of "data mining," which is often inalienable from the legacy of colonialism to this day. It was this nature of the "extractive industry" of academia that Martha was afraid of. She had seen too many times when Indigenous knowledge and experiences had been conveniently truncated and plugged into market economies or instantly turned into private property after being detached from their appropriate cultural contexts. Almost always, a plan of benefiting the local community never was part of this enterprise. "It takes a long time to earn your place in this village," she continued. "You will get a degree after talking with us and writing a paper using our stories. What will we get from you in return?" I went silent, feeling awkward and uncomfortable. Then Martha smiled subtly and asked me to swear that I would commit myself to cultivating a long-term relationship with her and her community before beginning work on my dissertation project. I agreed to make the commitment. Now, fourteen years later, I am still in the process of earning my place, and the process of relationship-building in the community has opened many doors to me that would have otherwise stayed closed. Many villagers graciously treat me as an adopted member of the Iñupiaq community and affectionately address me with my Iñupiaq names. When I completed a PhD a few years later, Martha congratulated me and said: "Now it's your time to pay us back." She emphasized that the best way for me to reciprocate with the Barrow community was to be a good teacher. In so doing, I would educate future generations of scholars about the importance of social justice, Indigenous sensibilities, ethics, community benefit, collaboration, and reciprocity so the future scholars "will never disappear." Martha has since passed away, but the wisdom she graciously shared with me manifests itself when I talk about the importance of reciprocity and relationship-building in the classroom at Oberlin College and beyond.

My doctoral dissertation was an ethnographic exploration of cultural adaptation and resilience of the Iñupiaq community with the effects of rapidly advancing climate change on the arctic environment. Iñupiat are the first people of the top of the world and known as the "real" (*piat* or *piaq*) "people" (*iñu*) or the authentic human beings. The term Iñupiat is plural, but it also handles the possessive; the singular and the adjectival form of the word is Iñupiaq. I specifically focused on relations between the Iñupiat and the bowhead whale, through subsistence activities including traditional whaling and various dimensions of expressive culture, especially music-making and storytelling (Sakakibara 2008, 2009, 2010). Through my fieldwork, Barrow became my "adopted" home, and the villagers generously incorporated me into their social and cultural fabric through the web of extended kinship and hospitality. I feel fortunate that I have been able to become part of this community on many different levels, including my collaboration with Columbia University's Center for Ethnomusicology for their community-partnered Iñupiaq music heritage project.

In this chapter, I describe how Aaron Fox—my colleague and principal investigator of the repatriation project—and I have been working together with the Iñupiaq communities of Alaska's North Slope to repatriate a collection of audio recordings of songs, oral narratives, and a related collection of photographs, made in Barrow in October of 1946 by the "music hunter" Laura Boulton (1899–1980). The Columbia collection includes the work of Boulton, who had, from the 1920s through the 1970s, traveled the world to record the work of traditional and tribal peoples. In her time, anthropology and ethnomusicology were frequently motivated by ideas of "salvage" ethnography, prioritizing the recording and documentation of "primitive" cultures before tribal peoples "vanished" through assimilation into dominant national cultures and identities. Boulton—an avid fan of what she considered "ancient" forms of Indigenous musical expression that were fast fading away—felt that it was her mission to record folk music before it perished. She produced numerous commercial releases of her recordings and several films. These materials are currently "owned" by Columbia University and Indiana University, respectively. Although nobody in Barrow today remembers her short visit, Boulton is an example of the scholars who left Barrow with "what they wanted" (songs, in her case) and disappeared.

Up to the end of the twentieth century, the relationships among Native Americans, anthropologists, archaeologists, and museums have been complicated and contested as a consequence of the conflict between two opposing worldviews with respect to the ownership of land, resources, and cultural and intellectual properties. To resolve such conflicts and misunderstandings (particularly those involving human remains, sacred objects, funeral objects, and objects of cultural patrimony that were displayed at museums or sold to collectors), the United States passed the Native American Graves Protection and Repatriation Act (NAGPRA) in 1990. The act requires US federal agencies and institutions to return culturally significant and sensitive items to their respective tribes and peoples. However, NAGPRA does not refer to "intangible" cultural products such as music and oral tradition. The issue of "ownership" over native music, performance, and knowledge had become a hot dispute on a global scale (Brown 2004). A central question is whether the ownership of field recordings and their associated intellectual property rights can be claimed by the non-Indigenous recordists or belong to the Indigenous artists who created them. In countless instances in the past, traditional and Indigenous music has been exploited by cultural outsiders for commercial and scholarly purposes, with very little concern for questions of ownership rights. Since many Indigenous musical traditions are orally transmitted, they simply fall outside the scope of Western copyright law, which depends on material inscription to establish "authorship." Although music and intellectual property rights are intangible, the idea of music repatriation indicates how understanding has grown to recognize the importance of ownership rights of Indigenous peoples, and the contribution of music creation to cultural identity.

The community-partnered Iñupiaq music heritage project aims to demonstrate an innovative model for reconceptualizing both archival practice and the place of archives of cultural resources for social science conducted with Indigenous communities. The ethically and culturally correct "giving back" process has to be based on reciprocity and mutual interest between multiple parties: Indigenous peoples, tribal members, scholars, and archives and museums that house institutional collections. As a premise, the transaction is expected to be complicated, because concepts such as "intellectual property," "property rights," "copyright," and "ownership" have colonial origins that have facilitated the exploitation of Indigenous cultural legacy, something that is inseparable from tribal and human well-being. We see "giving back" as a two-way collaborative effort with the community rather than simply handing over the recordings and reestablishing the "ownership" in a legal and academic way. Specifically, we are working together to (1) better situate the songs and other materials collected by Boulton in the community by recovering detailed contextual information about the materials that were not recorded by Boulton; (2) develop community-wide consensus on the proper disposition and future uses of these materials and related rights; (3) restore community access to the materials; and (4) encourage, support, and enable contemporary and innovative uses of these materials by Iñupiaq artists, educators, cultural activists, and by the community more generally to support Indigenous sociocultural activism. Through collaboration and fusion of diverse perspectives, this project shows that Indigenous communities and individuals can work together in discovering or recovering community resources from institutional collections in a less adversarial and more dialogic and equitable way. With this approach, the repatriation facilitates the true "giving back" to the community, about how such collections should be best managed, used, preserved, promoted, and understood in the light of Indigenous resilience in collaboration. It is our hope to demonstrate the significance of giving back as a form of cultural and social justice based on a sustained relationship between Indigenous and academic communities.

Collaborative Reciprocity

Resilience is the capacity of an individual, entity, or organization to maintain and renew itself when its existence or viability is challenged or threatened. The term "resilience" can be used with many different modifiers, such as ecological resilience, cultural resilience, and psychological resilience. Iñupiaq society exemplifies cultural resilience because the people have successfully survived on the northern rim of the world by retaining and building on their subsistence practices for thousands of years. The notion of "collaborative reciprocity" is crucial for understanding Iñupiaq cultural resilience as reflected in traditional whaling and associated cultural events. Central to the Iñupiaq notion of collaborative reciprocity is the belief that humans and animals physically and spiritually constitute each other—that the souls, thoughts, and behaviors of animals and people interpenetrate in a collaboration of life (Fienup-Riordan 1990). This relationship is fundamental to many Indigenous moral philosophies, a cornerstone for an appropriate way of life (Momaday 1974; Nelson

1980; Basso 1996). For example, many Indigenous groups in the Arctic understand that animals willingly give themselves to hunters in response to receiving respectful treatment as "nonhuman persons" (Nelson 1980; Fienup-Riordan 1990; Brewster 2004).

Furthermore, collaborative reciprocity should be understood as an adaptive strategy that is essential to Arctic life. Adaptation is a key to resilience for the people, a way of renewing and reconsidering their way of life for a hopeful future. Not only does it link human welfare with that of animals, but it affords people a means of expressing their concerns about social and environmental changes, and for coping with and living through such changes. This interrelationship is demonstrated in various ways, most of them publicly visible. In Iñupiaq society, collaborative reciprocity is revealed in the way whale hunting is organized and conducted, in the manner in which food is prepared and consumed, in the use of whale body parts in the built environment, and in the content and performative styles of Iñupiaq music, storytelling, and many other aspects of ceremonial and everyday life.

In the current era, when modernity intersects with socio-environmental uncertainty, it is important to revisit the notion of collaborative reciprocity to further explore the Iñupiaq resilience in a contemporary context. Resilience, as discussed earlier, can be defined as simply the ability to cope with shocks and keep functioning in much the same way (Walker and Salt 2012). In a cultural context, this capacity allows us to retain and, if necessary, strengthen our identity. Rather than being static or unchanging, resilience requires continuously reforming relationships with the environment, nonhuman animals, new people and ideas through the elasticity of culture and worldview. On the Arctic Slope, music plays a vital role in resilience through the exchange and communication among people and between people and environment, integrated into the structures of material and emotional reciprocity. Music serves as an icon of cultural empowerment and sovereignty by helping villagers reconfirm the meaning of relations, collaborations, and reciprocity.

Recent environmental degradation and the consequent disruption of traditional lifeways is linked with critical social problems facing Indigenous populations in the circumpolar Arctic: addiction, suicide, depression, violence, illness, poor access to medical care, and low motivation. These problems threaten the future of the community. At this time of heightened stress and oppression, resilience is linked to the power of cultural solidarity through traditions: hunting, religious worship, language retention efforts, and a variety of manifestations of expressive culture such as arts, music, and dance complemented by heritage education. Such efforts constitute new forms of collaborative reciprocity.

Music in particular has the power to resuscitate cultural and collective memories among Iñupiat—memories that play an important role in the community's responses to environmental uncertainties and their related emotional difficulties. In northern Alaska, music unites people just as the whales do. Following the whaling cycle helped me understand how dance and song are powerful cornerstones for cultural survival. In particular, dance reveals a strong sense of social integration and moral development. As Aaron Fox writes, "Put simply, young people who dance are less likely to die. Because so many do, dancing really matters for community health. Dancing saves lives" (2014, 544). In the Iñupiaq world, songs, drumming, and dances are inseparable from making music, and this integrity enhances the traditional understanding of collaborative reciprocity. Music enables a form of collaboration with human and non-human beings, as well as the reciprocity between different age groups, genders, and other communities in the circumpolar region.

The Music Hunter

In 1946, the end of World War II was already pointing to a new sustained military tension that would become the Cold War. In the Alaska Territory, exploration of the Naval Petroleum Reserve Number 4 began near Barrow, and construction of the Naval Arctic Research Laboratory (NARL) began near Nuvuk, just north of Barrow. With America's insatiable desire for natural resources and its intensifying conflict with the Soviet Union, Alaska was suddenly and strategically drawn into world history. In October of the same year, the music collector Laura Boulton landed in Barrow, accompanied by the young photographer John Klebe. She had become intrigued with the landscapes and the people of the North during a prior trip to the Canadian Arctic in 1943, in the course of producing wartime films for the Canadian government, and she must have had similar expectations about this trip to northern Alaska. During the one-week visit, Boulton recorded 115 Iñupiaq songs and oral narratives on aluminum discs, to which she added rudimentary notes. She later published an account on her trip to Barrow as part of her autobiography, *The Music Hunter* (1969), and released several songs from this expedition on her 1955 Folkways album *The Eskimos of Hudson Bay and Alaska* (Folkways FW04444). This recording featured six songs recorded by Boulton in Barrow in 1946, as well as thirteen tracks recorded on an earlier trip to the Canadian Arctic, with liner notes by Boulton and a print of the only known photo of all of the performers taken during her Barrow expedition. The record has been commercially available ever since, most recently as a download for purchase on the Smithsonian Institution's "Global Sound" website, as well as through Apple's iTunes platform. However, neither the original performers nor their descendants were ever notified of these commercial releases of their community's music.

In the early 1960s, Boulton sold most of her collection of field recordings from all over the world to the library of New York's Columbia University, including her Barrow recordings. But the collection was poorly documented, and the Iñupiaq recordings appear to have rarely been accessed in the intervening years. In other words, the 1946 songs had been sitting on a shelf at Columbia University, which has technically held the publication rights to these recordings as well, for over six decades.[1]

My involvement in the repatriation of the Boulton materials from Barrow began over a decade ago, when I was a graduate student. To trace the transformations of traditional Iñupiaq music over time and put it in a perspective of arctic environmental history, I wanted to listen to historical recordings made in northern Alaska—the older the better. This search eventually connected me with Aaron Fox, then the new director of the Center for Ethnomusicology and curator of the Laura Boulton Collection at Columbia University. Aaron was planning a large-scale effort to repatriate the center's entire inventory of Native American recordings. He had been engaged with the Navajo recordings made at the Century of Progress Exhibition in Chicago in 1935 and had worked closely with the descendants of the Navajo singer Pablo Wellito. Through his effort, the center was awarded the Academic Quality Fund grant in 2003. This award was distributed by the provost's office at Columbia for innovative development of educational resources with a goal of making sense of the Boulton archive and beginning a process of systematic repatriation. When Aaron received my inquiry, he was making plans to spend these funds completing the digitizing process, designing another attempt to systematically describe the collection, and identifying prospective repatriation projects. My brief email inquiry about the collection had Aaron generating a single-spaced, three-page memo detailing the nature of the Iñupiaq music collection housed at the center and its broader agenda to repatriate its Native American and Indigenous holdings. The Iñupiaq songs and oral narratives from Barrow made up a small part of this larger collection. Aaron's letter went on to say that, since the beginning of his directorship in 2003, the Center for Ethnomusicology had begun working on a project to "repatriate" the center's collections "to the descendants and communities from which this music was, in a frank word"—he emphasized, and, referring specifically to the aggregation and sale of intellectual property rights by Boulton—"stolen."

The idea of giving back the historical music recordings to my adopted home was thrilling beyond words. Aaron's words conveyed the urgency of the situation. The first step was to find out the lineages of the singers. Boulton's notes had the following names/spellings: Joe Sikvayunak, Guy Amiyurok, Alfred Koonaloak, Leo Kaleak, Otis Ahkivigak, Jonas Oyoowak, Mary Ahvik, Harold Kagak, and Eddie Orson. Through my earlier fieldwork, I had learned that almost all songs in the Iñupiaq tradition are part of the whaling cycle. And the Iñupiat respect for elders and their interest in ancestry also convinced me that finding descendants of the 1946 singers was feasible. With the scrap paper on which I had hastily written down these names, I went to the house of my adopted parents—Jeslie Kaleak, Sr. and his wife, Julia—to dine with them. When I brought up the names that I had copied on the paper, I saw an awkward expression on Jeslie's face. Then he opened his mouth: "What do you want to do with all those old names? Leo Kaleak is my father." My jaws dropped open. "Your father's songs are in New York City," I responded to Jeslie, my adopted father. At the same time, I realized that, as an adopted daughter of Jeslie and Julia, I was about to deal with my own ancestor's songs. Jeslie and Julia, and many other friends and family members, helped me connect to other offspring of the recorded singers. As a result, one person led me to another, and the web of friendship, excitement, and goodwill developed like a snowball rolling down a very steep hill. I knocked on doors of many houses, showed up at the Senior Center, Heritage Center, fire station, hospital, and called and visited many North Slope Borough offices to draw family trees and connections. Each time, many people were delighted to hear the news that their ancestors' songs were in New York, and better yet, they were coming home to Barrow.

As I identified descendants and other interested villagers, I emailed their names and contact information from Barrow to Aaron in New York. Aaron, in turn, sent CDs of the recordings to all who requested them. I later heard that Aaron had originally anticipated that the process would be a slow one that would develop into something only in the distant future. On the contrary, as soon as the people of Barrow became aware of the recordings, they took enthusiastic action themselves. Aaron recalls the level of surprise he had then: overnight, his email inbox was colonized by messages from an arctic village that he had never dreamed of visiting.

Bringing Songs Home: Photographs, Music, and Cultural Memories

Aaron and I joined up in Barrow the evening before Thanksgiving in 2007. This trip marked the very first of the many to follow, which was greatly facilitated by National Science Foundation funding we received in 2009. We conducted many extensive interviews with descendants of the performers on the recordings, and with other Iñupiat who love dance and music. Our hope was to begin a conversation about a formal return of Columbia's "ownership" rights in the recordings to the community and the people. With "community-partnered repatriation" in mind, we wanted to involve descendants of the performers Boulton had recorded and their contemporary communities—various stakeholders such as Arctic Slope Regional Corporation (ASRC), North Slope Borough (NSB), Iñupiat History, Language and Culture Commission (IHLCC), Iñupiat Community of the Arctic Slope (ICAS), and the Native Village of Barrow (NVB)—in deciding how the recordings should be returned, how and to whom the rights should be assigned, where recordings should be deposited, and how they should be preserved for the future. We also hoped to introduce people in Barrow more deeply to the project and the recordings, identify more descendants of the original singers, develop better genealogies for the singers, and begin amplifying the supporting notes and materials prepared by Boulton in the 1950s and 1960s by interviewing local elders and experts.

"Thank you for bringing back the songs to us." At the beginning of our collaboration, one of the most unforgettable memories was when three boys approached us and thanked us for what we were trying to accomplish with the community. During our initial visit, we kept up a hectic pace in Barrow. We made presentations on our project for descendants, young people, and community leaders and elders at the Hopson Middle School, at Barrow High School, at the Heritage Center, and at the Barrow Arctic Science Consortium's Outreach Program, with Iñupiaq translation help from Priscilla Sage. We also appeared on radio station KBRW so that we could reach out to the community, and across the North Slope, with news of the repatriation project and an invitation to participate. We met with dozens of descendants, elders, bilingual educators, and community leaders. We recorded a rehearsal of the Taġiuġmiut Dancers, and actively helped serving bowhead whale meat, muktuk (whale blubber), and other types of Native food in the Thanksgiving feast at the Presbyterian Church.

By the end of our first trip, we realized that the project had grown bigger than we had imagined possible. We saw how important these recordings were to many descendants, to elders, and to the educators and activists we spoke with, and especially how important they were to young people. We even met teenagers with songs from the Boulton recordings on their iPods, mixed in with hip-hop and pop songs. It was as if these recordings, long forgotten on a shelf in an archive, had come back to life in just the few years since they started their journey home to Barrow.

A few months following our first trip together, I received another full page email from Aaron, who was in Bloomington, Indiana. Aaron had discovered a collection of approximately 120 photographs gathered at the time by Boulton, which now belong to the Indiana University Archive of Traditional Music, where Boulton's correspondence and other materials, left to the archive after her death, are stored. While most of the photos were probably taken by John Klebe, some of the photographs, which show Barrow in the spring (Boulton visited in October) and are in a decidedly different style from the others, may have been taken by Marvin Peter, a noted Iñupiaq photographer of the time, and had somehow been acquired by Boulton. As interested as the people were in the recordings of the drummers, we found that they were even more captivated by the photos of their relatives and fellow Iñupiat, most of them now departed. Sometimes, a viewer would gaze on and study a single image for close to an hour at a time. The late Martha Aiken's hands stopped flipping the photos when she saw a photo of two boys standing in front of a storage building. The older boy holds a long baleen in his hand and the younger boy in a fur parka smiles at the camera. She looked lovingly and longingly at the picture, and then she spoke softly through her tears. "That's my Robert," she said, referring to her husband Robert Aiken, who had preceded her in death. Martha joined Robert in heaven in 2009, at the age of eighty-three. She and the late Warren Matumeak were our principal collaborators, and they generously shared their time, knowledge, and memories with us as they listened to the recordings and looked through the photos. Martha was losing her eyesight toward the end of her life, but with the assistance of Percy, her son, she always remained strong. Having known Martha for nearly five years, it was my first time to see tears in her eyes. Witnessing such a moment was an empowering and transformative experience for me. Through the effort of giving back, I felt that our relationship with the community has become stronger and more intimate, and that we were becoming more Iñupiat (real human beings) ourselves.

Taġiuġmiut Dancers

While dance has been an integral component of the whaling cycle since time immemorial, the tradition has been strongly reinforced with the emergence of contemporary struggles and a new sense of Iñupiaq identity. The active keepers of the musical heritage at Boulton's time were also *umialik* (whaling captains) and community leaders. For example, Guy Okakok (Amiyurok) served as the president of Iñupiat Paitot (meaning People's Heritage), the organization that was established in 1961 to claim Indigenous rights to the land, natural resources, and hunting wildlife. Cultural survival, subsistence, and music are inseparable in Barrow and other whaling communities in northern Alaska. In this sense, and contrary to the assumptions of Boulton and many anthropologists in the mid-twentieth century, Iñupiaq music had never perished or faded away, but remained the spine of communal well-being. It has indeed grown stronger and more central than ever before as an outward-facing symbol of collective identity, as has been the case for Alaska Native music and dance more generally. The mid-twentieth century was an era during which the Iñupiaq society experienced the brutal force of modernization, including continuous missionization and implementation of the boarding school system. Traditional dance and music performance had been suppressed continuously since the early twentieth century, as they were associated with shamanism and paganism. Disease, starvation, and misguided efforts to transform the people from subsistent hunters to reindeer herders and sedentary settlers also negatively influenced the community with deep trauma. The fear of losing the robust heritage motivated community leaders like Joe Sikvayugak to reinstate the dancing tradition. Other community leaders (also whaling captains) joined Joe's lead, and this effort culminated in successful attempts toward Iñupiaq sovereignty and civil rights in the 1960s and 1970s (Fox 2014).

After making a few trips together to Barrow, Aaron and I often talked about how Bolton's fear about the disappearance of Indigenous music and traditions was off the mark. Rather, drummers and singers that she met during her short trip foresaw the renaissance in Iñupiaq music, which would become intertwined with the Alaska Native sovereignty movement as an organized and outward-facing political expression of Iñupiaq identity. Being bilingual, Joe Sikvayugak devoted to the traditional music, served as the community liaison for Boulton. He also called out to other performers to set up drumming and recording sessions for Boulton. Sikvayugak, as the leader of the drum orchestra, must have seen Boulton as a colleague instead of a superior being from the south, and intended to collaborate with her to promote his active agenda by helping her collect traditional music.[2] In this context, the photographer Marvin Peter was another visionary who eagerly documented Iñupiaq life with an Iñupiaq perspective to promote visual sovereignty[3] at the time (Wooley et al. 1992). His photographs passed down to Boulton clearly show the connection to community, connection to land, and a vision of continuance, and nicely complement the activism pursued by Sikvayugak through music-making.

At the inception of our Barrow repatriation, our ultimate goal was to reintroduce the traditional songs to the community they came from. We hoped but never fully expected that the music might then be reincorporated back into the whaling cycle immediately. In reality, however, the process was apparently organic—the reenactment and revitalization of the historical performance had taken place even before we knew it. In fact, the inspiration for forming a new dance group came to Vernon Elavgak, grandson of Joe Sikvayugak, when he listened to the historical recording of his grandfather for the first time on Boulton's recordings. Vernon said: "When we listened to the recordings of our *aapa* [grandfather] singing in 1946, we thought it was cool. Great songs. . . . It was almost too scary to hear them because old music is so important and precious to us. We wanted to make our own dance group to put a new life into these tunes." The new dance group was named Taġiuġmiut (People of the Sea), and was founded on January 4, 2007, by three Iñupiaq youths: Vernon, his wife Isabell, and Riley Sikvayugak, Vernon's brother.

The young performers had diligently listened to, transcribed, and learned the 1946 songs and had begun to develop and practice motion dances put to those songs. In 2007, Taġiuġmiut won first place in the Eskimo Dance category at the World Eskimo-Indian Olympics (WEIO) in Fairbanks, and was invited to perform at the 2008 Gathering of Nations intertribal pow-wow in Albuquerque, New Mexico. The group has since grown in size, skill, and repertoire and connected Barrow with the rest of the world. Various events in the Iñupiaq calendar are inevitably connected to whaling, and a musical celebration and community dance takes place after each successful capture of a whale, sponsored by the successful crew. While they are creative and innovative in their exploration of contemporary Iñupiaq music, their musical foundation has its roots in the traditional drum dance and tunes performed by their ancestors, and their performances exude respect for this history.

The village of Barrow currently has six dance groups—Barrow Dancers, Nuvugmiut, Suurimaaŋitchuat, Ovluaq Dancers, Iñua Aġġirit, and Taġiuġmiut—all of which are active keepers of Iñupiaq traditions. As one of the newest of the groups, and almost certainly the one with the youngest average age of its members, Taġiuġmiut currently enrolls thirty performers in addition to thirteen young apprentices, and the number is growing. At the moment, the youngest member is two years old, and the oldest is in his late forties, which makes the group exceptionally young in the Iñupiaq musical tradition in which most dance groups are formed by and around elder dancers and musicians.

The drums Taġiuġmiut use specifically have whale-liver or stomach membranes, which was also the case for the drums played by their ancestors on the 1946 recordings. The performers place drums at the center of their creative force. In this sense, Iñupiaq music is drum music, and the drum is cared for, respected, and ritually nourished with fresh water in between songs, just like the whale who gave the people the drum along with sustenance.

Taġiuġmiut's regalia was designed and sewn by the group's female members. Isabell Elavgak, an active role model for the younger women, said, "The color blue represents the Arctic Ocean, and the white symbolizes the sea ice." Images of vital marine mammals were cut out and sewn on the trims across the fabric: the bowhead whale, polar bear, seal, and walrus. Behind male drummers sit female singers to support them in chorus. Dancers stand in front of them. The movements and choreography of the hands, arms, head, and legs characterize their performance, evocative of and inspired by animal behavior. The hands are covered by gloves to retain dancing spirits in their bodies.

"The 1946 songs were too fast for us," many elders pointed out as they listened to the historical songs. Although no one can ascertain the cause of this sped-up quality, this difference in speed might have been caused by the characteristics of the recording technology in the 1940s. Boulton used a Fairchild aluminum disc recorder that allowed her to record only a few minutes at a time. As a result, the singers might have been asked to sing faster to save disc space, or to fit a single song onto a single disc. More likely, the recordings were sped up either by a miscalibration of electricity in the original recording (since it was a diesel generator, entirely possible) or in a subsequent transfer.

Members of Taġiuġmiut, however, decided to put all their energy into these songs to keep up with the recording's speed. Audiences applauded as they generated a passionate response from their fellow villagers, including traditionalists and elders. In this respect, the songs are not only reenacted, but are also imbued with a new set of life and power.

Conclusion: Insights

In 1946, Boulton took songs and stories away from Barrow and disappeared. These songs and stories were steeped with memories, emotions, and stories of Iñupiaq lives, and they eventually found their way home all the way from Manhattan. The recent revitalization of Iñupiaq music and dance tradition through the incorporation of the 1946 music confirms the ability of Sikvayugak to see a long way ahead into the future of his community. By generously sharing his time, expertise, and music with Boulton, he must have seen the value of reciprocal benefits for his community despite the commercially oriented discourse that Boulton maintained till the end of her life. In arctic Alaska, traditionally, music served as a vehicle to connect people and whales. At this time of unpredictable socio-environmental transformation, music is metaphorically and actually bringing the community together—in terms of cultural, linguistic, and musical traditions, environment, human-human relation, and human-animal interaction. This adversity is strengthening the Iñupiaq cultural foundations through the repetitious reinstatement of resilience in a form of collaborative reciprocity. As several elders have shared with me, the spirits of the songs are the souls of the whales. They sustain, nourish, and develop Iñupiaq kinship with their universe as the whaling cycle rotates through seasons. I am just a humble witness of this process.

Participating in this project has been an eye-opening experience for everyone who is involved, including me. The recordings were taken away from Barrow, but, as it turned out, we have recently learned that the actual ownership of the 1946 recordings has never left the Iñupiaq land.[4] According to the United States Copyright Act of 1909, master sound recordings were not recognized as intellectual property. This means that a recordist (Boulton) could not claim the ownership of the recordings she made in her entire career as the music hunter. Such sound recordings would not gain federal copyright protection until 1972 for profit-making and reproduction. The US Copyright Act of 1976 defers explicitly to state statute or common law on the subject of pre-1972 recordings. In 1946, Alaska was still a territory of the United States. Now Barrow is recognized as a part of the sovereign territory of a federally recognized tribe—thus the recordings should be treated in the traditional legal framework of traditional Indigenous law, and it is now the time for the songs to officially return to their home and people.

At a meeting of the IHLCC in Barrow in August 2013, Aaron, along with Professor Kenneth Crews (then director of Columbia's copyright office) and I reported on the state of the project and sought advice and approval to continue the project by developing it into a digital publication for primary use by the North Slope communities, as well for as broader education and scholarly use. A committee to oversee the project's progress was successfully formed, to include several Iñupiat History, Language and Culture Commission (IHLCC) commissioners from various North Slope villages. Through a partnership with the IHLCC and other agencies in Barrow, Columbia has developed an agreement that would give the IHLCC—acting on behalf of the Iñupiaq community—significant control over the future publication of these recordings and related materials for teaching, research, and cultural heritage preservation.

Working in this fashion with archival collections can benefit a much broader range of social scientific objectives, and also the relationships between social scientists and Indigenous communities in which we work more generally. By working closely with members of the Iñupiaq community to describe, interpret, translate, and identify the historical features of Boulton's collected materials, we have gained extensive insights into more specifically geographical, historical, and ethnomusicological problems and questions that extend far beyond the materials themselves, suggesting that such archival materials, when treated as the basis for building relationships and developing dialogues with members of Indigenous communities, can become newly relevant for contemporary social research based on collaboration in Indigenous communities.

Last but not least, I will be a proud keeper of my promise with Martha and the Barrow community as long as my life goes on—I will never disappear.

Acknowledgments

Humans are tuned for relationship. The continuing relationship with my Iñupiaq colleagues, friends, and family turned Barrow, Alaska (the town whose precontact name was officially reinstated on December 1, 2016, Utqiaġvik [oot-kay-ahg-vik]), into my adopted home. I am eternally grateful for their love and support throughout the time that I was able to share with them. Special thanks are due to the late Martha Aiken, who played an instrumental role in my life to watch me grow up as a person and scholar. She was my teacher, mother, friend, and inspiration. I am indebted to the support, guidance, inspiration, and collaboration with Aaron Fox, the project leader of the community-partnered music heritage repatriation project. I have benefited immeasurably from his mentorship, support, generosity, and inspiration. Aaron is a strong believer in cultural resilience nurtured by Indigenous traditions, and his dedication to the Iñupiaq culture informed and fueled our collaboration on this project. The many trips that I have made with Aaron to the North Slope have undoubtedly deepened my relationship with the community in many unexpected ways, and for this I can never thank him enough. I would also like to acknowledge the financial and logistical support provided by the Iñupiat History, Language, and Culture Commission, Center for Ethnomusicology, at Columbia University, as well as Oberlin College, Barrow Arctic Science Consortium, and the National Science Foundation. Continuous rapport from the friends across the North Slope Borough of Alaska has generously poured the whale oil into my heart for continuous collaboration—special thanks are due to Fannie Akpik, Kathy Ahgeak, Jana Harcharek, Lollie Hopson, Julia and Jeslie Kaleak Sr., Jacob Kagak, Darlene Matumeak-Kagak, Roy and Flossie Avaiyak Nageak, Eileen Boskofsky, and the late Warren Matumeak, along with the members of the dance groups in Barrow. I also benefited immeasurably from friendship with many individuals in Barrow, now officially Utqiaġvik. I know the list could go on forever, and I offer my deepest apologies to anyone I may have overlooked. I want to sincerely thank all of these souls, because writing a chapter like this can be such a collaborative effort; but I also want to acknowledge that the mistakes in the text are mine to keep. *Quyanaqpak*.

Chapter 5 References

Basso, Keith. 1996. *Wisdom Sits in Places: Landscape and Language among the Western Apache.* Albuquerque: University of New Mexico Press.

Boulton, Laura. 1969. *The Music Hunter: The Autobiography of a Career.* New York: Doubleday.

Brewster, Karen, ed. 2004. *The Whales, They Give Themselves: Conversations with Harry Brower, Sr.* Fairbanks: University of Alaska Press.

Brown, Michael F. 2004. *Who Owns Native Culture?* Cambridge, MA: Harvard University Press.

Fienup-Riordan, Ann. 1990. *Eskimo Essays: Yup'ik Lives and How We See Them.* New Brunswick, NJ: Rutgers University Press.

Fox, Aaron A. 2014. "Repatriation as Reanimation through Reciprocity." In *The Cambridge History of World Music: Volume 1, North America*, edited by P. Bohlman. Cambridge, UK: Cambridge University Press.

_____. 2017. "The Archive of the Archive: The Secret History of the Laura Boulton Collection." In *The Routledge Companion to Cultural Property*, edited by Haidy Geismar and Jane Anderson, 194–211. London: Routledge.

Gray, Robin R. R. 2015. Ts'msyen Revolution: The Poetics and Politics of Reclaiming. PhD diss., Anthropology, University of Massachusetts, Amherst.

Lidchi, Henrietta, and Hulleah J. Tsinhnahjinnie, eds. 2009. *Visual Currencies: Reflections on Native Photography.* Edinburgh: National Museums Scotland.

Momaday, N. S. 1974. "Native American Attitudes to the Environment." In *Seeing with a Native Eye: Essays on Native American Religion*, edited by W. Capp, 79–85. New York: Harper and Row.

Nelson, R. K. 1980. *Shadow of the Hunter: Stories of Eskimo Life.* Chicago: University of Chicago Press.

Sakakibara, Chie. 2008. "'Our Home Is Drowning': Iñupiat Storytelling and Climate Change in Point Hope, Alaska." *Geographical Review* 98 (4): 456–478.

_____. 2009. "'No Whale, No Music': Contemporary Iñupiaq Drumming and Global Warming." *Polar Record* 45 (4): 289–303.

_____. 2010. "Kiavallakkikput Aġviq (into the Whaling Cycle): Cetaceousness and Climate Change among the Iñupiat of Arctic Alaska." *Annals of the Association of American Geographers* 100 (4): 1003–1012.

Tsinhnahjinnie, H. J., and Veronica Passalacqua, eds. 2006. *Our People, Our Land, Our Images: International Indigenous Photographers.* Berkeley: Heyday Books.

Walker, Brian, and David Salt. 2012. *Resilience Practice: Building Capacity to Absorb Disturbance and Maintain Function.* Washington, DC: Island Press.

Wooley, Christopher, Karen Brewster, Jana Harcharek, Dorothy Edwardsen, and Mabel Panigeo. 1992. "Marvin Peter's Iñupiat Family Album." *Alaska: The Great Land: Alaska Geographic* 19 (2): 64–67.

Notes to Chapter 5

1. This is a very shortened history of the recordings. The aluminum discs that Boulton recorded the original songs on were copied to tape only in 1973 by the Library of Congress, which then received the discs on permanent loan, while sending tape copies back to Columbia and Boulton. For more information on the history of the Laura Boulton Collection, see Fox 2014.
2. See Fox 2014 for more information on this discussion.
3. For contemporary manifestations of visual sovereignty by Indigenous artists, see Lidchi and Tsinhnahjinnie (2009) and Tsinhnahjinnie and Passalacqua (2006).
4. For more information on the following discussion, see Fox 2017. Additionally, Ts'msyen anthropologist Robin Gray's (2015) work on Boulton's Ts'msyen recordings illustrates how to reconstruct and bring into the present the traditional legal frameworks for song ownership and rights in Indigenous terms.

6

Giving Back after Fifty Years

Connecting, Returning, and Reflecting—New Research in Old Settings

RICHARD HOWITT, DAVID CREW, JANICE MONK,
CLAIRE COLYER, AND STEPHANIE HULL

O UR CHAPTER REVISITS communities studied in 1965, both to repatriate original research materials and to engage the communities in follow-up work on the original study. This addresses multiple layers of change—not only within the towns themselves, but in research ethics, methodologies, values, relationships, and responsibilities in the overall context of national and institutional frameworks, as well as in ourselves and in our engagements with the communities.

Janice Monk surveyed Aboriginal people in various rural communities in New South Wales (NSW) Australia as part of her PhD research (Monk 1972, 1974) (figure 6.1).[1] Some of her original survey materials were developed in consultation with the landmark project initiated by Social Science Research Council of Australia under the leadership of Charles Rowley (Rowley 1970, 1971a, 1971b), contributing to policy development of the era. They were not, however, returned to community participants. She personally retained the original survey forms, field notes, and photographic, print, correspondence, and statistical materials.[2]

Monk's research was unusual in the Australian academic scene of the time in exploring relationships between Aboriginal people and the larger society, culture, and economy (Howitt 2007). The link to Rowley's larger policy project also anticipated a more applied research orientation. The absence of direct feedback to local participants and their marginalization from wider research and policy processes typified the framing of research and government decision making in Indigenous settings at the time.

A chance 2005 conversation between Jan Monk and Richie Howitt in Tucson, Arizona, highlighted the potential value of these original surveys as a benchmark data set, pre-dating key policy initiatives in Indigenous affairs. We proposed to combine the return of her original materials to appropriate descendants of the original participants with a new study that would engage local Indigenous groups directly in assessing changes in social, economic, and environmental circumstances. We sought to integrate Jan's historic data with a wide range of more recent sources, including contemporary local field research, with a view to improving understanding of the diverse, competing, and even contradictory narratives of change that have shaped policy settings, material circumstances, and community understanding across the past fifty years.

This goes beyond "giving back" archival materials and historical information: it addresses new ethical, political, and methodological perspectives, new data opportunities, and new institutional circumstances. New theoretical and critical approaches to social research, including the development of Indigenous methodologies and participatory approaches, have displaced and challenged the privileging of academic and disciplinary framing of research. These changed circumstances all required attention and response.

Our current project has benefited not only from deliberate research design, but also from being open to opportunistic and serendipitous circumstances, such as developing relationships, the interplay of local activities, and the skills, interests, and capacities of the researchers. As local circumstances change over time, we recognize that ethics, research design, social theory, and politics form a crucible in which the politics of "giving back" demand attention. This cannot be limited to or driven by funding agencies and research institutions and their regulatory protocols and strategic priorities.

Context of Monk's Original Study

Monk's undergraduate education at the University of Sydney in the late 1950s did not address research on Aboriginal communities, nor the ethics of cross-cultural research. Yet at this time, Anglo-Australian society was experiencing new social relations and encounters with racial and ethnic diversity, including post–World War II immigration, which challenged widely held assumptions underpinning "white" Australia. Policies related to Aborigines had evolved during the twentieth century, from "protection" of an assumed "dying race" to "assimilation," and were then within the purview of state rather than national governmental legislation (see, e.g., McGregor 2011). Until the 1960s, Aboriginal people did not generally have voting rights, except where they qualified for and sought "exemption." It was not until after a national referendum in 1967 (Attwood and Markus 2007) that Aboriginal people were formally included in Australia's national census data (in 1971). Access to social security and other forms of citizenship entitlements were also not generally available until the early 1970s. Nevertheless, some non-Aboriginal people were concerned with Aboriginal well-being and rights (see, e.g., Reynolds 1998, 1999) via bodies such as Aboriginal advancement organizations, and welfare projects such as the house-building work camp in which Monk participated in 1961. Political activism around Aboriginal rights, such as the 1965 Freedom Ride in northern New South Wales undertaken by students from Sydney University, was also drawing press and public attention (Edmonds 2012).

On taking up graduate studies in geography in the United States, Monk was exposed to the 1960s civil rights movements. This new academic environment offered opportunities beyond the discipline of geography to take courses in social history, race relations, and cultural ecologies within sociology and in anthropology. This blending of personal and academic experience shaped Jan's choice of theme and methods for doctoral research in 1964–1965—a comparative analysis of the social and economic situations of Aboriginal communities in rural New South Wales. She selected towns that were demographically comparable though located in different regional economic contexts. Residential patterns of Aboriginal households were identified—on reserves, within town residential areas, and in marginal camping or informal settlement sites. From these she selected at random one-third of households for detailed survey (including housing conditions, economic resources, employment, education, health, migration history, and social networks). Jan also connected with non-Aboriginal residents engaged with Aboriginal people, including temporary residents in various organizational roles in schools, churches, health services, employment, government agencies, and volunteer community groups such as Aboriginal advancement organizations, and collected materials from local historical archives and records.

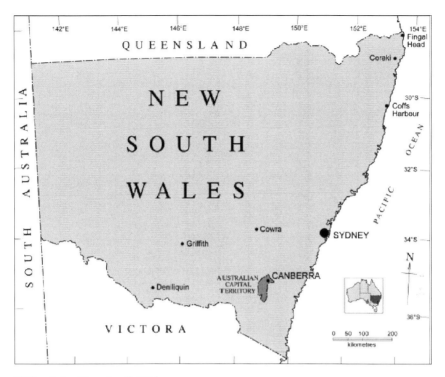

FIG. 6.1—New South Wales

The Current Study

We wanted our work to contribute to sustainable futures in Aboriginal communities in rural NSW. In particular, we aimed to assess the impact of government policies on the lives of Aboriginal families in rural towns in NSW over fifty years. We hoped this would improve both local people's and policy makers' understanding of past failures and successes, and contribute to discussions about foundations for building alternative futures.

We therefore needed to do much more than simply return the original household surveys to the communities. A process was required that would simultaneously look both backward and forward. We aimed to contribute to a hopeful geography for change (Lawson 2005). The first task was to produce an accessible archival record from the original data. This required careful negotiation of the terms for returning it to individual communities and depositing it into a national Aboriginal archive, where the material would be more widely accessible and able to be drawn into a range of uses in future.

Our goal was to work with policy makers, key local decision makers, and Aboriginal community groups to support new thinking about prospects for just and sustainable livelihoods for Aboriginal people in rural towns in NSW. To do this, we had to build a *longitudinal view of social and economic change* and a *conceptual framework* linking patterns of social, economic, and political inclusion, exclusion, and participation in such settings. Our project's modest ambition was to invite others to join us in reflecting on what the past has meant, and what currently needs changing, in the towns involved in the study. From that perspective, we introduced participatory methods to build local research skills and rigorously assess social consequences of conditions prevailing in Coffs Harbour, Deniliquin, and Griffith, three of the original study's sites where the opportunity to engage arose. Although the funded research activity has been concluded, the project was never solely academic in orientation; it was always intended that it would respond to opportunities as they emerged rather than insisting on an academic agenda as decisive. Thus, we continue to be open to further (and different) engagements over time.

Indigenous Research Ethics in Australia

In the mid-1960s, social research on Australian Indigenous communities was usually colonial and extractive, without ethical oversight and with little regard for the rights and interests of Indigenous[3] research "subjects"— at least as more recently envisioned. Access to communities relied on personal relationships with and approval from government agencies.

The intervening period encompasses almost one-quarter of Australia's post-invasion history, and many quite monumental changes in the framing of Indigenous peoples' recognition, rights, and position in Australian society, politics, and economy. This period has also seen multiple epistemological, conceptual, and methodological revolutions in the social sciences—a sea change noted, for example, by Toussaint in her engagement with Kaberry's ethnographic research in the Kimberley region during the 1930s (Toussaint 1999), and in Wolf's (1992) reconsideration, in the early 1990s, of her ethnographic notes on an incident in Taiwan in 1960. Substantial debates and rethinking of ethical frameworks for research with Indigenous Australians have been influential across disciplines and in key journals (Davis 2010; Davis and Holcombe 2010; Coombes, Johnson, and Howitt 2014, Australian Aboriginal Studies 2010; Qualitative Inquiry 2007; TAJA 2014). In parallel with stronger ethical oversight of social research generally (Hammersley 2014), Australian universities must comply with legislation and guidelines interpreted by institutionally based human research ethics committees (HRECs) (NHMRC, ARC, and AVCC 2007). They must demonstrate how research designs protect "vulnerable" Indigenous participants from exploitative research (Howitt 2005a, 2005b; Howitt and Suchet-Pearson 2006). Compulsory national guidelines for research with Aboriginal and Torres Strait Islander people were introduced in 1991 and revised in 2003, with further revision currently in development (NHMRC 2003; Lowitja Institute and AIATSIS 2013a, 2013b).

National guidelines introduced in 2000 (AIATSIS 2012)[4] direct researchers to explore opportunities for collaborative research partnerships with local Indigenous partners based on genuine reciprocity. Thus, returning Monk's materials was not simply a matter of repeating the earlier research and doing a longitudinal comparison—although some political figures urged us to do exactly that.[5] The legacy of academic paternalism, however, has meant that power and authority typically remain with academic researchers (Dudgeon, Kelly, and Walker 2010). Indeed, academic constructions of Indigenous vulnerability have created a policy discourse that suggests Indigeneity (Haalboom and Natcher 2012), rather than the slow-moving disasters of colonialism, dispossession, and injustice (Howitt, Havnen, and Veland 2012) is the prime driver of "vulnerability." Indigenous criticism of non-Indigenous research and its effects on Indigenous peoples has been powerful (Smith 1999, 2005; Johnson and Madge 2016). Even well-intentioned research often represents Aboriginal peoples "as passive victims succumbing to wave after wave of government oppression rather than as a cultural group reacting to external forces and accommodating changes" (Owen 2008).

Giving Back

"Giving back" needs to consider how research creates benefit as well as how it minimizes harm. Our iterative approach to research design and negotiation of cultural protocols recognizes that appropriate methodologies needed to challenge taken-for-granted privileges of academic and dominant culture researchers. Our team includes the original researcher, participants identified in the original surveys and their descendants, community-based and current university-based researchers, and current community members involved in a variety of roles from governance of the research to management of local activities and training as interviewers. We have adapted our approach as the project developed. Both the details of the work and its pace have been quite different from what we anticipated in our initial proposals to revisit Monk's study.[6]

Framing the research in wider-than-local contexts has also shaped how it "gives back" and negotiates reciprocity. Presenting local data in comparison to other places at the same local scale (and in comparison to wider Indigenous and total national populations) has given the statistical narrative new meaning and prompted engagement with audiences that a local-only framing of the research would not allow.

We foreshadowed working with published statistics and other information from state and national governments, local councils, Aboriginal organizations, and other sources to develop an account of social conditions since 1965. We would use interviews and focus groups to consider specific events, locations, and relationships, and local workshops to provide feedback and invite iterative interpretation of emerging evidence. We aimed to link local experiences to changes in public policy and practice in Indigenous affairs.

Initial responses varied among locations. In Deniliquin and Griffith, local Aboriginal reference groups were established to oversee the research and develop governance protocols that were incorporated into the formal ethics approvals. These cultural protocols address concepts such as cultural and intellectual property rights; prior informed consultation and consent; secret and sacred material, privacy, and attribution; legal recognition and protection; and rights to access information. In Coffs Harbour, where no reference group emerged, the project has generally been limited to returning the archival material to relevant families.

Interestingly, the formal ethics review process was intensively attentive to the rights and interests of Aboriginal participants, but almost disinterested in the rights and interests of non-Aboriginal participants in the original research. It has been much harder to frame mechanisms for engagement with them or their descendants than for the Aboriginal families.

The Community Contexts

The term "community" inevitably raises the question of just what is referred to across a period of five decades. The term labels a geographic location (a settlement or town), but too easily elides the social complexities of mobility, stability, and change within a local Aboriginal population (and the socioeconomic and cultural contexts of the towns where they are situated). We avoid the term as much as possible to avoid conflating local Aboriginal people with the concept of a singular coherent entity and eliding the complexity and difference that affects not only individual and family histories and experiences, but also diverse attitudes to and experiences of key elements of social, economic, and policy changes in these locations. There are communities in each of the research locations, but we do not seek to simplify them into a single, united, and common identity or experience.

Memory of the original research varies. Some recollection remains, but the local fieldwork was relatively brief and, from the participants' perspective, ephemeral. Return of materials to participants' families as an archive was welcomed, but differently in each place. This reflects the complexity of demographic and economic changes over five decades and across space (table 6.1).

Repatriation

The material returned to each of the original families consisted of a copy of the original survey data sheets and personal and district photographs from Monk's fieldwork to allow families to print and circulate the material as they wished.

The archival data recorded both personal and judgmental information that had potential to cause distress if released without careful reference to the participants and their descendants. Its relevance to contemporary circumstances needed to be established rather than assumed. Connections to current community organizations and their aspirations and priorities were also needed if our intention to use the serendipitous preservation of the archival data as an opportunity to look back and look forward was to be realized. This meant that the project could not simply arrive in the towns and begin research. Connections of trust, respect, and understanding needed time to develop.

The project's ethical framing privileged local Aboriginal people in determining what would be returned, how it should be returned, and what conditions should be placed on returned materials. This local authority was tempered in two ways. First, Monk lodged materials in the archives of the Aboriginal and Torres Strait Islander Studies (AIATSIS) in Canberra. This included household survey data collected in each of the communities in which she had conducted research. AIATSIS maintains a very large archive of original research materials. Creation of the Monk Archive at AIATSIS preserves the original data from all six of the communities studied in 1965 in a single location under access conditions developed by AIATSIS after wide consultations with Aboriginal and Torres Strait Islanders. This ensures that family members and local groups can have access to the data independent of our academic project. Second, Monk's original field notebook (a precious historical artifact in its own right), correspondence, and other materials concerning her engagement with both Aboriginal and other people, including press clippings and minutes of Aboriginal advancement organizations that existed in some towns, were not included in the Monk Archive at AIATSIS, nor in materials returned to local communities in this project. Some of these items raise sensitivities outside the scope of AIATSIS's Indigenous-specific ethics guidelines. We have digitized the notebook and draw on the field notes in the broader policy research elements of the project. Should the confidentiality of data obtained from non-Aboriginal informants be protected? In some of Monk's records, currently controversial values that were commonplace fifty years ago are attributed to identified individuals and thus may have consequences for those individuals and their descendants. We discussed these issues with local reference groups, but their addition to the central or local archives remains an open question at this point.

Project Approaches

We aimed to establish an ethical way of depositing Monk's historical data, particularly the household and individual survey forms, both in a national archive and to appropriate local recipients. Monk initially considered providing de-identified household survey forms in accordance with current ethical practice regarding confidentiality. AIATSIS, however, requested lodgment of the original identified survey forms because the greatest call on its collection is for family data. The survey data contained detailed information that was collected when few community records of this sort were kept, and this added to its significance and value. After negotiation with community reference groups, it was clear that de-identifying such historical records would contradict local Aboriginal groups' aspirations to narrate their own stories. How different national narratives would be if all historical records were de-identified.

Participatory methods have become the preferred approach to research in Indigenous geographies (Coombes, Johnson, and Howitt 2014), but we also recognize they carry their own limits and burdens (Svalastog and Eriksson 2010; Mistry et al. 2015). Responses in each town varied widely. Negotiating local engagement was at first slow and uneven, developing through multiple return trips that, first, built interest, then gradually, understanding and trust.

While in each town there was generally strong interest in the return of the 1965 survey data, there was not universal agreement about participating in a contemporary research project. General mistrust of academic research and its purposes, along with enormous pressures and demands on individuals who had local responsibilities, meant they had to see real merits of becoming involved and sharing capacities with us, or drawing on our capacity. In many ways, this required quite a leap of faith that the research was capable of and likely to return something of value to their community.

Deniliquin in 1965 was the most prosperous of the towns Monk studied. In 2011, it was little changed in size or demography, but had a significantly reduced economic base. Since its establishment in Deniliquin in 2003, the Yarkuwa Indigenous Knowledge Centre had been collecting past research, archival materials, and Aboriginal community knowledge to build strong local identity and purpose. When approached to be involved in our project, Yarkuwa quickly moved beyond the archival documents to the wider questions being canvassed and established a reference group to draw Macquarie University researchers into the organization's existing work. In 2012, Crew, a senior manager at Yarkuwa, commenced doctoral research under a negotiated agreement to investigate whether Aboriginal families in Deniliquin considered themselves better off than they had been in 1965. Yarkuwa was keen to identify the research questions and for its members to take part in an academic process documenting their experiences over the past fifty years. Some members of Yarkuwa, including chairperson Jeanette Crew, were included in the 1965 data.

In contrast, agricultural development in the Murrumbidgee Irrigation Area had significantly transformed Griffith. Since 1965, its population has tripled, and it is now the regional focus for government and community services and a center for food processing and other agricultural industry. In late 2011, the Griffith Aboriginal Community Working Party[7] discussed the project. There was interest, but no engagement until mid-2014, when a connection made through Yarkuwa in Deniliquin offered the Macquarie project team an opportunity to participate in an Aboriginal Family History Day in Griffith. This event opened a space for further

Table 6.1: *Key community statistics 1965[a] and 2011*

Key statistics	Coffs Harbour 1965	Coffs Harbour 2011	Cowra 1965	Cowra 2011	Deniliquin 1965	Deniliquin 2011	Griffith 1965	Griffith 2011	NSW 1966 [b]	NSW 2011
Total population	6,996	68,414	6,407	12,147	5,472	7,122	7,590	24,363	4,248,042	6,917,659
Number of Aboriginal people	159	2,817	149	793	114	257	165	1,001	14,219	172,621
Indigenous persons as % of total	2.27%	4.12%	2.33%	6.53%	2.08%	3.61%	2.17%	4.11%	0.33%	2.50%
Mean age of Aboriginal population (years)	19.7	25.4	18.9	28.6	21.5	28.2	17.5	26.7	21.0	26.5
Aboriginal population under 15 yrs	51%	38%	54%	33%	42%	37%	61%	51%	48%	36%
Aboriginal population in the workforce	20%	53%	18%	44%	42%	42%	25%	51%	48%	51%
Aboriginal men employed	78%	44%	45%	33%	78%	35%	69%	46%	64%	45%
Aboriginal women employed	0%	40%	25%	37%	67%	37%	45%	38%	15%	40%
Mean household income ($A/yr)[c]	22,031	56,042	24,468	50,083	40,150	39,044	29,152	53,015	-	66,128

Notes:

[a] 1965 Aboriginal population figures are drawn from Aborigines Welfare Board data provided to Monk, her fieldwork observation, and other government data. Monk concluded the Welfare Board estimates probably understated populations in the towns (Monk 1972, 190)

[b] Source: 1966 Australian Census of Population and Housing. The 1966 census data are the best available source to indicate population counts in the mid-1960s.

[c] Includes income from all sources including government benefits and is adjusted for inflation to 2011.

Sources: Monk 1972 and ABS 2011 census

discussions about our project. The Yamandhu Marang[8] Griffith Social Research Project, led by a reference group of senior community members, was established in late 2014.

In both Deniliquin and Griffith, the local reference groups negotiated research and governance protocols and coordinated local project support. They oversaw return of all the 1965 family surveys and development and delivery of local research skills training. They led the way as participants in local research and contributed to a national workshop on collaborative research.

The northern coastal city of Coffs Harbour presents a contrast to the others. It grew tenfold between 1965 and 2011 to become a service center for a rapidly growing and economically diverse tourism region. Project team members visited in 2012 and 2013 for meetings that produced some interest but no momentum to engage until a further opportunity arose in 2014, again following a connection made by Crew with the local Nguralla Aboriginal Corporation. Nguralla hosted a series of meetings with descendants of the families that had taken part in Monk's research, but while there was strong interest in return of the 1965 surveys to the families and to the community through some form of local archive, there was little interest in developing new research. Nguralla's coordinator and another community member, drawing on personal networks and community knowledge, worked with the project team to identify and contact appropriate individuals to receive family data folders in person. Coffs Harbour City Library requested deposit of a small collection of published materials (including Monk 1972, 1974; Howitt 2007; Howitt et al. 2016; and notes about the 1965 project). This collection would lay a "trail of crumbs" to allow future interest to be guided toward the AIATSIS archive in Canberra and to connect to the research team at Macquarie University if desired.

The project also brought together three distinct narrative threads: a policy narrative that reflected the changing approaches of governments to Indigenous affairs; a statistical narrative built on the public data and records that have informed policy making; and community narratives of change over this important period of Australian history.

National census and other published statistical data have influenced the development of government policies affecting Aboriginal people in rural NSW, but have been uneven in coverage and quality over time (Taylor 2005; Biddle 2014). Their influence was reinforced when the Council of Australian Governments (COAG) agreed that it was necessary to "close the gap"—to "close the [statistical] gap in life expectancy, early childhood, health, education and employment [between Indigenous and non-Indigenous Australians] . . . to focus effort for sustained change" (Commonwealth of Australia 2011; see also Pholi, Black, and Richards 2009).

Together official statistics, social policies, and differences in patterns of local economic activity profoundly affect the well-being of rural Aboriginal people. The geographies of inequality, poverty, and disadvantage have become highly racialized in rural NSW. Opportunities for rural Aboriginal groups to secure inclusion and participation in prosperous and sustainable local economies are deeply constrained both by racialized patterns of exclusion and disempowerment and wider processes affecting rural well-being more generally.

The development of the community narratives was guided by the project reference groups in each community. In Griffith and Deniliquin, the reference groups decided to conduct interviews with local Aboriginal people and with representatives of service providers, government agencies, and other non-Aboriginal stakeholders to build local narratives of change over time in each place. Local training programs were developed in association with local education service providers to build local research capacity, identify local audiences for the research, and provide input into our wider-scale analysis of policy and statistical narratives. After considerable discussion, both reference groups requested that the university researchers undertake the interviews with a range of local decision makers and service providers, as they felt the university researchers would be perceived to be independent and less subject to the influence of local patterns of paternalism and privilege.

The Complexities of "Giving Back"

As discussed in chapter 1 and elsewhere in this volume, reciprocity or "giving back" means moving from the "data mining" approach to decolonizing frames in which partnership, collaboration, and reciprocity frame research as a relationship as much as a service. This shifts the grounds on which researchers operate. Funding agencies and university administrations are slower to respond. Their bureaucratic terms easily reduce reciprocity to a one-off transaction such as return of data, completion of a report, or delivery of an agreed service. In our experience, local people see reciprocity as a longer-term relationship, changing the positionality of researchers, bringing them into continuing engagement less focused on a project and more oriented to ongoing engagement. Our team has built a range of relationships with local people and organizations, changing institutional relationships with people and places and the issues they raise. We have become teachers (and learners) as well as researchers; current friends rather than archival entities; and implicated into local thinking in ways that will have longer-term implications than any of us really understood when serendipities framed our project around the Monk Archive. Our Aboriginal colleagues have begun to reframe their own approaches to research, policy, and community development. Involvement has been more than an investment of time and has become an emotional investment in and connection to family history. Community interviewers in both Deniliquin and Griffith interviewed many members of their own families, learning about their experiences across the last fifty years. Consequently, they have greater understanding of the way government policies have affected their families and communities. This understanding has created new ways of examining the role of policy in the local context and built confidence to question "better-off-ness." It opens questions of power, control, and autonomy as matters for local debate rather than leaving such issues as the province of academic theorizing or in the hands of distant policy makers.

Moving from intention to practice, however, is always fraught. The politics and processes of giving back are not simple; a variety of audiences are always implicated. We have faced challenges and complexities arising from both ethical and practical issues. Even the apparently straightforward task of lodging the 1965 data sheets and photographs with AIATSIS confronted key questions: Who owns (and who should own) the data? Who should determine access conditions? What should be confidential or restricted? Who should determine restrictions and enforce them? We quickly learned that the household data was a record of high importance to the descendants of the families Monk surveyed and was seen that way by others. In each town, family members shared their pleasure in having materials returned. For example, one young participant expressed how her family valued now having a photograph of her grandmother when the latter was a child—a resource they had never had.

In Monk's 1965 project, as was then current practice, neither the householders surveyed nor other informants were asked for, or gave, formal consent regarding future management and confidentiality of their information or how it might be interpreted in other times or by other audiences. Difficult questions arose regarding return of the 1965 survey data, photographs, and other information to the groups we work with and individual family members. Giving back carried with it significant responsibilities: What might be the consequences for communities and individuals if some of the detailed confidential family survey data were made available? Who should have access rights to the data? What protocols should be followed? Who was entitled to photographs of people, places, and living conditions taken in 1965?[9] Balancing the accuracy of the information being archived and maintaining the integrity of the historical documents required attention to detail, sensitivity, and recognition of the possibility that incorrect information may have been supplied, knowingly or unknowingly, at the time; that information may have been misunderstood; or that inaccuracies in recording may have occurred.

Return of the family surveys was an important objective, but giving back, in this sense, could not easily form an end point of the relationship established by the existence of the archival data. Although we have been able to return 1965 data to nearly every family in the towns we are working in, and the project allowed considerable flexibility, in practice time and project resources are finite, and so not every community and family that participated in 1965 could be approached. A booklet was prepared (Howitt et al. 2016) so that knowledge of the 1965 and the current project will continue to be available to each of the six towns in which Monk worked, along with information about how to access the Monk archive deposited at AIATSIS. The booklet has been widely distributed to community organizations, policy makers, and decision makers as well as local libraries, councils, and academic outlets.

Conclusion: Negotiating "Giving Back" to Move Forward

This project of "giving back" in rural NSW demonstrates that simply returning information is not enough. We integrated archival, statistical, and policy sources with current interviews. The statistical, policy, and community narratives cover a fifty-year time span. In doing this, we had to consider how research data may constrain, or even determine, the narratives of change and to debate this with local people whose temporal and policy horizons have been stretched by the project. Building audiences, both locally and in wider policy discourses, for this sort of longitudinal and critical work is an important challenge. We have grappled with the conceptual, methodological, and logistical complexities of working across spatial and temporal scales, managing multiple data sets, responding to local diversity, and negotiating changing ethical and historical imperatives and expectations.

We responded to the people with whom we have worked, and have built wider audiences to discuss policy frameworks in ways that might nurture more sustainable and equitable well-being for Aboriginal people across rural NSW. We also sought to be accountable to locally negotiated cultural protocols and develop ethical standards while meeting robust disciplinary research discourses. As researchers, we had to be prepared to listen and respond, to cocreate spaces for reflection. We invested in processes and relationships, and asked local Aboriginal people to do the same. This evolved differently in each location, bringing different concerns and capacities to the fore in each set of relationships and issues. One key message from this work has been how appreciative individual families have been to connect back fifty years to an earlier time, and to connect or reconnect with Jan and hear personal stories from the time.

Giving back is about a larger project of reciprocity, of working together and combining capacities to empower community members to speak to policy makers directly. Of the three towns, Deniliquin's Yarkuwa Indigenous Knowledge Centre had unique capacity to house and take responsibility for management of the materials. In contrast, a much slower process and longer-term investment in time and relationship-building was needed in other places. In Deniliquin and Griffith, new skills and community capacity has developed as local Aboriginal people have participated in training to collect data and conduct interviews. This goes beyond returning archival materials. We have learned that there is no singular way to "give back," nor a singular way to move forward.

Acknowledgments

The research is supported by a grant from the Australian Research Council (Grant No. ARCDP110101721 Social conditions of Aboriginal people in rural NSW). We acknowledge the support and guidance of Yarkuwa Indigenous Knowledge Centre Aboriginal Corporation in Deniliquin; Yamandhu Marang Griffith Social Research Reference Group in Griffith; and Ngurrala Aboriginal Corporation in Coffs Harbour; and the research and administrative support from Macquarie University and Association of American Geographers. We also thank the generous engagement with our work from Indigenous families in Coffs Harbour, Deniliquin, and Griffith; the Australian Institute of Aboriginal and Torres Strait Islander Studies;

and colleagues in various conferences (Institute of Australian Geographers, Association of American Geographers, and International Geographical Union). Our work is approved under Macquarie University Human Research Ethics Committee approvals 52014000647, 5201200210, and 5201500110.

Chapter 6 References and Recommended Reading

AIATSIS (Australian Institute of Aboriginal and Torres Strait Islander Studies). 2012. *Guidelines for Ethical Research in Australian Indigenous Studies*. Canberra: Australian Institute of Aboriginal and Torres Strait Islander Studies.

Attwood, Bain, and Andrew Markus. 2007. *The 1967 Referendum: Race, Power and the Australian Constitution*. Canberra: Aboriginal Studies Press.

Australian Aboriginal Studies. 2010. "Themed Issue on Ethics in Aboriginal Studies, edited by Michael Davis and Sarah Holcombe." *Australian Aboriginal Studies* 2010 (2): 1–125.

Biddle, Nicholas. 2014. "Data about and for Aboriginal and Torres Strait Islander Australians." In *Close The Gap*. Clearinghouse Issues Paper No 10. Canberra: Close The Gap Clearinghouse.

Commonwealth of Australia. 2011. *Closing the Gap Prime Minister's Report 2011*. Canberra: Attorney-General's Department.

Coombes, Brad, Jay T. Johnson, and Richard Howitt. 2014. "Indigenous Geographies III: Methodological Innovation and the Unsettling of Participatory Research." *Progress in Human Geography* 38 (6): 845–854.

Davis, Michael. 2010. "Bringing Ethics Up to Date? A Review of the AIATSIS Ethical Guidelines." *Australian Aboriginal Studies* (2):10–21.

Davis, Michael, and Sarah Holcombe. 2010. "'Whose Ethics?': Codifying and Enacting Ethics in Research Settings." *Australian Aboriginal Studies* (2): 1–9.

Dudgeon, Pat, Kerrie Kelly, and Roz Walker. 2010. "Closing the Gaps in and through Indigenous Health Research: Guidelines, Processes and Practices." *Australian Aboriginal Studies* (2): 81–91.

Edmonds, Penelope. 2012. "Unofficial Apartheid, Convention and Country Towns: Reflections on Australian History and the New South Wales Freedom Rides of 1965." *Postcolonial Studies* 15 (2): 167–190.

Haalboom, Bethany J., and David C. Natcher. 2012. "The Power and Peril of 'Vulnerability': Lending a Cautious Eye to Community Labels in Climate Change Research." *Arctic* 65 (3): 319–327.

Hammersley, Martyn. 2014. "On Ethical Principles for Social Research." *International Journal of Social Research Methodology* 18 (4): 433–449.

Howitt, Richard. 2005a. "Editorial: Human Ethics, Supervision and Equity: Ethical Oversight of Student Research." *Journal of Geography in Higher Education* 29 (3): 317–320.

———. 2005b. "The Importance of Process in Social Impact Assessment: Ethics, Methods and Process for Cross-Cultural Engagement." *Ethics Place and Environment* 8 (2): 209–221.

———. 2007. "Hidden Histories in Geography: A Politics of Inclusion and Participation." *Gender, Place and Culture* 14 (1): 51–56.

Howitt, Richard, Claire Colyer, Janice Monk, David Crew, and Stephanie Hull. 2016. *Looking Forward—Looking Back: Changing Social and Economic Conditions of Aboriginal People in Rural NSW, 1965–2015*. Sydney: Macquarie University Department of Geography and Planning.

Howitt, Richard, Olga Havnen, and Siri Veland. 2012. "Natural and Unnatural Disasters: Responding with Respect for Indigenous Rights and Knowledges." *Geographical Research* 50 (1): 47–59.

Howitt, Richard, and Sandra Suchet-Pearson. 2006. "Changing Country, Telling Stories: Research Ethics, Methods and Empowerment in Working with Aboriginal Women." In *Fluid Bonds: Views on Gender and Water*, edited by Kuntala Lahiri-Dutt, 48–63. Kolkata, India: Stree.

Johnson, Jay T., Garth Cant, Richard Howitt, and Evelyn Peters. 2007. "Creating Anti-Colonial Geographies: Embracing Indigenous Peoples, Knowledges and Rights." *Geographical Research* 45 (2): 117–120.

Johnson, Jay T., and Clare Madge. 2016. "Empowering Methodologies: Feminist and Indigenous Approaches." In *Qualitative Research Methods in Human Geography*, 4th ed., edited by Iain Hay, 76–94. Oxford, UK: Oxford University Press.

Koch, Grace. 2010. "Ethics and Research: Dilemmas Raised in Managing Research Collections of Aboriginal and Torres Strait Islander Materials." *Australian Aboriginal Studies* (2): 48–59.

Lawson, Victoria. 2005. "Hopeful Geographies: Imaging Ethical Alternatives —A Commentary on J. K. Gibson-Graham's 'Surplus Possibilities: Postdevelopment and Community Economies.'" *Singapore Journal of Tropical Geography* 26:36–38.

Lowitja Institute and AIATSIS (Australian Institute of Aboriginal and Torres Strait Islander Studies). 2013a. "Evaluation of the National Health and Medical Research Council Documents: Values and Ethics: Guidelines for Ethical Conduct in Aboriginal and Torres Strait Islander Health

Research 2003 and Keeping Research on Track: A Guide for Aboriginal
and Torres Strait Islander Peoples about Health Research Ethics 2005."
Canberra: National Medical and Health Research Council. http://
www.nhmrc.gov.au/_files_nhmrc/file/health_ethics/human/issues/
nhmrc_evaluation_values_ethics_research_on_track_150513.pdf.

Lowitja Institute and AIATSIS (Australian Institute of Aboriginal and Torres
Strait Islander Studies). 2013b. "Researching Right Way—Aboriginal
and Torres Strait Islander Health Research Ethics: A Domestic
and International Review." Canberra: National Medical and health
Research Council. http://www.nhmrc.gov.au/_files_nhmrc/file/
health_ethics/human/issues/nhmrc_evaluation_literature_review_
atsi_research_ethics_150513.pdf.

McGregor, Russell. 2011. *Indifferent Inclusion: Aboriginal People and the
Australian Nation*. Canberra: Aboriginal Studies Press.

Mistry, Jayalaxshmi, Andrea Berardi, Elisa Bignante, and Céline Tschirhart.
2015. "Between a Rock and a Hard Place: Ethical Dilemmas of Local
Community Facilitators Doing Participatory Research Projects."
Geoforum 61:27–35.

Monk, Janice. 1972. Socio-Economic Characteristics of Six Aboriginal
Communities in Australia: A Comparative Ecological Study.
PhD diss., Department of Geography, University of Illinois at
Urbana-Champaign.

———. 1974. "Australian Aboriginal Social and Economic Life: Some
Community Differences and Their Causes." In *Cultural Discord in the
Modern World: Geographical Themes* edited by L. J. Evenden and F. F.
Cunningham, 157–174. Vancouver: Tantalus Research.

NHMRC (National Health and Medical Research Council). 2003. *Values
and Ethics—Guidelines for Ethical Conduct in Aboriginal and Torres
Strait Islander Health Research*. Canberra: NHMRC.

NHMRC, ARC, and AVCC (National Health and Medical Research Council,
Australian Research Council, and Australian Vice-Chancellors'
Committee). 2007. *National Statement on Ethical Conduct of
Research Involving Humans—Updated May 2015*. Canberra: National
Health and Medical Research Council. http://www.nhmrc.gov.au/
guidelines-publications/e72.

Owen, Chris. 2008. "Publish and Be Damned!" Native Title Conference
2008. http://aiatsis.gov.au/sites/default/files/docs/presentations/
publish-and-be-damned.pdf.

Pholi, Kerryn, Dan Black, and Craig Richards. 2009. "Is 'Close the Gap' a Useful Approach to Improving the Health and Wellbeing of Indigenous Australians?" *Australian Review of Public Affairs* 9 (2): 1–13.

Qualitative Inquiry. 2007. "Special Issue on IRBs, Ethics and Qualitative Research." *Qualitative Inquiry* 13 (3): 315–444.

Reynolds, Henry. 1998. *This Whispering in Our Hearts*. Sydney: Allen and Unwin.

———. 1999. *Why Weren't We told? A Personal Search for the Truth about Our History*. Ringwood, Victoria: Viking.

Rowley, Charles D. 1970. *The Destruction of Aboriginal Society: Aboriginal Policy and Practice*. Vol. 1. Canberra: Australian National University Press.

———. 1971a. *Outcasts in White Australia: Aboriginal Policy and Practice*. Vol. 2. Canberra: Australian National University Press.

———. 1971b. *The Remote Aborigines: Aboriginal Policy and Practice*. Volume 3. Canberra: Australian National University Press.

Smith, Linda Tuhiwai. 1999. *Decolonizing Methodologies: Research and Indigenous Peoples*. Dunedin/London: University of Otago Press/Zed Books.

———. 2005. "On Tricky Ground: Researching the Native in the Age of Uncertainity." In *The SAGE Handbook of Qualitative Research*, edited by Norman K. Denzin and Yvonna S. Lincoln, 85–107. Thousand Oaks, CA: SAGE.

Svalastog, Anna-Lydia, and Stefan Eriksson. 2010. "'You Can Use My Name; You Don't Have to Steal My Story'—A Critique of Anonymity in Indigenous Studies." *Developing World Bioethics* 10 (2): 104–110.

TAJA. 2014. "Soapbox Forum: Ethics Review Regimes and Australian Anthropology (Themed Section) (edited by Lisa Wynn)." *Australian Journal of Anthropology* 25 (3): 373–375.

Taylor, John. 2005. *Tracking Change in the Relative Economic Status of Indigenous People in New South Wales, CAEPR Discussion Paper 277/2005*. Canberra: Centre for Aboriginal Economic Policy Research, Australian National University.

Toussaint, Sandy. 1999. *Phyllis Kaberry and Me: Anthropology, History and Aboriginal Australia*. Melbourne: Melbourne University Press.

Wolf, Margery. 1992. *A Thrice Told Tale: Feminism, Postmodernism and Ethnographic Responsibility*. Stanford, CA: Stanford University Press.

Notes to Chapter 6

1. Monk's 1965 research investigated six rural locations in NSW (see figure 6.1): Coffs Harbour, Coraki, Cowra, Deniliquin, Fingal Head, and Griffith.
2. Current procedures often routinely require destruction of research data after a specified period as a condition of ethical approval. The community value of the retained data used in this research highlights the importance of retaining rather than destroying primary source materials such as surveys and interviews.
3. For many Indigenous Australians, their preferred identifier is the language group with which they affiliate. In referring to broader geographical groupings in the Australian study areas involved in this project, we adopt the local protocol to refer to Aboriginal people.
4. These guidelines were further revised in 2010 and are currently undergoing further revision.
5. The then Opposition spokesperson (now Commonwealth Government minister) on Indigenous affairs in the national parliament urged us to ignore the ethics procedures governing research and repeat the original survey so he could see what had changed (Crew and Howitt, field interview, Canberra, October 2012).
6. The proposal funded by the Australian Research Council in 2010 anticipated recruitment of local research students in each town and the development of local steering groups for each local project in the first year of funding. In its fifth year of funding, only one PhD student has been recruited and only two community-based reference groups have been developed, for reasons we explain.
7. The Griffith Aboriginal Community Working Party is an interagency coordination group involving Aboriginal community organizations in medical, legal, and community services, and a range of government agencies.
8. Yamandhu Marang means "Are you well?" in Wiradjuri language.
9. The delicacy of this process was evident at an early meeting in one community, when a family member, shown survey data relating to his family, was distressed to find that deeply personal information, understood by local people to be incorrect, had been recorded in the survey and was now at risk of being permanently "on the record."

7

Portrait, Landscape, Mirror

Reflections on Return Fieldwork

KENDRA MCSWEENEY

RECENTLY, A GRADUATE STUDENT asked me how long she should stay in the field while conducting research on rural livelihoods in Latin America. I suggested that it was important to stay long enough to ensure reliably close ties with local collaborators, develop a solid knowledge of the area, and, ideally, observe the dynamics of life through every season. Upon reflection, however, I think that the *length of time* in a given research site is arguably less important than the ability to *go back* to a place of research. Indeed, geographers have argued for the importance and rewards of recurrent visits to particular landscapes over long periods. Return visits can yield better understanding of place-shaping processes and offer new perspectives on old problems. As James Parsons (1977, 14) found, "it pays to keep going back to an area, a people." Other geographers have found the same rewards, but also point out some of the responsibilities and commitments implied by research that involves "many rounds of returning to communities over many years" (Stevens 2001, 66).

This chapter is a personal reflection on the issues and insights that arise from repeated visits—what I call "return fieldwork"—to a research base in an Indigenous Tawahka community on the Patuca River in eastern Honduras. From June 1994, I lived in this community for twenty-two months as half of a research team that included a Honduran biologist.[1] I returned again for much shorter periods, in 1998, 2001, 2002, and 2011, and I plan to return again in 2016.

Some of the benefits of returning are obvious. These include the immediate familiarity of place, people, and language. There is also tremendous personal gratification in returning to work with old friends, to watch children grow whose birth I witnessed, to be able to bring gifts for a specific person or family. There is also no doubt that by returning to this particular place I accord its residents tremendous respect. I cannot count the number of times that villagers emphasized that they were delighted that I had *come back*. Especially after Hurricane Mitch, people told me that my return contributed to their feeling of not being "forgotten."

As Parsons (1977) noted, returning also offers tremendous opportunities to look with new eyes on a place. For me, every visit has yielded insights into some whole new aspect of life or landscape that I wonder I never saw before. This is as much because *I* have changed in the interim—grown older, had children of my own, or been influenced by the latest things I have seen or read—as it is because of the ways that the people and place have changed. These changes have sometimes been profound, such as devastation by Hurricane Mitch, the governance changes catalyzed by the ratification the Tawahka Asangni Biosphere Reserve, or the relentless encroachment of the cattle frontier into Tawahka territory. For those who study the dynamics of land use change, repeat visits are therefore an excellent opportunity to chronicle their dynamics up close. In fact, long-term, sequential insights are often professionally rewarded by the academy, where in-depth longitudinal studies can be rare (Kates 1987).

Of course, returning repeatedly to a research site also demands some form of "giving back." When I found that villagers had used the pages of one of my research articles to patch over holes in the bamboo walls of an outhouse, it became very clear that English-language reprints were woefully insufficient in this respect. Much more meaningful has been my ability to lend my time and my position as a US-based university professor to work in solidarity with Tawahka on the projects that they identify as most pressing. Over the years, this has included helping fight a proposed hydroelectric dam, writing grants for development funding, gathering data for a co-management plan, acting as legal adviser, working to channel Mitch relief funds to the mid-Patuca area, helping fund medical interventions, and contributing to the financial support of Tawahka students in Honduran cities. Many geographers do much more (see

Stevens 2001; Herlihy and Knapp 2003). These collaborations are typically long distance, and would be impossible without email and, now, Skype. It is personally rewarding to me to invest time and effort in these projects, and by doing so I maintain close ties with my research collaborators during the long interludes when I have been unable to go to Honduras. When I am in the field, however, these efforts can considerably complicate a research project. For example, villagers who are aware that I have previously raised money on their behalf (particularly after Hurricane Mitch) showed some bitterness when I failed to continue to regularly do so. Similarly, the more fluent I became in the regional lingua franca (Miskitu), the more comfortable villagers felt in pulling me aside and articulating their needs to me—for cigarettes, for cash, to borrow a mirror, for a little sugar, some aspirin, or simply to lament the various ways in which their lives are difficult. These distractions sometimes consumed whole days in the field, and left me emotionally drained. Yet they represent a trivial price to pay for the tremendous access that local peoples offer into their lives and homes—access on which I have relied heavily in building my academic career.

What is much more disturbing, however, is what the luxury of being able to contemplate such trade-offs implies about the deep asymmetry of research relationships with profoundly marginalized populations. During my doctoral research, when I was occasionally faced with what I considered excessive financial requests, I would protest that I was a mere student. But residents were always quick with retorts that combined something of the following: *If you fly in an airplane to Honduras and live in our world, you have far more money than we could dream of. If it were not so, we would be visiting your country.*

Simply put, my mere presence in their community speaks volumes about the massive gulf of power and privilege that allows me to be the visitor, and they the "visitees"—an imbalance that I reassert with every return. Further, this power is closely associated in local minds with that manifested by the visits of all gringos. (Both "gringo" and its Miskitu equivalent, *miriki*, are used in the Mosquitia to denote white, non-Hispanic people, regardless of their national origin or mother tongue. Outsiders' efforts to distinguish themselves as German or Canadian, for example, are usually met with ambivalence.) In effect, I contribute to the legacy of the steady stream of privileged outsiders—researchers, NGO employees, explorers, ecotourists, businesspeople, or missionaries—who have come and gone in the Patuca Valley for hundreds of years, and will no doubt continue to do so. Whether I like it or not, as a returning fieldworker I am still an actor in what some would call a fundamentally (neo)colonial project of exploring, converting, consuming, and researching this place.

Here, I hope to illustrate one way in which these power relations shape the research endeavor, and the ways they can be reasserted even when the intention is to undermine them. I do so by describing aspects of my research trip to Tawahka territory in 2002, when I attempted to give back historical photographs of Tawahka individuals. This exercise in giving back revealed far more than I had expected. For example, it forced me to finally recognize key nuances in the ways that Tawahka thought about cultural identity, production of knowledge, notions of time, and relations of power—four issues of central importance for my broader research agenda that I had previously completely missed. Below, I describe my foray into visual methodology and the insights it provoked, particularly by bringing into sharp focus what for me are some of the most pressing, if ambiguous and conflicted, aspects of return fieldwork and the forms of giving back it can entail.

Historical Photographs in Geographic Research

The incorporation of historical, oblique (side-looking) photographs in geographic research is not new (Humbert 2001; Sidaway 2002; Jakle 2004). In Latin America, oblique landscape photographs from the early twentieth century have been paired with contemporary shots in fine-grained assessments of changes in land use and land cover (Works and Hadley 2000; Bass 2004). Others have used old photographs to re-create the travel paths of eminent geographers (Walker and Leib 2002), and to solicit migration narratives (Price 2001). But few geographers appear to have used historical photographs explicitly as a means to access local residents' own perceptions and interpretations of changes in their social and biophysical environment.

This is what I had in mind when I returned to Tawahka territory in 2002 with copies of thirteen historical photographs. Most of them were portraits of Tawahka individuals, rather than the landscape shots more commonly used in geographic research. They had been taken in 1933 by Allen Payne, a member of a Smithsonian expedition to the middle Patuca that was led by the noted archaeologist William Duncan Strong (Strong 1934; see also Cuddy 2000, 2007). I had chosen the images from about 180 that were taken during the team's stay in the mid-Patuca. The images are preserved in the expedition's annotated photo album, which is now housed in the National Anthropological Archives in Maryland.[2] The existence of these photographs had been brought to my attention in 2000 by anthropologist Thomas Cuddy, then a Smithsonian Research Fellow. Only two images from the Tawahka series had ever been published (see Strong 1934); the rest, as far as I knew, were unknown in Honduras.

My plan was to repatriate these long-lost photographs to the descendants of those pictured—an act I vaguely envisioned as "decolonizing." In the process, I hoped that Tawahka individuals' own interpretations of both the images and their temporal context might shed some light on their perceptions of how their lives, livelihoods, and environments have changed across the past seventy years.[3] In effect, I wanted to tap in to what the anthropologist Gow (1991, 3) has termed "history from within." Although I had previously shared many conversations with Tawahka about the past, it seemed to me that the immediacy and detail of the photographs might awaken deeper and more specific reflections on local perceptions of time and change, based on the naïve assumption that Tawahka would see the photos as I did: an unproblematic, legible record of Tawahka life in the early twentieth century.

The photographs seemed to hold particular promise in this regard, for several reasons. First, they depicted a time that the historical record suggested to be one of particularly rapid change for Indigenous communities in eastern Honduras. For example, the photographs include images of Tawahka individuals, families, and villages some years after their population was apparently brought to its lowest point by a smallpox epidemic (see Cuddy 2000), and when the group's extinction appeared to be imminent (Harrower 1925; Conzemius 1932). But against all odds, the group was to survive, culturally, linguistically, and territorially (Davidson and Cruz 1995). The photographs therefore depict not the "last Tawahka," but a core of survivors that were to eventually keep the Tawahka ethnicity alive by selectively intermarrying with neighboring ethnic groups (McSweeney 2002a). So it is significant that the photographs also depict Nicaraguan Miskito refugees as recent arrivals to the mid-Patuca. Fleeing the conflicts between Sandino and US Marines along the Río Coco (see Brooks 1989), the Miskito were just becoming a significant cultural and territorial presence in the mid-Patuca when Strong's expedition met them (Cuddy 2000). It is no coincidence that Tawahka genealogies show this to be a time when Tawahka families increasingly incorporated Nicaraguan Miskitu. At the same time, Payne's photographs of the Miskitu are also a reminder of a particularly overt phase of US intervention in the Mosquitia region, which would foreshadow the contra-Sandinista conflict that profoundly disrupted lives along the river fifty years later.

Second, although Strong's expedition notebooks suggest that he held what were typically normative and paternalistic views of the people he encountered (i.e., "our first Sumu" [Tawahka]; "a real Indian at last!"; in Cuddy 2000, 11), Payne's photographs seem unusual. For one, many are portraits that were shot surprisingly close up (figures 7.1–7.3), rather than at the mid-range distance preferred by ethnographers of the time (Johnson 1998). The effect is a high degree of intimacy and visual detail that is heightened by the fact that the names of the subjects were recorded, as were detailed notes on their relations to one another. The overall result is an unusually personal and accessible set of photographs. Third, the photographs appear much less staged than might be expected from contemporaneous images of native peoples (Harlan 1995). Most of the subjects appear to be relaxed; some are smiling. Not that some of the pic-tures are not *posed*: most of the portraits taken on the beach at Krautara show an identical background, as though individuals were asked, in turn, to briefly step in front of the fixed camera (e.g., figures 7.1 and 7.2). The spontaneous nature of the photographs may reflect the fact that the expedition stopped only briefly in each community, where they "spent some time getting photos, trading . . . and fooling around" (in Cuddy 2000, 10). These shots appear to be the only visual record of Tawahka individuals taken in the half century between 1919 and 1970 (see Adams 1972; Girard 1979 [1948]).

For all of these reasons, I was excited at the thought of returning the photos—or at least copies of them—to the descendants of those pictured. Tawahka families had often asked me for any pictures I might have of their recently deceased children, parents, and siblings. In fact, photographs had always been one of the most tangible products of my research and widely appreciated as gifts. I therefore anticipated that photos of long-gone fathers, grandmothers, and great-grandparents would be particularly appreciated, especially by older folk. Further, the Tawahka's remarkable internal growth since the 1930s meant that most of the more than 1,300 Tawahka then living along the Río Patuca could claim some blood connection to those in the photographs.

At the same time, I hoped that the photographs would advance my own research in specific ways. Specifically, the research grant that had allowed me to pay for the photographs' reproduction ($25 each) proposed

FIG. 7.1—Is this Ramón Sánchez? Krautara beach, Río Patuca, Honduras, 1933. Photograph by Allen Payne (William Duncan Strong Papers, Box 67, National Anthropological Archives, Smithsonian Institution).

to explore links between the Tawahka's demographic growth and land use change in the region. In previous research on the group's demography, I had paid little attention to how Tawahka themselves perceived their own population history, particularly regarding the increasingly interethnic nature of Tawahka marriages. So I looked forward to using the photos to explore categories of identity used by local peoples themselves. I was particularly curious about whether the complex interplay of interethnic mixing, ethnocultural persistence, and interethnic contests over land that *I* perceived to be important would echo in local people's own interpretations of the images of their forebears.

FIG. 7.2—Francisco Ordoñez and wife Victoria, Krautara beach, Río Patuca, Honduras, 1933. Photograph by Allen Payne (William Duncan Strong Papers, Box 67, National Anthropological Archives, Smithsonian Institution).

Little did I realize how much the photographs would reveal, although in ways quite different from what I had anticipated.

Tawahka Interpretations of the Strong Expedition Photographs

In six weeks along the Patuca, I eventually showed the photographs in both impromptu and scheduled meetings with individuals, families, and elders, and in random gatherings in the five Tawahka communities. I spread the photographs out on porches, under trees, and at the local church and school, where they were viewed by daylight, candlelight, and flashlight. Some observers—especially those with little formal education—required several moments to get a photo right side up. I estimate that I was present

FIG. 7.3—Unnamed Nicaraguan Miskitu refugee and child, on beach at Krautara, Río Patuca, Honduras, 1933. Photograph by Allen Payne (William Duncan Strong Papers, Box 67, National Anthropological Archives, Smithsonian Institution).

when some two hundred people first saw the photos. In each community, I left a complete set of the thirteen images with a community designate, and individual photos with closest relatives of those pictured. (Ironically, I took no photographs of these meetings because my own camera succumbed to humidity after less than a week in the field.)

During each meeting, I briefly explained that the photographs had been taken by a visiting gringo seventy years before, who then brought the pictures home to the United States. I explained that, when he died, his effects had been left to an institution (which I described as a cross between a museum and a library) in Washington, DC. I said that copies of the photographs were now available at the archive to anyone who wished to pay for them. I then listened, and sometimes videotaped or voice-recorded, as the photographs were interpreted and discussed. Depending where we were, conversation comprised a mixture of either Tawahka and Spanish, or Tawahka and Miskitu. Occasionally I'd be asked to clarify something about the photographs: Was anyone pictured still alive? Were there more? Who was "selling" them? Because the obvious newness of the paper on which the images were copied led to some confusion about the actual age of the photographs, I often had to clarify the issue of their provenance, upkeep, and reproduction.

Not surprisingly, the images provoked considerable discussion. Older people were pleased to see that the photos confirmed what they remembered of how clothing had been worn by their grandparents. Many people considered the loincloths worn by children in the photos to be hilarious. Although today Tawahka are known for their modesty, the bare-breasted women in the photos were only remarked on as offering evidence of the "styles" of that time. For many, looking at the portraits was obviously moving. One young man remarked, "It's like they're alive, and I'm looking at them." One woman cried silently at the sight of her long-dead father. The patriarch of one family, whose parents were depicted in one photo (figure 7.2), said, "My mother, my father—they died a long time ago. And now I have them again."

Some responses to the photographs also suggested that viewers perceived some qualitative changes in their lives since the photographs had been taken. There were several comments about the previous abundance of fish and game compared with their paucity today. These comments were primarily stimulated by the picture of a member of the Strong expedition near the village of Yapuwas holding up a recently caught freshwater shark—a species that has not been seen in the river since the 1970s. On the other hand, several women were quick to remark on how "dirty" people looked in the photographs; and how "sad" life appeared. "How much has changed in seventy years!" said a Tawahka nurse. One man specifically asked that I not show the photos elsewhere, particularly not in Miskitu villages downriver. He was worried that the images might confirm old prejudices about Tawahka as "bad people, dirty Sumitos" (a derogatory term for Tawahka used primarily by neighboring Miskitu and mestizos).

Discussion also spontaneously turned to particular issues that I had been interested in, but in unexpected ways.

Cultural Identity

I was surprised at how repeatedly comments about the photographic subjects' skin tones cropped up, and how discussion shed light on the ongoing affirmation of Tawahka identity. One portrait was frequently, and approvingly, said to represent a "*puir*" (pure) Tawahka. I had never remarked the use of this term before, which appeared to acknowledge the high degree of interethnic mixing that had apparently diluted these *puir* features in generations since. But even as this was acknowledged, the importance of ethnic purity was as quickly refuted by comments asserting that culture is "carried" by people, it is not inherited. One man stated categorically, "To have the culture, that is worth the most; blood isn't worth anything."[4] I had never heard such a clear distinction made between genetic and cultural ascription, and it struck me as one that has been probably been central to the Tawahka's linguistic and cultural persistence against tremendous assimilative odds.

The Nature of Knowledge

I was disappointed by the relatively few comments that identified specific ways in which people thought life and landscape had changed since the 1930s. As people talked about the photos, however, I was reminded that in both Miskitu and Tawahka, "to see" and "to know" are the same word. This linguistic flag marks the degree to which, as in many cultures, knowledge is considered to be derived primarily from firsthand experience (see Gow 1991, 168). Thus if one has not experienced a particular time, it is impossible to truly know it, nor, by extension, to have an opinion about it. As a result, most of the people who looked at the photographs were reluctant to assess how life must have been in the past. As I was frequently told, "*Como yo no miraba ese tiempo, no puedo decir*" (Since I didn't see that time, I can't say). Instead, they suggested I talk to the one woman whose life *did* span both periods: a Tawahka matriarch known to be well over eighty. When the opportunity finally arose to show Doña Rufina the pictures, however, she only squinted at them with failing eyes and declared, "Can't see a damn thing."

Notions of Time

Another factor that hindered any clearer articulation of the differences between "then" and "now" was that such comparisons imply a linear and unidirectional view of time. As I heard people talking about the photos, it became clear that a simple timeline did not order most people's thoughts about the past. Thus places and people that the Strong expedition had photographed within a week of each other were not necessarily accepted as contemporaneous. For example, there appeared to be a common conviction that the village labeled as "Pitabila" belonged to a more distant time than did the remembered faces in the other photographs. That is, no one questioned the photograph's representational authority (i.e., that the picture showed Pitabila), but they summarily rejected its implicit temporal claim. Further, Pitabila was said to belong to a "bad" time with which the people in the portraits were not considered to be associated. Interestingly, the hex experienced by that particular village was said to be of the sort currently visited on Krausirpi (in which a relatively high number of people had died since Hurricane Mitch). The photograph of Pitabila, then, became a referent through which to understand modern goings-on. The photograph therefore suggested a much more multidimensional view of time than the simple one that shaped my research questions.

Power Relations

As much as the photographs' *content* shed new light on how Tawahka perceive identity, knowledge, and time, the most disquieting insight for me arose from discussions of the photographs' *provenance*.

One memorable exchange was sparked by the portrait reproduced in figure 7.1. Strong and the photographer had written in their notes that the picture represented a young man in his early twenties named Ramón Sancis (or Sánchez). Soon after I arrived in a Tawahka village in which many residents have the surname Sánchez, a group assembled to look at the old photographs. No one, however, recognized the face, so after a while I offered the name. After some consultation, they called over an older woman, probably about forty-five or fifty, who had been otherwise uninterested in joining the group. They told her that this was a picture of her father. She looked at it for a while, and then declared,

"That's not my father. My father had a beard."

People urged her to look again: the camera might have been at a strange angle; here, he is younger than when you knew him—[5]

But she would not budge: "*No creo* [I don't believe it]."

At this point, I interjected, and suggested that perhaps Strong had gotten it wrong: perhaps there had been some confusion, and that this was *not* a picture of Ramón Sanchez. At this point the discussion took a revealing turn.

Impossible, they said. Gringos are smart, and they write things down properly. There was no mistake. Hadn't the man who took these pictures been clever enough to see that they continued to be sold, even after his death? Thus ensued a lively discussion about how gringos held on to other peoples' photos, and took care of them. We Tawahka would have let them rot long ago—and *then* how would we have known what our ancestors looked like? One woman summed it up: "*Los gringos mandan* [gringos are in charge]." I demurred. She persisted:

> If it wasn't for gringos, Honduras would have nothing. . . . The money for this Reserve, it's sent by foreigners [*de afuera*]. It's a political thing of the gringos, this reserve. You guys bought it. If it were [really] ours, we'd all have a paper [title]. Where are the papers? . . . . The money comes from the US. This land belongs to the gringos! As long as it is like this, there are no papers, we will live like we live now [i.e., poor].

I had never heard—or rather, listened for—such an interpretation of land ownership in the region, or of the Tawahka Asangni Biosphere Reserve. In subsequent discussions of the photographs, I therefore paid closer attention to this train of thought. As long as the discussion was in Miskitu or Tawahka, I heard several echoes of this sentiment regarding exogenous control over Tawahka lands. For example, I heard mention that the management rules for the reserve (which were generally understood to involve prohibiting the sale of forest goods, and in rendering some areas off-limits to extraction) were designed so that gringos could come and enjoy the environment, even if it meant keeping Tawahka poor.

I did not get the impression, however, that these ideas constituted most peoples' *primary* reaction to the photographs, nor that these ideas encompass *all* understandings of the reserve's management. But I did get the distinct feeling that this was not an uncommon view stirred up by the photographs, and that for many it constituted a reasonable assessment of their ongoing experiences of foreigners' interests in the region.

Conclusion: Historical Photographs as Mirrors, not Windows

It has now been several years since I gave back the photographs to Tawahka families. I don't know if the images still represent mementos of gringo power; it does appear, however, that the photos may appear in a history of the Tawahka people coauthored by several Tawahka bilingual education students. I also know that the experience has caused me to rethink the very notion of "return fieldwork" and of "giving back."

First, it has made me think much more deeply about the persistence of foreign influence over Tawahka lands that I embody, consciously or not, with every return visit. After all, the photographs that I had naïvely thought I could "give back" ultimately served to reinforce the impression that all documents of value to Tawahka lives are out there somewhere in gringo hands. In essence, the photographs did not act alone as passive windows into the past (as I thought they would). Instead, they acted in concert with me and with Strong to align us in asserting gringo control over Tawahka pasts and futures.[6] This was a troubling realization to me, because I had always envisioned my engagements with Tawahka as qualitatively different than that of other visitors: I told myself that I had lived there, I had returned, I had given back. And yet clearly my presence was deeply conjoined with that of other outsiders who preceded and will follow me into Tawahka lands. This insight humbled me to the complexity of my research position, and has since inspired me to acknowledge that while I may always have something to offer Tawahka, I will always have far more to learn from them. Further, I am more likely to learn (and thus be a better collaborator) if I am willing to slow down and listen more—what Grandia (2015) refers to as "the subversive slowness of grounded community research [that] creates a temporal space that facilitates mindfulness in observing the subtle, incremental, yet terribly profound transformations of human and social relations" (304).

Second, the experience has somewhat undermined my confidence in interpreting the changes that return fieldwork allows me to see. Previously, the longitudinal nature of my research lent conviction to my assertions about the dynamics and drivers of what seemed to me to be the most urgent and proximate types of changes occurring in the Tawahka landscape: emerging land scarcity, an encroaching deforestation frontier, rising local populations. But the priorities and schedules within which I and other researchers have discursively framed and explained these events may be seriously out of synch with local perceptions and explanations of change. For one, discussions arising from the photographs suggest to me that my linear sequencing of specific events, and the priority I place on certain ones, may only partially reflect the temporal order and relative importance with which local people experience and prioritize changes in their lives and landscapes (see also McSweeney 2002b). These mismatches in temporal perceptions are far from trivial. Most "collaborative" research initiatives—particularly in the arena of conservation and rural development—are premised on the unexamined assumption that all stakeholders hold a common way of thinking about the nature and pace of landscape changes such as forest conversion. Yet a common understanding should *not* be assumed. Geographers, whose interests in landscape *change* put *time* (as much as space) front and center in their work, must therefore be particularly prepared to listen for—and, through discussion, reconcile—differences in local and outsider narratives about history, chronology, and change. Without such attempts, local people are unlikely to comply with management edicts that rest on assumptions they do not hold.

Finally, the unexpected responses I received to the return of the photographs reminded me of just how restricted were the knowledges that I held about the people and places of the mid-Patuca. After all, I had completely failed to anticipate what this particular research method would do, and what it would reveal. I would probably have been less surprised, however, had I been more familiar with visual anthropology (e.g., Banks and Morphy 1997), critical visual methodologies (e.g., Rose 2001), or the fascinating work in native studies that unpacks not only the "colonial grammar" in photographic representations of Indigenous people, but how that legacy is resisted and subverted when Indigenous peoples themselves reinterpret those old images and produce new representations of their own (see, e.g., Harlan 1995; Tsinhnahjinnie 2003; Goeman 2014).

In fact, as I "friend" a growing number of urban Tawahka youth on Facebook, I marvel at the enthusiasm and panache that they exhibit in representing themselves online. Via Facebook, we exchange photos of friends, children, offer birthday wishes, and share news. This visual reciprocity far eclipses my former, clumsy efforts to give back photographs. As such, I have come to think that it offers an apt metaphor for the direction in which my research is, and should be, moving. That is, away from merely "giving back," toward sustained, reciprocal relationships founded on long-term political solidarity and care.

Chapter 7 References

Adams, William G. 1972. Mosquitia: A Honduran Frontier. Unpublished ms. Eastern Kentucky University Department of Geography.

Banks, Marcus, and Howard Morphy, eds. 1997. *Rethinking Visual Anthropology*. New Haven, CT: Yale University Press.

Bass Jr., Jerry O. 2004. "More Trees in the Tropics." *Area* 36 (1): 19–32.

Brooks, David C. 1989. "U.S. Marines, Miskitos, and the Hunt for Sandino: The Río Coco Patrol in 1928." *Journal of Latin American Studies* 21 (2): 311–342.

Conzemius, Eduard. 1932. *Ethnographical Survey of the Miskito and Sumu Indians of Honduras and Nicaragua*. Smithsonian Institution Bureau of American Ethnology, Bulletin 106. Washington, DC: United States Printing Office.

Cuddy, Thomas W. 2000. The Sumu of Northeastern Honduras: Classic Ethnography by William Duncan Strong. Unpublished ms.

———. 2007. *Political Identity and Archaeology in Northeast Honduras*. Boulder: University Press of Colorado.

Davidson, William V., and Fernando Cruz. 1995. "Delimitación de la Región Habitada por los Sumos Taguacas de Honduras en el Período de 1600 a 1900." *Mesoamérica* 29:159–165.

Girard, Raphael. 1979 [1948]. *Esotericism of the Popol Vuh*. Trans. Blair A. Moffett. Pasadena, CA: Theosophical University Press.

Godoy, Ricardo A. 2001. *Indians, Markets, and Rainforests: Theory, Methods, and Analysis*. New York: Columbia University Press.

Goeman, Mishuana R. 2014. "Disrupting a Settler-colonial Grammar of Place: The Visual Memoir of Hulleah Tsinhnahjinnie." In *Theorizing Native Studies*, edited by Audra Simpson and Andrea Smith, 235–265. Durham, NC: Duke University Press.

Gow, Peter. 1991. *Of Mixed Blood: Kinship and History in Peruvian Amazonia*. Oxford, UK: Clarendon Press.

———. 1995. "Land, People, and Paper in Western Amazonia." In *The Anthropology of Landscape: Perspectives on Place and Space*, edited by E. Hirsch and M. O'Hanlon, 43–62. Oxford, UK: Clarendon Press.

Grandia, Liza. 2015. "Slow Ethnography: A Hut with a View." *Critique of Anthropology* 35 (3): 301–317.

Harlan, Theresa. 1995. "Creating a Visual History: A Question of Ownership." In *Strong Hearts: Native American Visions and Voices*, edited by Peggy Roalf, 20–32. New York: Aperture Foundation.

Harrower, D. E. 1925. "Rama, Mosquito, and Sumu, of Nicaragua." *Indian Notes (Museum of the American Indian, Heye Foundation, New York)* 2 (1): 44–48.

Herlihy, Peter H., and Gregory Knapp. 2003. "Maps of, by, and for the Peoples of Latin America." *Human Organization* 62 (4): 303–314.

Humbert, André. 2001. "The Aerial Field." *Geographical Review* 91 (1/2): 273–284.

Jakle, John A. 2004. "The Camera and Geographical Inquiry." In *Geography and Technology*, edited by S. D. Brunn, S. L. Cutter, and J. W. J. Harrington, 221–242. Dordrecht: Kluwer Academic.

Johnson, Tim, ed. 1998. *Spirit Capture: Photographs from the National Museum of the American Indian*. Washington, DC: Smithsonian Institution Press.

Kates, Robert W. 1987. "The Human Environment: The Road Not Taken, the Road Still Beckoning." *Annals of the Association of American Geographers* 77 (4): 525–534.

McSweeney, Kendra. 2002a. "A Demographic Profile of the Tawahka Amerindians of Honduras." *Geographical Review* 92 (3): 398–414.

———. 2002b. "Two Years after Hurricane 'Mix': Indigenous Response in the Rain Forest of Eastern Honduras." *FOCUS on Geography* 46 (4): 15–21.

Normark, Don. 1999. *Chávez Ravine, 1949: A Los Angeles Story*. San Francisco: Chronicle Books.

Parsons, James J. 1977. "Geography as Exploration and Discovery." *Annals of the Association of American Geographers* 67 (1): 1–16.

Price, Marie. 2001. "The Kindness of Strangers." *Geographical Review* 91 (1/2): 143–151.

Rose, Gillian. 2000. "Practicing Photography: An Archive, a Study, Some Photographs, and a Researcher." *Journal of Historical Geography* 26 (4): 555–571.

———. 2001. *Visual Methodologies*. London: SAGE.

Sidaway, James D. 2002. "Photography as Geographical Fieldwork." *Journal of Geography in Higher Education* 26 (1): 95–103.

Stevens, Stan. 2001. "Fieldwork as Commitment." *Geographical Review* 91 (1/2): 66–74.

Strong, William Duncan. 1934. "Hunting Ancient Ruins in Northeast Honduras." *Explorations and Field-Work of the Smithsonian Institution* 1933:44–53.

Tsinhnahjinnie, Hulleah J. 2003. "When Is a Photograph Worth a Thousand Words?" In *Photography's Other Histories*, edited by Christopher Pinney and Nicolas Peterson, 40–54. Durham, NC: Duke University Press.

Walker, Johnathan, and Jonathan Leib. 2002. "Revisiting the Topia Road: Walking in the Footsteps of West and Parsons." *Geographical Review* 92 (4): 555–581.

Works, Martha A., and Keith S. Hadley. 2000. "Hace Cincuenta Años: Repeat Photography and Landscape Change in the Sierra Purépecha of Michoacán, Mexico." *Yearbook, Conference of Latin Americanist Geographers* 26:139–155.

Notes to Chapter 7

1. We were both working as researchers for the NSF-funded Honduras Forests Project of the Harvard Institute for International Development (see Godoy 2001).
2. These archives are part of the National Museum of Natural History. The annotated album from the Strong expedition is filed with the William Duncan Strong Papers, under "Smithsonian Archaeological Expedition to Northeast Honduras and the Bay Islands, [January–July] 1933." The entire collection includes some 407 images, with an associated list of photographic subjects; Strong's notebook contains further details relevant to image interpretation (summarized in Cuddy 2000, 2007).
3. My optimism in the potential for using historical photographs for this purpose was also fueled by the remarkable book *Chávez Ravine, 1949: A Los Angeles Story* (Normark 1999). At the time, I was not aware of the National Museum of the American Indian's own efforts to connect their collections of old photographs of native peoples to the subjects' descendants, and thereby stimulate new narratives about what the pictures represent (see Johnson 1998).
4. Interestingly, this same man is locally considered to come closest to bearing the characteristic features of a *puir* Tawahka. The view he voices regarding the reproduction of culture is also remarkably similar to that reported among Amazonian peasantries by Gow (1991).
5. Such comments were typical: most people were remarkably astute regarding the potential distortions produced by the camera.
6. Rose (2000) and Gow (1995) describe similar ways in which photographs and paper documents act as objects that assert particular forms of authority.

PART 3

Telling Their Stories

8

"Are You Making a Million Dollars?"

Reciprocity as Cultural and Environmental Reconnection

MARIA FADIMAN

"**A**RE YOU MAKING A million dollars?" Don Jorge asked.

"No," I replied.

He laid his hand on the bark of the tree and said, "We heard that a researcher in the next village made a million dollars," he paused, "and didn't give any to the people."

"No money for me."

"Then why are you doing it?" he asked.

That was a good question.

Why do I what I do? I am an ethnobotanist studying the relationship between plants and people. My overall goal is to promote conservation and cultural retention from within communities. Through helping local people maintain their own plant knowledge, this can lead to a more concrete reconnection to the plants themselves and raise the value of the ecosystems in which these plants live (Fadiman 2007). One of the issues I need to address on every project is how do I compensate people for the time they take out of their daily schedule working with me and sharing their information?

How to give back to the people with whom we work? Is "giving back" even the best terminology? I have worked with everyday compensation, such as daily working wages (complicated), candy (popular but morally dubious), and photographs (which I still do) to reimburse people for time and energy. What I gave back before I started in academia, and to which I am now coming full circle, are accessible records of their information. These are collaborative endeavors returned to the locals in an absorbable medium. This does not come without complications and, depending on the kind of research one does, may or may not fit. I myself am still learning how to most effectively execute these projects. Each mission has progressed as I learn more about what communities want and what I can—and cannot—facilitate. The attempt is to find a meaningful way to work with people while shifting the dynamic away from them giving to me and my compensating them to something we create together from which we all benefit, culturally, ecologically, and academically.

This chapter is about how versions of my projects—ethnobotanical booklets—are evolving to aid in conservation through reconnecting people to their own culture and the land from which it sprouts, and in so doing, how this becomes in and of itself a form of reciprocity. Working jointly with local people, I convert oral knowledge into written words and images so that when elders pass away their information is not lost with them. This is not without consequences, as putting another culture's wisdom into a Western context can affect the information itself. Deciding that the risks are worth the results, I maintain that written information takes on a particular validity through the fact that it is a tangible representation of thought. It is important to note that I wish I could say I have done this every time, but I have not. Over the years, I have still handed out many mini-Snickers during my research.

Looking at the overall method and impact of this kind of reciprocity, these are the categories this paper addresses:

1. Creation of a lasting record: The final product of a written document (in their own language is best), punctuated by illustrations or photographs, validates the information of the elders for themselves and the youth.

2. Lasting book benefits: The community not only has a book of their ethnobotanical knowledge, they have the intangible effect of elders' cultural and ecological knowledge celebrated. These elements remain in a community indefinitely.

3. Including maximum number of plants and people: Through happenstance and then later with more intention, I have tried

to continually include more plants and kinds of people, such as women, children, teenagers, and distinct ethnicities, in an attempt to empower more people and age groups.
4. Recognizing the role of language: A central way to give back to people is with their own words in their own language.
5. Giving back: Most importantly, these booklets are a form of giving back to the people with whom I work in an equitable and beneficial way for all parties.

Using examples from personal experience, I address my trajectory in making these forms of reciprocity. The increased understanding and incremental development of methodology draws from community reactions and input coupled with chance situations. I draw from my research with the Kichwa in the Amazon in Ecuador; the Lacandon in Chiapas, Mexico; mestiza women on the Osa Peninsula, Costa Rica; the Ndeble in Zimbabwe, Southern Africa; and the Ha in Tanzania, East Africa.

Ethnobotanical Giving Back: The Beginning

Don Jorge, a Kichwa *curandero* (healer) in the Ecuadorian Amazon, asked me the "million dollars" question while stopped at a mahogany tree. Although income was not my goal, it was important that I give him something for the time he spent with me. We walked the forest each day as he taught me about medicinal plants. We clarified that I was not working for a pharmaceutical company or anyone else with designs on his knowledge, and he agreed that he wouldn't tell me anything secret anyway. I was making a booklet of his plants for him and his children so that his knowledge would not be lost when he passed away. "When an elder dies a library burns" is an African proverb, with variations of the same sentiment said in numerous cultures (Samuelson 2010). I was trying to do my small part to not only prevent that disappearance, but to also try to reverse the trend. I hoped that young people would be encouraged by the activity and take an interest in the use of their own ecosystem. This was my way of ensuring that the local residents "got" something out of the exchange. Later, I learned through academia how to give these works meaning beyond the immediate people and communities. At this point however, I was not yet an academic. With Don Jorge I was just getting started, and in so doing, learning about how to "give back" as well as I could.

Earlier that month I had arrived at the biological station Jatun Sacha in Ecuador as a volunteer with the goal of pursuing ethnobotany. As soon as I managed to extricate myself from raking leaves in the rain forest, I followed Don Jorge for the next few months, taking notes and tying a piece of flagging tape onto a sample of each plant discussed and popping it into my bag. All the plants we collected were medicinal, as I assumed that was what ethnobotany was. Healing plants are indeed a large part of the plant/people relationship, and over the years I have opened my research to pursue the many other kinds of plant uses that exist as well.

I attempted to illustrate the collections to make the booklet more aesthetically alluring and so that illiterate people could also connect with the finished product. Although the concept of drawing the plants was sound, the main hindrance stemmed from my inability to draw. However, with much erasing on damp paper in the rain forest, pencil marks emerged that resembled plants. In hindsight, it was a bonus that I had not yet studied botany and thus felt satisfied with a single leaf. I justified my pitiful renditions with the fact that the Kichwa recognized the plants, and the booklet was for them. It was not until I entered graduate school that a botany professor brought to my attention that proper botanical illustrations required fruits and/or flowers, and perhaps, on a really bad day, at least two leaves.

Ignorant of such details at the time, I balanced in the canoe on the Napo River on the way to the photocopy machine that was located in the small town downriver that had electricity. Wrapped in a plastic garbage bag, my typed work was protected from the water spray, each page including the plant name in Kichwa, the habit, the Latin name, use, and preparation, accompanied by a drawing taped beneath the text. Earlier that week Don Jorge had sat with me as I double-checked the spelling of the plant names in Kichwa, and I began to realize what it could mean to people to see their own language written.

After a successful round at the copy machine, I handed my mentor the finished project. When I saw the look on Don Jorge's face as he turned each photocopied page, spiral-bound with a sheet of plastic as a cover, his appreciation let me know this mattered. He and his family now had his information in a lasting format. Admittedly unprofessional and botanically limited, this was my "giving back" for our many months in the forest together.

Gender and Ethnicity: Validating *Mestiza* Women and Their Expertise

After getting a taste of the rain forest, I followed my interests and worked as a naturalist guide on the Osa Peninsula, Costa Rica. The more I learned about the mass of green through which I led people, the more I realized the level at which humans are inextricably integrated into the ecosystem. If I was interested in conservation, I had to include the people who lived in the forest. It also became clear that the most successful way was through collaboration that the locals felt was worth their time. With my still fledgling skills, I decided to give back another booklet of information.

The people with whom I worked on the peninsula were not Indigenous; they were *mestizos* (a mixture of Indigenous and European). I had idealized Native people, their role in the forest, and their knowledge. This was in no way lessened while I was in the Amazon with Don Jorge. However, now in a distinct setting, I was learning that the ethnicity of those with whom I worked was not the most relevant factor, but that whoever lived in and from the forest were the notable people in the equation. In this case, the mestizos were the individuals whose knowledge deserved to be preserved.

In order to increase the pool of information and to increase the number of people who felt connected to the project and the forest, I wanted to expand the work beyond just the knowledge of one person. I chose to research with a whole community. Setting out during the daylight hours, I knocked on doors beneath thatched roofs. The people who answered my knuckle taps turned out to be exclusively women. The men were in the fields.

Gender had not been the intention of my study, but since these were the only individuals available to speak with me, and they were excited to do so, the work shifted to a female-centered study. I clarified what I intended to give back to them, and they readily agreed. The women's eagerness was initially a surprise. Perhaps my own shock was due to the fact that most visitors addressed husbands and fathers, especially for this kind of information. The women quietly also had knowledge. For this particular booklet, I decided to include a photograph of each collaborator to promote not only their knowing the information, but also to recognize each individual herself. This seemed a proper form of reciprocation.

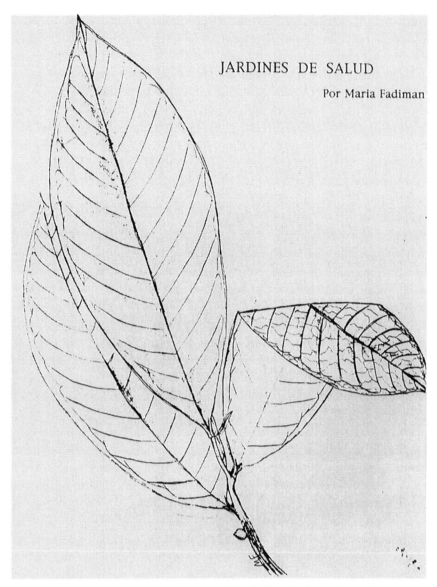

JARDINES DE SALUD

Por Maria Fadiman

FIG. 8.1—Cover of the booklet *Jardines de Salud*, made for and with the women of the Osa Peninsula, Costa Rica.

I not only saw this as a chance to empower women and the wisdom they held, I also started to see patterns that I could analyze academically, such as the trends of gender differentiation that emerged. For example, data demonstrated that women focused on plants for cooking and children's health. Moreover, the spatial relations of the plants used in the majority of their remedies grew close to home, and included a high ratio of cultivated species from their gardens. I ended up naming the booklet, *Jardines de Salud* (Gardens of Health). Informal interviews with men emphasized the gender-specific aspect of these findings, as I learned that men mostly gathered wild forest plants, often located at great distances away from home.

Validating her knowledge through the written word, each woman could now be respected for what she knew. Additionally, others could also see that someone from outside made a booklet of women's information concerning health and plants. This was before scanning, so the pictures were photocopied and dark, and the drawings—although larger and including more of the plant—were still but a gesture toward recognition. However, for these women and the time they spent with me, to hold the final project was a solid form of reciprocity. These women now owned a tangible item that dignified their culture, their plants, and themselves. One woman said, "I'm going to show this to my kids ... especially my eldest daughter."

Age: A Surprising Group of Experts

Understanding the importance of giving back to more people in the community, especially to underrepresented groups such as women, I wanted to increase the kinds of people who were involved in the projects. Through unexpected circumstances I found myself working, not with a gender balance, but a new age group, teenagers. Researching with the Lacandon, a lowland Indigenous group in Chiapas, Mexico, in 1996 was a challenge. They lived in the Selva Lacandon (Lacandon Forest), where the Zapatista Army of National Liberation, commonly called the Zapatistas, was also headquartered—a revolutionary group mostly comprising Indigenous peasants. In 1994 they swooped into various municipalities, one of which was San Cristóbal, on New Year's Day, and took over the city. The soldiers were hung over and unprepared and the Zapatistas scored a temporary success. The Mexican army eventually drove the rebels back into the mountains (Duncan 2005). Although there was still tension in the area, two years later the media coverage and the major action seemed to have subsided. I was going to Chiapas to work for a peaceful cause: the preservation and promotion of Lacandon ethnobotanical information. The Lacandons themselves were not a part of the rebellion. However, two weeks before I headed out in 1996, paramilitaries had massacred a group of Indigenous people while they worshipped in the local church, and the region was tense. Despite obstacles to our research group, including entering a now-guarded wooded area and continually needing to show our passports to teenage boys cradling machine guns, we eventually entered the forest.

When I arrived in 1996, there were only about 650 Lacandon-speaking members in existence (Hernandez Cruz et al. 2014). Many wore traditional robes, white for the men and flowered for the women, and both genders wore their hair mostly long. I talked with the community about the possibility of a booklet, gauging local interest to see if they felt this was a fair exchange for their time and knowledge. After seeing their enthusiasm, I asked who wanted to do the work with me. Expecting older men, and trying to figure out how I would also ask for women, to my surprise, the ones who came forward turned out to be teenagers. More commonly in my experience, elders knew how to use the forest and, through working with them, I tried to entice the youth into being interested and respecting this information. In this case it seemed the opposite.

Why the young people? The boys told me that there were no longer *curanderos* or shamans in the villages, no specific older people who held the plant knowledge. Although this may or may not have been fully accurate, it highlighted the need to preserve what was still intact. Furthermore, the tensions in the regions may have occupied the energy of the elders, while this group of youth was relatively free. Partially, I also suspected that the teens' initial interest in working with me was due to my outsider status. They had already formed a group to lead tourists to the waterfalls, and time with foreigners appealed to them. However, tourists rarely came, and since the Zapatista conflict, there were almost none. I was their chance for outside connection. In the collaborative setting I was espousing, it was up to me to respect the community's decision and embrace the situation. Thus, they took it upon themselves to work with me, and were forthcoming with the information about their plants.

The plant knowledge they did possess, which despite my initial doubts was substantial, seemed to take on a new importance as the foreigner—me, who was a curiosity to them—was curious about what they knew. They placed high value on the outside world and the items that it contained,

Nombre:
Maya-   Nikte a'ak
Español-   Barba de viejo
Científico-   *Clematis doica* L. (Ranunculaceae)

Hábito: Bejuco maderable

Lugar de colección: Bosque primario, a 1 kilómetro de la comunidad.

Descripción: Flor blanca, pequeña. Fruta: frijol color verde.

Uso: a) Catarro. b) Tos. c) Artritis.

Preparación: a) Se hierven en dos litros de agua 5 hojas con una cucharadada de la corteza del bejuco raspada durante 15 minutos. b) Se cortan 15 hojas frescas c) Se hierven 20 centímetros de la corteza en una olla de agua durante 20 minutos.

Dosis: a) Se toma una taza 3 veces al día. b) Se comen dos hojas cuando empieza la tos. c) Se toma una taza diaria.

Número de Colecta: 23

FIG. 8.2—A page from the booklet made for and with the Lacandon in Chiapas, Mexico.

such as blue jeans and cars. Initially they peppered me with questions on these topics. However, as the time advanced, and they recognized that my attention was focused on them and their ethnobotanical knowledge, discussions became based more on their experiences, not mine.

When I completed the booklet, spiral-bound and photocopied, it contained plant names in Latin, Lacandon, and then English, with the preparation and dosage written in Spanish. The illustrations were now more detailed, some with flowers and fruit and all with at least numerous leaves. Scanning had also become accessible technology, and more details were captured from the drawings to the page.

When the boys held their own words in print, and thanked me as I thanked them, it was a step in reconnecting them with the importance of their own information. They now not only had a physical record, but they had been the main players in the process of their own compensation.

It would make a tidy story to say that they no longer valued blue jeans and fantasized about cars, but they did. I at least like to think that their world widened to include more of a fascination with their knowledge of their world in addition to the Western world. This booklet turned into a more wide-ranging project in terms of age; however, as all of the young people were male it lacked the gender component. Furthermore, the range of plants still covered only medicinal. Thus, it was more inclusive in some ways, and still exclusive in others.

On the Side: Booklets in Addition to Other Research

Zimbabwe in 2007, although not how Chiapas had been, was a different kind of tense. Robert Mugabe, the first democratically elected black leader after independence, had over the years of his rule become increasingly dictatorial. He eventually exerted his power through ethnic cleansing and then burned down rural shacks and roadside stands, inflicting extreme poverty on those who were already poor (Hoffman 2012). Inflation turned to hyperinflation as people took a "brick of bills" (a stack of Zimbabwe dollars the size of a brick) to buy a piece of fruit. As the local situation became more desperate, I noted how many people sat beneath trees carving. I learned that such a high number of individuals were out of work that they learned to carve decorative items for a living. As one man told me, "Starvation taught me art" (Fadiman 2008). I ended up researching woodcarving and tree poaching. This time as a side project, I learned about medicinal plants.

My study was not about making a healing plant record, but was an academic ethnobotanical analysis of tree use. The booklet I made was a hasty addition. The final edition was not as polished as others: photocopied pages with the plant names and uses with dosage and collection, stuffed into a three-ring red plastic binder. But the looks on the faces of the adults as they flipped through the pages, and the children's reactions as they hovered to try to get a good look, emphasized my deepening realization that this can be a powerful form of collaborative giving back. Independent of the product's level of sophistication, the information mattered.

Years later I received an email from a stranger who had been to the village and wrote to me that when Mpisi, the carver with whom I stayed, saw her he proudly brought out the photocopied sheets in the same red binder and said, "These are our plants." And he pointed to the first one and said, "The names are in our language." This work included only medicinal plants, and the people who shared with me were older men. So, there was still a bias in the book, as it lacked a level of botanical and human inclusivity. Furthermore, it was more rudimentary than any of the other ones I had made previously. However, it was a form of giving back to the people who had worked with me. I also returned to them the academic article, but that was of far less interest. I learned that even if plant knowledge records are not my main project, it turned out to be a meaningful aspect on which to focus some attention, as it was an appreciated way to give back.

Inclusivity: Language, People, and Plants

To embrace the academic aspect of recording plant use and to be more inclusive in terms of age, gender, and flora, I pursued a new opportunity. During my sabbatical year, I collaborated with Grace Gobbo, a Tanzanian ethnobotanist, on recording the useful plants of the Ha people in the village of Bubango, Tanzania. This time, I was clear to include categories beyond medicinal, to encompass more kinds of people, and to translate all of the text into the local language.

The importance of working with the Ha culture and the environment was particularly important not only for its own sake, but also because of external pressures. Sharing the region with the Ha were immigrants from Burundi who had settled in increasing numbers as a consequence of political unrest in their own country (Milner 2014). Thus local knowledge and language perseverance were situationally challenged. Moreover, interest in sustainable forest use extended beyond their own community to their immediate neighbors with whom they shared a forest border, Gombe Stream National Park. Gombe is home to the chimpanzees with whom the Jane Goodall Institute works. Thus traditional and sustainable use of the forest was important not just for village livelihood, but also for notable fauna. Reciprocation in this context would be multilayered.

Having noted the interest focused on the few words I had included in the local language, albeit just plant names, and after having worked on an ethnobotanical project in the highlands of East Asia in which we emphasized local dialect, the power of native vernacular was clear. Understanding this, I wanted not only for the project to include more plants and more people, but also for language to play a prominent role. If we were going to give something back, we wanted it to matter.

In order to apply for the grant, we needed a formal letter from the community asking us to come. This was a new level of collaboration, as we were there at the village's request. The explicit goal of this project was the booklet for the people. Additionally, as I was now part of the university system, I had a more thorough understanding of how to academically combine the recorded information with the research itself. With informed consent, the data we collected through interviews and observations such as demographics, plant species and families, habits, plant parts used, collection methods, preparations, accessibility assessments, locations, and sustainable aspects were all facts we could analyze, taking it beyond just the item we gave back. Furthermore, adding depth to the quantitative data, we gathered qualitative information, as each person and plant had its own story.

Expanding beyond medicine—although it was certainly included—we inquired about vegetation for food, music, construction, crafts, and rituals. Opening up the categories helped us include more kinds of people, as multiple uses were important to the larger community. Furthermore, this expansion also provided us with the opportunity to include more of a gender balance. Although women were healers, in this situation they were less likely to have come forth, or been brought forward by the community. However, when talking about cooking and crafts, and our specific request to include two genders, the community and the women themselves were more comfortable about being a part of the project. Although their numbers remained small, we did speak with them.

Part of the idea of reciprocity is that what we gave back would have an effect beyond the booklet itself. We wanted a specific element that would have meaning for the next generation. Despite the fact that the teenagers held the information with the Lacandon, which may in part be because they no longer had designated healers in the community, elders were still those who usually held the knowledge. When we arrived in the study village, Bubango, a village elder said in reference to the youth, "The young people don't care about plants. They just care about their cell phones." In a village without electricity, a high percentage of young people did have phones, with which they were often occupied. In order to actively include young people and children, we held a drawing contest of the plants that the older people had discussed. In this way, I—the researcher—was not the illustrator, the community was. The level of connection that a person can obtain when drawing a plant, studying the shape and details such as the texture of the leaf margin and the bend of the petiole, increases while transferring these to paper.

To pursue this part of the plan, we proposed the concept through the schools. We spent time explaining the importance of the project with the head of village education, who then became interested himself. The next step was to ask the teachers to be the judges. Thus they learned not only about which plants were useful, but also to think about the importance of the subject as a whole. We gave school supplies as prizes to all participants, and while buying the pens and paper, we explained the purpose to the curious stationery vendor, incorporating more unforeseen individuals.

Children also connected to the elders' information in ways that we did not orchestrate. While we interviewed the senior members of the village, youngsters literally hung on to the window sills, gripping with their fingers and pulling themselves up to peek. The fact that we were asking about the community's own plant culture elevated the status of that information in the eyes of the onlookers. The impact of the process became even more evident as others, such as motorcycle drivers, neighboring villagers, and people of the larger city, began to take interest.

As the motorcycle owners positioned us on the backs of their bikes to ride into the village each day, the drivers would ask why we were there. Over the music from their flash drives, the wind, and, for me, the barrier of not knowing how to say much more than "banana" in Swahili, we explained the project. They would usually shout back a few plants that they knew, as it became clear that was wisdom we valued. Moreover, while the drivers waited to take us back to the city, these young men came along as we collected plants with the elders. The drivers themselves began to ask questions of their own people. Our concentration on their world seemed to pique their own interest in their knowledge of their own place.

Language raised the level of inclusivity and the importance of what we were giving back. We wanted language to go beyond just the names of the plants and to occupy its own role, as language retention is a central aspect of cultural integrity (Salzman, Stanlaw, and Adachi 2014). We made the product trilingual: Kiha (the local language), Kiswahili, and English. We

FIG. 8.3—The schoolchildren of Bubango, Tanzania, seeing the finished booklet for the first time.

made sure that Kiha was first, and that English was last. At a group meeting of all the participants, they elected one of their men to translate with us. We worked with the text, transforming the ideas into three languages. Adding their linguistic sense of self was a new step for me in incorporating the locals and how they think and communicate. The project for us was about ethnobotany, and creating a lasting record, so when the elders passed away the knowledge would not be lost and forest practices could stay intact. And this was all true. However, as the project began to take form, in many ways language seemed the element with which the locals most connected.

Usually, the giving back of the booklets I made over the years had been to individuals without much fanfare. The pages themselves were the exciting parts. However, in order for this project to have a larger impact, the actual "giving back" itself became its own event. We decided to make the booklet presentation public and grand. Beyond the idea of mere reciprocity, it became a celebration of communal project completion. We not only wanted to honor the people whose knowledge was in the book,

Plant name: **Oncoba spinosa**

Izina mgiha: Umuyebhe

Ingene yibhiti: Ni giti chu muyebhe, kilakula kikamako ibhintu vyumu viringo bhiteye ngakuya kwa mabhungo.

Akazi bhikola: Ugukolako amayebhe yi usambele

Luhande: Amatunda

Akazi bhikogwa: Avuze shuusha musumari, uhweje kuteka utobholetobhole, ukulemo bhiyabhilimo, uhweze utole imbegu zu bhulengo ubhikemo; ushileko numugozi wambale, utangule kuvyina.

Ukulonkekana: Ni bhikeyi

Tabia za mmea: Ni mti wenye miiba na uzaao matunda makubwa saizi ya yai la kanga

Matumizi yake: Kutengeneza njuga kwa ajili ya ngoma ya Usambele

Mahitaji: Matunda makavu, mbegu za Bhulengo na msumari

Jinsi ya kutayarisha: Chemsha tunda kutoa ngozi ya juu, na mbegu, ikishakauka toboa matundu madogo; ingiza mbegu za Bhulengo kwenye matunda, unganisha matunda mengi na kamba ili upate njuga

Upatikanaji wa mmea: Hupatikana porini na mashambani

Plant Type: Tree

Use: Musical instrument, anklets for the Usambele dance.

Part Used: Fruit

Collection: Take desired number of fruits from the tree

Preparation: Put the whole fruit in the bucket where keep drinking water, and then dry each one on a nail. Then, put the nail in fire and heat it in order to make small holes in the fruit.

Accessibility and Location: Rare and found in the village and in the forest.

FIG. 8.4—A page from the more professional booklet in Tanzania, with the full Kiha text.

and the children with their drawings, but we also wanted the whole village to see that this information was important. The community brought in dancers who wore ankle seed rattles, which happened also to be plants included in the document. After the singing and stamping, we called up each person who had contributed information to the book to come up in front of the community, honoring each one individually.

For the schoolchildren, having already held their individual prize ceremonies at their classrooms, we brought them forward as a group with their teachers. As they clambered over each other to look at the finished product, the excitement was tangible. They could see, accentuated with colorful photos, their own information in a written format.

I keep referring to this work as collaborative, and there were different levels of who did what. In terms of the information, it was all the community's. For the actual book-making process, they helped us with photographs, taking us to the plants and, in some cases, taking pictures themselves after a quick lesson with the camera. Now that digital photography was available, each plant was depicted with a color photograph. For the actual making of the book, Grace took it to the capital, Dar es Salaam, where she had it printed in color on shiny thick paper, and thus the item itself turned into something of which to be proud. It looked professional and added to the importance to the content.

The spatial impact of the booklet extended out of the village itself. The stationery man in the city of Kigoma who sold us the children's prizes asked for a copy. When we brought it to him, from the back of the store we heard "I want a book in Kiha!" so we gave one to his helper. Through an interest in the Kiha language, he at least would be exposed to the plants and the value of conservation. Other people in town heard about it from the stationery worker, and they too wanted a copy. There was some ill will, as there were not enough copies for all. But through their desire to have copies, the local people and city dwellers endorsed the information. And, it was not just the ecological plant knowledge—our initial goal—but their cultural sense of self that came through the pages.

People in other villages then asked if we would do books with them. The interest was the beginning of concentric circles of knowledge and forest valuation. In comparison with my other works, this booklet had more people, plants, and language, although it was certainly not comprehensive. The women represented were fewer and were still relegated to realms of traditional female knowledge of cooking and crafts. Although not fully representative, it was an evocative giving back for us all.

Conclusion: Refining Collaborative Books to "Give Back"

In terms of compensation, giving back, or reciprocity, the making of booklets of people's own ecological and cultural information morphed over the years from a simple conglomeration of lists, into deeper interviews, more participants, promotion of local language, and the gathering of ecological information. In the future, I look to include not just pictures of the plants, but symbols for use categories, so that people can connect with the book more easily whether they can read or not. Thus, the project itself is about giving back. In the future, I would like to facilitate young people to do the interviews, so that they have their own ability to retain their information. Thus, the reciprocation would start from within the community.

As well as these items' function as a form of exchange, it is important to note the drawbacks as well. As mentioned, this is a western way of retaining information, and that can differ from local traditions. Furthermore, a record with supposed longevity is susceptible to the physical elements such as humidity, rain, and dust, as well as insects that may eat the books. Furthermore, how long they last is still dependent on the community, as eventually people could toss them aside, converting them into litter. In addition, I have used the resource of paper to make them, perhaps at odds with sustainable tree use. Socially, there has been jealousy by some who were not interviewed and/or did not receive copies. Some people still wanted to be paid for their time, and we had to look at cultural norms and how that fit into what we saw as our objective and the justice of the larger situation. We discussed the idea of putting this information on the web with informed consent. In some ways computer networks and the cloud are more ephemeral, although in others more permanent. However, until the people with whom we work have access to computers so that they can get their own information, we are keeping that as a concept in progress.

Given all of these aspects that deserve consideration, I maintain that, through my personal experiences, the positives outweighed the negatives. The photocopied pages and sketches evolving into slick magazine presentations connected people to the research, to the forest, and to themselves. Having a written record can be an avenue for mutual interchange. Although these examples are from ethnobotanical research, many aspects of a culture can be captured and presented in this or similar formats. Rudimentary or professional looking, this is one way as researchers to recognize the people with whom we work, and to facilitate ways to give back to them, from us, and from themselves.

Chapter 8 References and Recommended Reading

Duncan, Earle, and Jeanne Simonelli. 2005. *Uprising of Hope: Sharing the Zapatista Journey to Alternative Development.* London: AltaMira Press.

Fadiman, Maria. 2007. "Exploring Conservation: Piguigua, *Heteropsis ecua-dorensis*, in Ecuador." *Papers of the Applied Geography Conferences* 30:427–436.

———. 2008. "'Starvation Taught Me Art': Tree Poaching, Gender and Cultural Shifts in Wood Curio Carving in Zimbabwe." *Ethnobotany Research and Applications* 6:335–346.

Hernandez Cruz, Rosa, Eduardo Bello Baltazar, Guillero Montoya Gomez, and Erin Estrada Lugo. 2005. "Social Adaptation: Ecotourism in the Lacandon Forest." *Annals of Tourism Research* 32 (3): 610–627.

Hoffman, John. 2012. "Reflections on the Concept of Progress—and Zimbabwe." *Journal of Contemporary African Studies* 30 (1): 139–145.

Milner, James. 2014. "Can Global Refugee Policy Leverage Durable Solutions? Lessons from Tanzania's Naturalization of Burundian Refugees." *Journal of Refugee Studies* 4:1–18.

Salzmann, Zdenek, James Stanlaw, and Nobuko Adachi. 2014. *Language, Culture and Society: An Introduction to Linguistic Anthropology.* 6th ed. Boulder: Westview Press.

Samuelson, Ralph. 2010. "Council of Elders: An Intergenerational Dialogue: Knowledge Pathways for Traditional Arts in the 21st Century." *Indian Folk Life* 36:21–23.

9

Pacific Worlds

Documenting Communities' Place-Based Knowledge for
Internet Dissemination

RDK HERMAN

I N THE LATE 1990S, the Smithsonian National Museum of the American Indian—then still without buildings of its own, much less exhibitions—entered into conversations with American Indian educators to determine what sort of project the museum could do that would best serve education in Indian country. Understanding the role of the museum to assist Indigenous communities to preserve their cultural heritage, language, knowledge, and values, these educators conceived a project called Geografía Indígena as a mechanism both for meeting that need and for technologically empowering Native communities to further this process themselves. This proposed "knowledge/technology transfer" was intended operate in a way that was culturally appropriate and useful. Technology was seen as the tool for achieving the goals of cultural preservation, while the content—coming from the communities themselves—was understood as the driving force behind the project.

Geografía Indígena emerged as a three-pronged program intended to (1) produce a web-based portfolio of Indigenous knowledge about Indian communities in the Western Hemisphere; (2) produce educational materials, curricula, and professional associations for teaching geography in accordance with national geography standards but as tailored to the

needs, values, and perspectives of Native America; and (3) develop internet and multimedia technological capacity within Indian communities
that would, among other things, allow them to preserve their own cultural
information and to expand on their community websites.

As stated about this project in an early grant application (NMAI 1999),

- It compiles and preserves an integrated package of information
  about these oft-overlooked and highly diverse communities.
  The project includes a very strong native-language emphasis by
  including native terminology for a range of data. Oral material
  is gathered and presented in such a way as to give voice to the
  community through these sites.
- It takes the community's perspective as primary, rather than imposing an external understanding on them (although quantitative
  and external data is included as well, but as secondary information).
  It is a "what can we learn from Native peoples" approach.
- It allows Native students to explore, compare, and understand
  other Native communities, and as with all geography study, this
  allows them to better understand their own communities. In
  doing so, this accomplishes the goal of reinforcing Native perspectives and values, and encourages cultural preservation.
  Empowered with computer technology, these students will be
  able to expand on, enhance, and contribute to the body of contemporary knowledge about their own cultures in a way that
  allows them to share with other Native communities.

Beyond these goals, a number of guiding principles made this project
particularly innovative and exciting at the time:

- It offers an exciting contribution to geographic knowledge and
  understanding as a whole by presenting Indigenous perspectives
  on how culture and experience influence the environment, and
  how the environment helps shape culture and worldview. This
  knowledge, previously dismissed by mainstream educators,
  enhances our understanding of the spatial aspects of human
  existence—the relationships between people, place, and environment. It might encourage students (and others) beyond the
  Native community to consider Native perspectives in their own

right, offering a valuable and effective vehicle to expand students' ways of seeing the world. This project therefore, it was argued, had a distinctive value to geography education as a whole.

The aims and intentions were good, but in the end the execution left plenty to be desired. The technology transfer never happened, there was no overall curriculum, and no association of Native teachers was ever encouraged. It became merely a platform for communities to tell their stories (though that in itself was worthwhile). After documenting seven communities, the project was terminated in 2009 and taken off-line.

At that time I had been working for NMAI on a short-term contract to get that project started. I participated in the field research for the pilot website on the community of Sipaulovi on the Hopi Second Mesa, and edited the interviews into essays. I also designed the initial web architecture. But a congressional shutdown in late 1999 froze the funds we anticipated getting, and with my contract over, I took a faculty position at Towson University in Maryland in late 2000. There I embarked on my own version of this project with a focus on Pacific Islands. With a very small seed grant and some parental support, Pacific Worlds was born.

Pacific Islanders represent the most widely scattered culture group on the face of the Earth, linked by an ancient heritage and a complex oceanic environment. They present a cornucopia of compact, distinct, yet related cultures, ruptured and divided by colonial administrations. The Pacific was one of the last frontiers of Western colonization, most of it taking place in the nineteenth century, with some islands relatively unaffected until World War II. Moreover, the Pacific was carved up into four colonial realms, known today as the American Pacific, the New Zealand Pacific, the Australian Pacific, and the French Pacific. Micronesia—islands from the Marshall Islands to Guam and the Marianas—fell under a United Nations mandate after the war, administered by the United States, which (aside from conducting atomic testing in the Marshalls) largely left these islands alone until the 1960s (figure 9.1).

Hence the older generation today still recalls the war, and has observed the changes of culture since that time. Cultural decay has led to higher rates of crime, teenage suicide (highest in the world), and other social problems among island youth. And this was clearly seen as due to the loss of traditional culture. Isaac Langal, an educator on Ulithi Atoll (Yap State, Federated States of Micronesia) remarked,

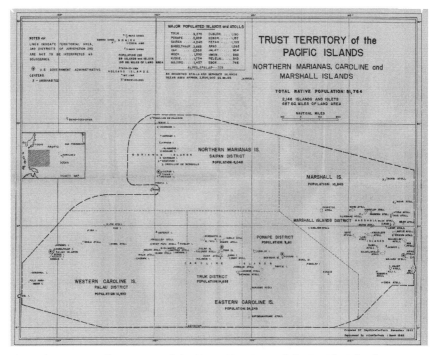

FIG. 9.1—US military map of the Trust Territory of the Pacific Islands.

When people started to focus on Western education, then the local education kind of slacked off, because people pushed their children to go to school: "Never mind learning these [traditional] things, because in the future you will not need them. You go and attend school." Right now there is only one person on this whole atoll that can make canoes. But before, there were a lot of old people that made canoes over here. And this passing down of knowledge from father to son, it's almost non-existent now. I think education should try to maintain the culture. And they should have started back when the Western education got introduced to the island. (Langal 2003)

The situation on islands of the American Pacific differs from that of Indian reservations: native governments in the American Pacific (the former trust territories, plus Hawaiʻi and American Samoa) have high levels of sovereignty over all of their islands (except in Hawaiʻi). In addition, the colonial legacy of the Japanese presence in the region (1914–1945) left a non-American imprint that, like the island cultures themselves, is at odds with the American doctrine of personal freedom and unhindered consumption. Nonetheless, the islands have in common with Indian reservations that the forces of colonization, including the introduction of Christianity, capitalism, and various new economic activities—as well as the American educational system—continues to push these peoples into global capitalism and modernity. Some islands, at least, are more insulated by their remote locations, small sizes, and relative lack of material resources.

It is both the connections and the disconnects among Pacific Island communities across the region that made this sort of web-based, cultural-comparison, education project seem like a perfect fit. Pacific Worlds follows the same principles and intentions as Geografía Indígena, but since it did not come about with the support of local educators, it was up to me to "sell" this idea: to convince people—initially, in the Hawaiian Islands—that it was a good idea, and that they should participate in it. Most important (aside from funding, of course), I needed some communities to be willing to be profiled. Between 2000 and 2005, I profiled seven communities—three in Hawai'i and four in Micronesia.

In another publication (Herman 2013), I describe the life trajectory that led me to this point. Among other things, I had been a student at the University of Hawai'i at a time of virulent Hawaiian-sovereignty activists. White male scholars in particular came under attack for cultural appropriation, colonization, inappropriate representations of Hawaiians and Hawaiian culture, and so forth. I managed to fly under the radar because I was studying Hawaiian language (up to that point, most Hawai'i scholars had little or no capacity in Hawaiian, and the language had nearly died out). But because of this tense climate, I was acutely aware that whatever I did, it could not be in any way exploitative. Better to let Indigenous peoples represent themselves than for me to do it, but as a trained scholar, I could help with that.

I would refine these ideas later, arguing in various publications about the need to decolonize the discipline of geography (Shaw, Herman, and Dobbs 2006) and on the importance of Indigenous knowledge (Herman 2008; Coleman and Herman 2010; Herman 2015). This draws on my own experience as well as the works of Cajete (2000), Deloria (2006), and Johnson and Murton (2007). Linda Tuhiwai Smith's work, *Decolonizing Methodologies* (1999) also had an impact. With my brief experience with the Geografía Indígena project, I was determined to craft a new web-based platform for presenting Indigenous knowledge in the words

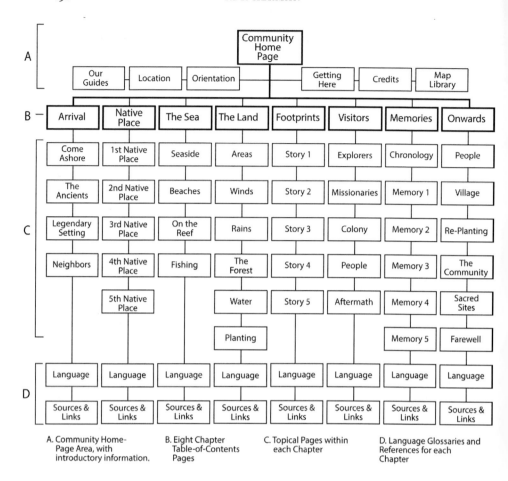

A. Community Home-Page Area, with introductory information.

B. Eight Chapter Table-of-Contents Pages

C. Topical Pages within each Chapter

D. Language Glossaries and References for each Chapter

FIG. 9.2 — Original web architecture for a Pacific Worlds community website.

of the people themselves, and to build curricula to teach young people Indigenous ways of knowing.

As noted in chapter 1, I have since published on research methodologies for working with Indigenous communities (Herman 2015). I would like to say that I followed all those principles, but in fact I was out of my depth. A weekend of interviews in Hopi, led by my colleague Jose Barreiro, was the only field experience I had had. I did have one thing to rely on—the element that I felt was most important—and that was my own integrity. I needed to convince Native Hawaiians that the project was worthwhile, and that they should share their knowledges with me for publication on the World Wide Web. In this chapter, I document my successes and failures, my lessons learned, and suggestions—to others, if not myself—about how it might be done better.

Structure of Pacific Worlds

The idea behind both Geografía Indígena (where it did not manifest) and Pacific Worlds (where it did) was that the website for each community would follow a consistent pattern or template to allow for "horizontal navigation." The reason for this is the educational component: to build curricula, there needs to be some regularity so that students can compare and contrast information about different communities. The template that emerged for Pacific Worlds is shown in figure 9.2.

With this consistent format, a curriculum can be built around a particular area ("The Sea," for instance) or even a very specific topic ("Fishing") and users can easily navigate from one community website to the next, staying on that same page. I call this the "horizontal" navigation across the overall website, as opposed to the vertical navigation within any given community website. This manifests on the website itself as a drop-down menu labeled "choose location" that allows viewers to go to exactly that same page for any of the other communities. I explain, in the "About this Site" section, that there are two ways to use the website: one is to compare certain topics across communities; the other is to read about any given community in depth, starting at the beginning and going through the entire community website. And if you do so, you will find that there is a consistent narrative that emerges.

For each community, there is a home page with a few sub-pages to orient the reader to the community. On one of these pages—"Guides"— the interviewees self-introduce. These speakers will be identified throughout the rest of the website, wherever their words are used. This is an important step away from the types of research where the information is mostly parlayed by the scholar, with some occasional quotes by interviewees who may not necessarily even be named. Here, the idea is that the information comes almost exclusively from the community members themselves, glued together when necessary with my input. (How this comes together is discussed below under "Methodology.")

After the community home-page section, there are eight thematic "chapters," each of which has a consistent set of sub-pages plus a glossary page and a "sources and links" page. Each chapter represents a layer of information; these are not exactly chronological, but mix time and space in a way that conveys movement and crossover from ancient origins to the immediate present and future. The overall format explicates mythological understandings, human-environment relations, cultural landscapes and practices, and historical impacts, as well as contemporary issues and mobilizations. It is, of course, just one of many possible models, and, as I will discuss later, I have created a new and larger template that incorporates more topics. The idea is to present a well-organized, holistic documentation of place-based community knowledge.

Each chapter, as mentioned, includes a glossary in the Indigenous language; this required contracting a language expert from each island entity. The glossary was intended to be not so much a list of words, but of categories of ideas and concepts, since there may be no one-to-one correlations between words from one language to another.

There is a section off the main homepage called "About This Site" that explains the principles (like those above) and the methodology underlying the project as a whole.

Finally, there is an "Education" portion of the website that includes the curriculum in various free-to-use formats, a discussion of how to use the project to meet specific US educational standards, and information on teacher-training workshops. There is also, built into the project as a whole, a set of short essays that explain the nature and purpose of each thematic chapter (these being the same across all communities). These essays try to explain how Indigenous knowledge and experiences differ from Western approaches, and how and why the content tries to elicit these Indigenous perspectives.

At the request of one of the project's sponsors—the Hawai'i Council for the Humanities—I started including thematic essays written by other scholars. Despite my emphasis on Indigenous knowledge and Native voice, I often found that funders wanted to see something a bit more "scholarly." Two of the essays that I included were essentially guides to doing oral-history research in Indigenous settings: one more general, and one specific for Hawai'i. These served my aim of making this project something that other communities could replicate for themselves. It was always hoped that one result of this project would be people from other communities saying "Hey, we can do this ourselves." Both the curriculum and these essays were aimed toward that end.

Methodology

The first step in doing this project, of course, is to choose a community. Initially, it was suggested that I connect with a Native Hawaiian colleague, Carlos Andrade, who was then working on his dissertation about the community of Hāʻena, Kauaʻi. Thus the community was selected. The second and third Hawaiian communities I chose myself, being in touch at the time with people who were working with (but not necessarily native to) those communities. This worked out better in one case (where there was a historical family tie) than the other (where there was not). For my work in Micronesia, the sponsor was Pacific Resources for Education and Learning (PREL), an NGO that received block grants from the US Department of Education to develop curricula for the "American Pacific" (most of Micronesia plus American Samoa). PREL had offices in all the locations they served, with local staff who worked with local historical preservation offices, education offices, and other relevant players to determine which villages I should work on. So these communities were chosen for me, except in the case of Palau, where I chose between two options presented to me. With PREL's on-the-ground support, I also had a preassigned community "guide" who made introductions for me and generally opened doors. That doesn't mean the community knew what I was up to when I arrived there, however, but the guides did a wonderful job of convincing (often in the native language), and I was able to get the interviews necessary.

For these interviews I have a two-part protocol: first, I ask permission to do the interview, assuring the respondents that I will make nothing public until they have had a chance to review the final material. I then follow up on that promise when I have a final draft, giving everyone copies to read and accepting any changes or corrections they request (there have rarely been any). At that point, they sign a release that permits me to make the material public. I have maintained that this two-part protocol is essential to ensuring my integrity—that I am not there to take from them and run, or to use their words against them. Yet I bear in mind that this "permission" is a Western protocol that does not embody the depth of my responsibility. As Carter, Pearce, and Jacobson point out (chapter 2, this volume), the real issue is my positionality in relation to these interviewees: my ongoing commitment to them and to the knowledge they share with me.

I also make absolutely clear before and during the course of every interview that I am not there to get any secrets. As is standard for interview protocol, I inform them that they may stop the interview at any time, or tell me to pause the recorder and keep something off the record, or change or delete information during the final review process. And I have heard some amazing things, off the record.

In addition to interviews, on-site collection involves what I call "walking the land": physically exploring the area to gain a first-person sense of place, an intimacy with sights, sounds, and smells, in order to be able to effectively reflect a sense of place when editing and composing the website. Some geographic field methods are also useful for framing the place in contemporary terms of relative location. Finally, extensive photography is performed to enable a strong visual presentation of this place.

After I return from the field, I engage in a massive editing job. First I go through each interview transcript and correct any errors, include any words in the native language that the transcriber didn't catch. Then I smooth out the text, glossing it into a more readable form. That is, this is not about verbatim oral-history documentation, with all the "um"s and "ah"s. It needs to be more polished than that. Then I cut up each interview into pieces that fit into the different boxes on the template. Once I have done that with all the interviews, I then work one "box" at a time, taking what I have in there to produce a smooth narrative.

At this point I may draw on bibliographic materials to supplement the oral material. Published versions of legends and other stories, proverbs and sayings, historical records and materials—especially those relating to changes in land ownership or use, and historical eyewitness accounts of the area—help add more content. Other images are also gathered as needed, and as available, to further the graphic presentation of information on the site. This can include historical photos, air photos, maps of all sorts (including those generated by geographic information systems), and iconography to create a theme for the visual navigation structure.

Without a doubt I find, in the course of this stage, that I have holes to be filled, and this requires a second research trip. The process is then repeated until I have a complete product. And, as previously mentioned, that product goes back to the community and to the participants for their review and corrections before the website is launched.

The result is a portfolio of thematic essays structured by the template, with most essays being composites of pieces from multiple interviews with different people. Each speaker is identified. So, for example, on the "Legendary Setting" page for the Yap-Ulithi website, the story of Yongl'aab and Liomarer is told alternately by Phillip Nery, Pitmag, Hosay, Alphonso, Stanley, and Yaad. When the speaker switches, the names are identified. The resulting essay reads as though these gentlemen were sitting around a table telling the story together, but in fact they were all separate interviews, or at most in pairs.

There was also information I gathered that did not fit into the template, but which I found too important not to include. For these I added separate pop-up windows. For example, on the "Fishing" page of the Kawaihae website, six separate pop-up windows include further explanations of related topics: the making of *aku palu* (a fermented fish product), sea currents off Kawaihae, traditional *olonā* fishing line, chumming, and *koʻa*— piles of rocks used as weights that accumulate on the sea floor in fishing spots. Like the main essays, each of these includes photos, text, maps, and illustrations, as available. In my thinking, every bit of documentation of community knowledge that I could fit should go in, if possible.

Giving Back?

I would like to think that the products of this work serve the communities—that these websites are as much for them as anyone else—more so, really. Unlike conventional scholarship, Pacific Worlds is not about me "data mining" from the community to produce a scholarly publication. Rather, the final product is a manifestation of all the data "coming back" in the form of the website. And I would argue that the website serves the purposes of documenting the community's knowledge for themselves and their descendants, as well as for the general public. It also provides a portal whereby their expatriate members—raising families away from their home communities—can teach their children about their culture in the words of their own elders and culture-keepers. Finally, it provides a means by which the rest of the world can come to understand these cultures better in their own terms, rather than in the terms of outsiders and tourist guide books.

I also feel that the teacher workshops are a form of giving back. From 2000 to 2006 (that is, while I had grant money) I conducted fifteen teacher workshops in a range of venues and locations. The first of these were sponsored by the Hawaiʻi Geographic Alliance and were held in the Hawaiian Islands. I also held multiple sessions at the Native Hawaiian Education Association conferences. For Micronesia, I held two workshops on Guam, two in the Marshall Islands, and two in Palau as part of PREL's Pacific Education Conference. Finally, I held two workshops in Samoa at the 2004 meeting of the Pacific Association of Teacher Educators. In all of these venues, my mission was to bring the project back to the larger community of Native Hawaiian and Pacific Islander teachers, and to provide them with a resource for locally derived education on Hawaiʻi-Pacific cultures and places.

The project as a whole has been kept strictly nonprofit and noncommercial. I did not get paid to do the work on top of my university salary, and I resisted numerous recommendations to find ways to make money out of the research I had done. I have kept banner advertisements and such off the website entirely. If there was money to be made, I asserted, it would have to go back to the community. But none was made, and I was fine with that.

Nonetheless, there were instances when the "giving back" element was questioned or became problematic. The first criticism I encountered was that the structure of the website (the template) did not derive from the communities. Why shouldn't each community shape their information their own way, to reflect their own worldview? The answer, as I explained earlier, is to allow the comparative tools for curriculum development. On the few times that this criticism arose, it disappeared once the speaker actually used the website, or once I had been able to explain what the project was about and how it worked. In Hawai'i, I got both barrels straight to the chest from a Hawaiian studies professor and sovereignty activist: "You haoles! You come in here with your colonial expropriation, and take from native communities, and . . . and . . . ." Half an hour of discussion later, however, she gave me a hug.

In Samoa, one community leader I tried to win over said flatly that the project's forms of giving back were not enough. If I were, for example, helping the village to develop a clean water supply, that would have convinced him. In another case, an elder sat me down and informed me that a researcher who had come through a year or so previously had given every informant $300. I replied that I did not have that money to give, and that in fact I myself did not make any money off of the project. "Then why are you doing it?" he asked. "So that I can come out here and talk to people like you," was the best answer I could give at the moment. But of course, aside from that small selfish goal, I would like to feel that my aims are more noble.

For the Hawai'i-based communities, I tried to hold aside a small pool of grant money to give honoraria to the participants. I never promised them any compensation, or even raised the topic, but at the end I would send a thank-you letter with a check (for maybe $100), saying it was a small gift for all they had given me. For Micronesia, my contact at PREL (who has since left) felt that was too problematic and difficult.

There were also the smaller encounters of trying to give back, such as bringing gifts. In one case, since I was coming from Washington, DC, I brought a handful of hats that had the seal of the president of the United States on them. My first day there I laid them out for my "guide" to choose the one he liked. A young man working nearby witnessed this, and came to me later, saying that he had talked about it with my guide and that I was to give him a hat too. I was dismayed, as this young man was not a contributor to the project, and I had only five hats. I was caught in a cultural bind that I did not understand, but I gave him one. A day or two later I saw that same hat on the head of the village chief. I had—as so many other field researchers have done—caused a minor sociocultural issue which the chief had resolved.

I have nonetheless worked out ways to give small gifts that show thanks without upsetting social balance. I now always bring a stack of the same gift—usually CDs of Native music and calendars from the National Museum of the American Indian, where I now work—and give these as gifts after I have concluded the interview. In Ulithi Atoll I was advised by my guide to give cigarettes, so I came with two cartons—much against my better judgment. Once I also brought some betel nut from Yap, which was in short supply on Ulithi, and discreetly gave some to people who had done me favors.

As recently as June 2017, I was in the field on Kaua'i when a Native Hawaiian colleague on the project wrote me: "I need to be honest with you that your approach does not always follow cultural protocols and has left a bad taste in some people's mouths." He went on to say, "It's generally not a good strategy to ride the coat tails of your own good intentions or that of the reputations of others. Not here at least. In the interest of the work that a great many of us have dedicated our lives to, I really need you understand that a foundation aspect of Hawaiian culture is the practice of giving before taking. Not taking with a promise of giving later (we've had enough of that already), nor taking and trying to convince someone that it will be in their best interests to do so."

Needless to say I was shocked by this—it shattered, temporarily, my sense of myself as a researcher and my project as a form of giving back. I have no idea who he was referring to as "some people," since the overwhelming response I had gotten in that community was appreciation and support. And I continued to get that on that very same research trip, from everyone except this one fellow. So I learned two things from this painful incident: first, a reminder that it is, in fact, wise to give first—as this fellow clarified later in our exchange, it's the principle of "*aloha aku, aloha mai.*" You give aloha out first, before expecting anything back. So since then,

I made sure to arrive with gifts of food—fish and poi, mostly—whenever I went to meet with someone. Second, as other Hawaiian colleagues assured me, sometimes these things are really about the person raising the issue, and not about you. Either way, we always need to be ready for such encounters. I learned from my painful experience aboard the *Hōkūleʻa* voyaging canoe that no matter how long and deep my Hawaiian cultural credentials may be, some people are always going to see just another "mainland *haole*," there to exploit them.

As for returning the raw data from my fieldwork, in some cases I made an effort to give the field recordings and complete interview transcripts back to the participants, but—I am embarrassed to say—mostly they remain in my office. I have thought about donating them to the Pacific Collection at the University of Hawaiʻi library, but that would require getting another round of permissions from the original interviewees, and that's logistically beyond my capability right now. Since I have come to learn much more about appropriate methodologies for working with Indigenous peoples, I see this as a significant shortcoming on my part. In every case, complete transcripts and recordings (copies, at least) should go back to the interviewees.

How It Could Be Done Better

When I began Pacific Worlds in 2000, I was unemployed and in debt—a situation resolved a few months later when I was hired by Towson University as an assistant professor. Nonetheless, the early grants were small, I had no team per se, and I was trying to do work in places thousands of miles away. The National Museum of the American Indian, with its Indigenous Geography project, had a team of people doing the work, and much larger financial and institutional resources—as well as a name and reputation that automatically opened doors, which (alas) "Towson University" did not. With minor exceptions, I did virtually all the work myself: the fieldwork, the editing, the website construction, the graphics, the maps. Now I would suggest other ways to do this that engage the community more, and in so doing, give back in greater ways.

In 2012 I was part of a small team from the Smithsonian that tried to work with the Menominee Indians in Wisconsin on what was supposed to have been a dual culture-science project. I was the culture person on the team, and I was proposing to do essentially this same kind of work as discussed here, with a newer and larger template I had since developed

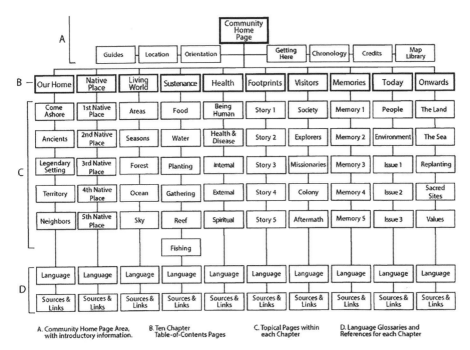

A. Community Home Page Area, with introductory information.   B. Ten Chapter Table-of-Contents Pages   C. Topical Pages within each Chapter   D. Language Glossaries and References for each Chapter

FIG. 9.3—Revised architecture for Pacific Island community websites.

for work with American Indians. This version includes more topics with a more clear focus on environment, with the intent that this project would help communities document place-based knowledge in the face of impending climate change, when such knowledge could be lost. I later readapted this new template for Pacific Worlds, and at this writing, am in the midst of implementing it for one community (figure 9.3).

There was a great deal of enthusiasm and support from the tribal college there. But I did not want to do all the work anymore. Though that project did not come together, here are the ideas I developed. These, again, are more easily done with greater institutional support and a larger team than doing it on one's own:

1. Meeting with the community. As discussed in the introduction to this volume, the notion of "community" is fraught, as any experienced field worker knows—communities are complex and multifaceted entities (Pain 2004). But there are methods for having community meetings, or for participating in such meetings, that

already exist. In more traditional cultures, "community" is a little more clearly defined, as is community leadership. In my case, going directly to people or going through the PREL offices, I never engaged the whole community. They learned about it bit by bit as I made my rounds doing interviews, and word spread. I would rather have a more formal engagement and understanding with the community (and its leadership) as a whole. But it is always complex. At Menominee, we were right away dealing with three different entities: the tribal college, the tribal government, and the tribal corporation that actually controlled the forest that was the focus of the study. Then, had the project gone forward, we would have presented our project at a series of open community meetings. I would also encourage the formation of a community advisory board to oversee the project and review the final draft of the website.

2. Running field camps to train students in the community how to do ethnographic field work. Rather than me doing all the interviews, perhaps it would be better to have young people from the community doing them. This way there would be direct oral transmission from elders to the younger generation. And the students would learn a skill. There are problems with this approach too, however. As a complete outsider, I was naïve enough to not know what they were on purpose not telling me. Ignorance was bliss, or at least it served the speakers. Insiders do not have that. Moreover, in some cultures, the speakers may not feel that certain younger people are worthy of the information, or there may be old conflicts or resentments. Finally, my ignorance served in another way: I asked the "stupid" questions. That is, people inside the culture are more likely to take certain things for granted that might be completely unfamiliar to outsiders. Since Pacific Worlds is for use by people outside the communities as well as in, it is important that basic concepts be explained. In one case, on Saipan, I pointed out an old Spanish-style brick oven (called a *hotnu* in Chamorro language), overgrown with vines, just off the center of the village. Most of the villagers walked by this every day. But once I pointed it out, there was a collective "oh . . . yeah," and as we ripped the vines off it for a photo, some elders came out and told stories about it from their childhoods. Had I—the out-

sider—not been there, this would not have happened. Still, I feel that engaging the community—especially the youth—in more of the fieldwork, including the photography and even making videos, would greatly increase the "giving back" aspect of the project.

3. Giving the community more control over the website. Pacific Worlds remains in my hands, and because of the structure necessary for the curriculum, I have been afraid to give others access to changing anything in it. I would rather see each community have control of their own website, and be able to update it as they see fit. At the very least, I am looking at having blog sections for each page, on which community members (only) may add comments, observations, and so forth.

In short, what I came to conclude, sixteen years since I started this project, were the principles I have only more recently learned from my research on participatory action research (wherein community members becomes partners in the research process) and feminist methodologies (empowering participants via their participation, thereby inverting the traditional balance of power in the research context), as discussed in chapter 1. Against the background of my indoctrination by those "radical" Hawaiian-sovereignty activists, which taught me to be extremely mindful of relations of power and the potential for appropriation in a research context, my personal experiences led me in the same direction as the emerging scholarship on decolonizing methodologies, and has enabled me to contribute to it.

Giving On

My dear friend and Hawaiian elder Mel Kalahiki told me a story, which is recounted in total on the Kawaihae website on Pacific Worlds. It concerns night marchers—ghostly entourages of ancient warriors who are reputed to travel at night:

There are the night walkers. I asked my Grandfather that, because I knew that when he built his house, he took the back section out because of the Night Walkers. They used to walk through the back end of the house. He explained to me that if you put anything in their path, they will walk though it! So he took that section of the house out. . . . He told me the direction that they came from and where they go to. So that path was out the back window, in the back of my bedroom and his bedroom. Then I asked him about night walkers, and my question to him, I said, "I can see?" He telling me, "Uhhh, yeah. Because you're *ohana* [family], it means you're in the line." . . . Sure enough, I was sleeping and woke 'cause I heard all the sounds like Grandpa said. I stood by the window looking out and there they were walking past outside my window. They were walking . . . and walking slowly. It was not spooky to me. Just knowing that I had a family connection within these marchers, kept me from being scared.

The thing is, Mel reminded me, that once you ask for knowledge, and get it, then *you become responsible for that knowledge*. And that is a lesson for us all.

Over the course of the work I have done for Pacific Worlds, and one hundred other interviews I have done in Hawai'i since coming to the Smithsonian, I have come to recognize more and more the responsibility that comes with what has been shared with me. Not just in what I publish in Pacific Worlds or other venues, or put on exhibition at the Smithsonian. These interviewees have opened up to me and shared their knowledge, their experience, their thoughts, their hopes, their traditions, their insights. All of that has profoundly shaped how I understand the world, and how I try to act in it. And all of it has given me a sense of responsibility to do right by that information. It's not necessarily a matter of giving back, but of giving on—to others.

This feeling came clear for me in 2006 when I was offered a position back at the National Museum of the American Indian. I had to contemplate whether this was a right move. One night as I pondered this and opened myself up to inspiration, I felt the presence of the many people I had interviewed for these projects—people who had shared their knowledge and stories with me. It felt like a great river, whose waters were gently but firmly moving me forward. Much as Roxanne Ornelas was told directly by one elder (chapter 10 of this volume), the message was clear: "We taught you. Now go forward and put this knowledge and wisdom to work."

In the course of my work on the Nu'uanu website, I tracked down every legendary, historical, or archaeological site that I could possibly find in that valley, and there were a lot. Some appeared to have been destroyed, but many I found. Then I found myself being called upon by other Hawaiians: can you show us where this particular site is? Sometimes I simply told them, another time I took a group on a field excursion to show them. Because through my work, I had become a knowledge-keeper in my own right, and now it was time to give back. To give on.

So I return to what I said in chapter 1: it is a matter of doing the good work ... or at least trying to. And we don't always know what that means. But we need to take responsibility for the knowledge that we gain, and to share it—or not share it—as is appropriate.

Chapter 9 References

Cajete, Gregory. 2000. *Native Science: Natural Laws of Interdependence.* Santa Fe, NM: Clear Light.

Coleman, Cynthia Lou, and Douglas Herman. 2010. "Ways of Knowing: 'Naked Science' or Native Wisdom." *National Museum of the American Indian Magazine* (Winter): 28–33.

Deloria Jr., Vine. 2006. *The World We Used to Live In: Remembering the Powers of the Medicine Men.* Golden, CO: Fulcrum.

Herman, RDK. 2008. "Reflections on the Importance of Indigenous Geography." *American Indian Culture and Research Journal* 32 (3): 73–88.

———. 2013. "In the Canoe: Intersections in Space, Time, and Becoming." In *A Deeper Sense of Place: Stories and Journeys of Collaboration in Indigenous Research*, edited by Soren Larsen and Jay T. Johnson, 55–72. Corvallis: Oregon State University Press.

———. 2015. "Traditional Knowledge in a Time of Crisis: Climate Change, Culture and Communication." *Sustainability Science* 11 (1): 163–176. http://link.springer.com/article/10.1007%2Fs11625-015-0305-9.

Johnson, Jay T., and Brian Murton. 2007. "Re/Placing Native Science: Indigenous Voices in Contemporary Constructions of Nature." *Geographical Research* 45 (2): 121–129.

Kalahiki, Mel. 2006. "Night Marchers." Pacific Worlds Kawaihae website. http://www.pacificworlds.com/kawaihae/stories/story2.cfm.

Langal, Isaac. 2003. "Education." Pacific Worlds Yap-Ulithi website. http://www.pacificworlds.com/yap/memories/memory5.cfm.

NMAI (National Museum of the American Indian). 1999. "Geografía Indígena (Indigenous Geography): A Project Concept of

Community Services of the Smithsonian Institution's National Museum of the American Indian." New York: National Museum of the American Indian.

Pain, R. 2004. "Social Geography: Participatory Research." *Progress in Human Geography* 28 (5): 652–663.

Shaw, Wendy S., RDK Herman, and G. Rebecca Dobbs. 2006. "Encountering Indigeneity: Re-imagining and Decolonizing Geography." *Geografiska Annaler* 88B (3): 267–276.

Smith, Linda Tuhiwai. 1999. *Decolonizing Methodologies: Research and Indigenous Peoples.* London: Zed Books.

10

Continue to "Tell Them about Us"

ROXANNE T. ORNELAS

I N   H I S   B O O K   *P E D A G O G Y   O F   H O P E : Reliving Pedagogy of the Oppressed* (2004 [1992]), Paulo Freire emphasized that teaching is essentially pointless if the concept of hope is not somehow attached to the practice. Those of us who are actively involved in research and teaching about Indigenous peoples are quite often intentionally drawing attention to these populations by lifting the historic cloak of silence that has accompanied their legacy of colonization, oppression, and subjugation by the state. For me, a clear decision has been to ride the slippery slope between academic research for scholarly tenure requirements and my own participation and activism within the communities I work with who are engaged in social and environmental justice actions.

Several years ago, while conducting research during graduate school with the Mandan, Hidatsa, and Arikara Nation at the Fort Berthold Indian Reservation in North Dakota, I was introduced to an Indigenous woman, Elder Celeste, who told me that she had decided to participate in an interview with me because she wanted to make sure that the youth and the future generations of her people knew about the "old ways" on her reservation. Specifically, she wanted them to know about the catastrophic environmental destruction on her reservation following the construction of the Garrison Dam in the 1950s. Elder Celeste asked me to promise to continue to "tell them about us. Tell them about us." During the interview, she explained that the "them" in the telling also included those who were not living on her reservation. In other words, she wanted it to be known to history, and to the rest of the world, what had happened to her people. Not only did they lose many of their homes, towns, businesses, and sacred places, as well as historic heritage as a result of the rising waters of the dam's reservoir—ironically, Lake Sacagawea—they also suffered devastating social consequences, including the disintegration of many families and community ties.

The promise I made in my commitment to carry on the telling of what had occurred at Fort Berthold has evolved into a whole new level of engagement that now includes teaching college courses about the Indigenous communities that I encounter during my research and in my personal life. With the passing of Elder Celeste into the spirit world, the promise that I made to her still endures, and my commitment has deepened over the years. But knowing how to begin to tell those stories has been most challenging, as well as most fulfilling and personally enriching.

Challenges in Teaching about Indigenous Peoples

Many academic researchers in the discipline of geography who are doing work related to the geographies of Indigenous peoples face ongoing challenges of acceptance. Academics trained in the Western tradition, including university administrators, sometimes find it problematic to accept scholarly work about the worldview of Indigenous peoples as being valid contributions to the academy. In recent years, however, I have witnessed a growing acceptance of the Indigenous Peoples Specialty Group within the American Association of Geographers. And, yet, there are few job announcements for or hiring of university faculty whose research expertise is focused on Indigenous peoples. The seeming rigid authority given to Western framings of truth and knowledge are the same sorts of barriers that continue to maintain systems of inequality in society at large and, most significantly, within our education curricula.

Early in my college teaching career—but not so much anymore—I was often surprised at the lack of knowledge my students demonstrated about Indigenous peoples upon entering my classroom. I surveyed the students during the first weeks of class, and they would share with me what they knew about these populations in the United States: after twelve to sixteen years of education, the most they could tell me was their spare knowledge of Pocahontas, having learned what they know from Walt Disney. And, maybe, just maybe, they know a little bit about "that Indian woman who traveled with Lewis and Clark," and that General George Custer was killed by Indians—but they do not know why. These spare bits of information are all they know of the first inhabitants of the North American continent. What I had thought was going to be continuing education, with advanced discussion about environmental challenges on reservations, or the ongoing struggle to protect the sacred lands of Indigenous peoples, has turned out not to be so, essentially forcing me to begin the courses I teach by spending several weeks reviewing the equivalent of Indigenous Peoples 101. This has to be done before I can even begin to dig into the subject matter of the upper-level course. So, how do I teach about Indigenous peoples in a way that gives me the best avenue to teach my course subject area? How can I continue to tell students about Indigenous peoples as a way of giving back, and following through on my promise to Elder Celeste?

Imagining Geographies of Hope

In figures 10.1 and 10.2, I share with you a pictorial sampling of my research journeys into the field. An important part of my ethnographic methodology is to go into the places I teach about, to experience the feel of being there and to report back through either my teaching or my scholarly written contributions. For, after all, the disciplinary origin of the field of geography has a long history of expedition. Early explorers voyaged into uncharted territories to learn about those places and the peoples who lived there.

A major focus of my personal research examines questions concerning environmental justice and the human rights of Indigenous peoples with regard to their relationship to those lands they believe to be sacred places. The protection, caretaking, and traditional ceremonies that minister to those sites are an integral part of their lifeways. As Indigenous legal scholar Vine Deloria Jr. (2003) describes, "We attribute sacredness because the location is a site where, within our own history, regardless of our group, something of great importance took place" (19). One cannot delve into these particular topics without being faced with the reality of the environmental and cultural dispossession that has occurred as a result of land loss, forced relocation, and the aftermath of generational trauma. In promising to tell about what has occurred, it is critical to discuss the misunderstood land ethic and Earth-identified spirituality that is a large part of the ontological and epistemological vantage of many Indigenous peoples. In addition, Tsosie (2006) notes that, "The central connection

FIG. 10.1 — Sacred Mato Tipila, Devil's Tower, Wyoming.

that unites all Indigenous peoples involves the relationship of the people to the land. Native peoples often describe themselves as 'belonging' to particular lands" (48). This way of Indigenous "seeing" (Fixico 2003) the world is a basic part of teaching about the geographies of Indigenous peoples, and, I have found, it is one of the most problematic concepts.

Geographer Victoria Lawson discussed the meaning of the term "geographies of hope" during an opening session of the 2013 American Association of Geographers Annual Meeting (AAG). She stated, "Hope can be a mobilizing force beyond the personal; it can be a mobilizing force for action" (2013). The promise we made to our various research participants, to tell the outside world about them, clearly establishes the dynamic link of reciprocity and, consequently, provides a space for hope to flourish.

Not only is the aspiration of hope tied to physical landscapes, hope includes the emotional or spiritual connection that must also be

FIG. 10.2—Working on the draft version of what would become United Nations Declaration on the Rights of Indigenous Peoples.

understood. Over the years of conducting field research within various Indigenous communities, I know that the fight for the protection of a sacred stream, for example, is more than about the place itself. The human connection to it includes centuries of stories and the ceremonies of the people who revere it. In a 2012 report by the United Nations Special Rapporteur on the rights of Indigenous peoples, Professor James Anaya wrote that "the desecration and lack of access to sacred places inflicts permanent harm on Indigenous peoples for whom these places are essential parts of identity" (UNSR 2012, 12). The infliction of permanent harm includes not only the detachment from the place; it must be understood that a part of cultural identity and heritage is being lost if access to the places is compromised. These sacred places reflect the continuity of hope and future health and vibrancy of the communities into the future.

The geographical sense of these multiple sacred places can be rich and evocative, yet conflict-laden, and as varied as the people and the terrains from which those beliefs are derived—but, generally speaking, Indigenous peoples have an understanding of the world that is often at odds with Westernized belief systems (Cajete 2000; Shaw, Herman, and

Dobbs 2008). Very often their spirituality and religious practices can be attached to natural landforms, such as to a river or a mountaintop. But resistance to these knowledge systems can be found in some of my fellow geographers. As Laura Pulido (1998) observed about the discipline,

> Moreover, our reluctance to acknowledge spirituality as a force for social change leads us to further deny our own spirituality.... For those of us dedicated to social and environmental justice, how can we profess to know and understand marginalized groups, let alone identify a path for social change if we consciously or unconsciously avoid spiritual matters? (719)

Pulido is referring directly to geographer David Harvey's (1996) response to the language of the 1991 Principles of Environmental Justice that were drafted at the First National People of Color Environmental Leadership Summit that "affirms the sacredness of Mother Earth" (369–370). About the principles, Harvey wrote that "it is not hard to see how many professionals might regard them as ... lacking the virtue of elementary let alone 'impeccable logic'" (370). This statement demonstrates the complete failure to acknowledge even the slightest possibility of a non-Western epistemology as being valid. Both my research and my teaching experience tell me that Harvey is not alone in this type of rationale, though perhaps over the years his perspective has changed.

Through engagement with Indigenous communities in public actions that are related to the rights of their communities to live in healthy and empowering environments, we teachers must not only engage with the idea of giving back by envisioning a scheme for the geographies of hope that helps provide a framework to tell about the places and the stories in teaching about Indigenous peoples, but we must also talk about other reasons why, for example, we all should care about protecting the sacredness of Mother Earth, too. By taking my students along with me on my research journeys, experienced through photographs or documentary film, I can report back to them what I have learned during my travels. Then they can begin to imagine other possible futures, by planting the seeds of knowledge in a cycle of reciprocity and relationship. As I tell the students about Elder Celeste, and the many others I encounter, the promise continues to grow. The associations made are similar to rhizomatic connections to the past, present, and future. All of us involved in the learning have the ability to link to an as-yet-unknown potential—an unforeseen network of possibilities that can provide the spark to ignite transformative change. The linkages of those associations have the power to create an atmosphere that supports teaching and mutual learning about other ethnicities or cultures within the United States and beyond. These nodes of connections create cognitive sites where one can begin to view and consider other ways of understanding life on Earth.

In the learning environment within a classroom, there is an expectation that all who are present are willing and open to new and different ideas about the subject area. I have found that many of my students who are coming to learn about Indigenous peoples are ready to be taken on a new adventure in learning. I create a classroom environment that ensures that they feel honored for who they are and for the decision that brought them to my class in the first place. This is important because I know that their experience in the class will not necessarily be an easy one. As time goes on, and they begin to learn about the hole in their own education with regard to Indigenous peoples, many of the students become angry upon realizing they have missed learning about this important history before they reached the university. Student comments in their course evaluations for the class include, for example, "I can't believe that it took until my senior year to learn about Native Americans in my own country. I thought they lived in the past" (Student 2014). What I wish for them to leave with is a sense of responsibility, not only for the present, but also for what can be, to inspire a belief and a deeper understanding to challenge the "dialectical relationship between the oppressor and the oppressed, of the process of the introjection of the dominator by the dominated" (Freire 2004 [1992], 122). We teachers who teach about social and environmental justice topics must aspire to provide a setting within the life of the classroom where it is safe to talk across our various differences, to want

> An education that challenges the status quo, on dialogue, on democratic initiatives; on the need, in a progressive educational process, for educands to have their curiosity challenged; on the critical presence of educators and educands who, while teaching and learning respectively, nevertheless, all learn and teach, without any implication either that their relationship is one of homogenous reciprocity, or that the teacher does not learn and the learner does not teach. (Freire 2004 [1992], 122)

The network of possible connections for addressing such topics in a supportive space is thus enlivened and able to constantly adapt to a hybrid of associated external influences. What was once a frame of mind filled with preconceived notions can be inspired, one way or the other. It would be utopian to think that all students will want social and environmental change. They have, after all, lived a life before they even walk through the doorway. Liberal and conservative, Independent and Green Party and other political influences have shaped the people who now sit in my classes. But at the core of it all is our shared humanity, and the teacher's experience is to guide them through the educational voyage of discovery.

Deconstructing Privilege

Teaching is a symphony of applied practice, all parts coming together to be played in a harmonious concert—or a grating dissonance. What is important most of all is that we teachers are facilitating partners in the education process of the class. We hold the rudder and can steer the direction by discussing the meaning of a tale or a historic occurrence. We can take time developing insights and prompting discussion about our mutual humanity. But what of the inevitable voyage steered into rough waters where, maybe for the first time, non-Indigenous students are struck by their own privilege in historical context?

As mentioned above, some students have expressed anger when they learn that they did not know the extent of the devastation experienced by Indigenous peoples after first contact with early European settlers. In telling them about their Indigenous brethren, the truth is often met with something similar to Dr. Elisabeth Kübler-Ross's five stages of grief: denial and isolation; anger; bargaining; depression; and, finally, acceptance (1969). Unlike the romantic teachings of precollege United States history classes, students must face the death of the concept of manifest destiny as a visionary quest for the growing American West; it takes some deep soul-searching to finally recognize that this national agenda led to the near genocide of millions of the original inhabitants of the North American continent. Once the impact of this awareness is processed, the result can be emotional and quite disconcerting. Even grasping the self-identifier term "settler" can be enough to move students into the stage of denial. But if the telling is to be sufficiently grounded in reality, this discomfort must be experienced in order to proceed to acceptance. As Richard J. F. Day observed,

While the horrors of several hundred years of colonialism in the Americas must never be forgotten, we must also remember that before the white Man could colonize anyone else, he had to decolonize himself. And so, before he can truly stand beside anyone else to confront the tasks of decolonization and resurgence, within, against, or outside of the dominant order, he must attend to his own decolonization at the level of both the individual and the community. (2010, 268)

It is therefore necessary for the students in a classroom to face their worst fears by acknowledging that which they find most distressing when first learning about the legacy of colonization and its devastating consequences for both Indigenous peoples and settler populations. Only then can we begin a healing process and start deconstructing the privilege that has allowed the truth to remain hidden beneath the consciousness of settler populations throughout their early education.

We teachers guide the course and create opportunities for giving back, over and over again. I have witnessed minds opening and expanding in my classes. Sometimes I receive notes from former students, years after they have left the university, telling me how what they learned in my class changed them forever. They have told me how they live their lives with renewed purpose and attention to other peoples and to the environment. Is not this result, then, the realization of the geographies of hope that we aspire to? This is the gift to the elders being realized as I continue to tell about them in the cycle of reciprocity.

Oral Tradition and Methodology

On that day so many years ago when I first interviewed Elder Celeste, tears streamed down her face as she recounted her personal story of loss and the associated pain that still clung to her and overshadowed her throughout the subsequent decades. While she spoke, I could not help but be moved, too, by the telling of her story. Those of us who attended the 2013 AAG, and who were fortunate to view the film *Gifts from the Elders* (Fortier 2013) on Wednesday, April 10, were reminded about the treasure trove of knowledge so many of our elders hold and what wisdom they have to share with us. We need but stop and take a moment to sit down with them for conversations to learn about each other's lives. Our elder relatives are us, and the oral tradition of passing on their stories is how we can learn to have a deeper understanding of our past.

Time and distance between families and communities in the twenty-first century places a burden on so many of us to maintain familial connections in order to be able to share family history. As a child, I can recall sitting with my elder relatives and asking them to tell me stories about my family. While teaching about the importance of the oral tradition of Indigenous peoples, I sometimes ask my students about their own elder relatives and whether or not they know their family histories and stories. Recently, in a class of over thirty-five non-Indigenous-identified students, I asked how many of them actually knew their own family's history over the generations. Only two of them raised their hands. When I asked about their elder relatives, most answered that they never saw their grandparents or other relatives at all. There is something to be said about this void of experience that is significant to one's sense of self. Sometimes students are motivated to ask their parents after class about their own family history. They then return to class with a report of what they have learned and how it made them feel. What I have found most significant is their sudden desire to learn more about the other elders in their families. Learning of the oral tradition in the lives of many Indigenous peoples finds resonance with others across cultures.

The passing of each elder into the spirit world represents a break in the link to our past that we can never learn from again. The knowledge they had of their time now becomes the next addition to the longer tale about one's culture and historic traditions. The gifts of their teachings are there for the rest of us to learn from in these modern times. We all have the ability to then reciprocate by passing on what we have learned from our own life experience. The hope that the stories can inspire should not be overlooked or forgotten. As Kovach (2009) has written, "Stories remind us who we are and of our belonging. Stories hold with them knowledges while simultaneously signifying relationships. . . . They tie us with our past and provide a basis for continuity with future generations" (94). Murton (2012) later emphasized the importance of such oral traditions when he wrote,

> We need to make more of "orality," as the communities in which Indigenous geographers do their work are, or until recently have been, oral. Persons brought up within literate cultures seem to speak about the world around them, while Indigenous people

often speak directly to that world, which speaks back, not necessarily in words but in a myriad of other ways. (17)

Giving back by continuing to tell the story, we all become another branch on the human familial tree.

Through the process of transforming perceptions about our social relationships, we are better able to awaken, as Anzaldúa (2002) described, "the potential of knowing within, an awareness and intelligence not grasped by logical thought" (540). In this system, Anzaldúa suggests that we engage in the process of transformation to expand our perceptions of reality: to create transformative hybrid experiences—inside eager spaces, in between the known and unknown—to bring form to conscious thought and to thereby increase understanding and perception of our lives and the richness that lies within our multidimensional relationships. If we can somehow facilitate this process as educators and researchers, the opportunity to give back to our research participants continues to grow exponentially.

Intentional Pedagogy

The potential for a limitless hybridity of changed social relations offers multiple possibilities for intentional pedagogical planning. Recognizing the characteristics of diverse cultures opens the way to consider alternative realities, such as those engaged in cross-cultural dialogues. Anzaldúa (1987) described a tolerance of ambiguity that broaches the problematic of "entrenched habits and patterns of behavior," and notes that "rigidity means death." In what becomes a transformational hybrid of perspective through developing education, growing awareness can reveal the type of thinking inclusive of difference and the flexibility that is needed to intentionally engage with the knowledge and belief systems of Indigenous peoples. In her description of the necessity for *la mestiza* (a Mexican Indigenous woman of mixed European heritage) to develop a tolerance of ambiguity, Anzaldúa writes,

> Only by remaining flexible is she able to stretch the psyche horizontally and vertically. *La mestiza* [italics original] constantly has to shift out of habitual formations; from convergent thinking, analytical reasoning that tends to use rationality to move toward a single goal (a Western mode), to divergent thinking, characterized

by movement away from set patterns and goals and toward a more whole perspective, one that includes rather than excludes. (1987, 79)

Anzaldúa's description of flexibility can be viewed as an attribute of giving back. It is a matter of opening up minds to divergent ways of thinking across cultures and across landscapes. Through the use of a layered plan for teaching, each new topic provides a mechanism to shift rigid ways of thinking where evolutionary processes can then be developed and learned. This requires an intentional pedagogical process that begins to deconstruct fear of the unknown "Other." By continuing to tell about my research with Indigenous peoples, connections begin to be made to their humanity in a way that may not have existed previously for those who are unfamiliar with them.

The epistemological and ontological traditions of Indigenous peoples' customs have historically been misunderstood and undervalued. It is through their traditional ways of making meaning and viewing others, nature, and the universe that they are often misinterpreted and not understood. In the twenty-first century, this misunderstanding includes the personal experience of many Indigenous students. Many of them entering universities today are on a steep learning curve when it comes to learning their own history—especially if they have not had the opportunity to learn from their families or from their previous education experiences. The process of their education can be not only transformative but also extraordinarily empowering. Archibald (2008) astutely observed that

> Indigenous peoples' history of colonization has left many of our peoples and our cultures weak and fragmented. Cultural knowledge, traditions, and healing have lessened the detrimental effects of colonization. Cultural knowledge and traditions have also helped us to resist assimilation. I believe that Indigenous stories are at the core of our cultures. They have the power to make us think, feel, and be good human beings. They have the power to bring storied life back to us. (139)

This insight is critical to understanding the multidimensional knowledge systems that many Indigenous people have. The fact is that all tribes have creation and belief systems as distinct as they are and as varied as their territories. It is important in teaching to build on the multiple layers of life experience. In order for non-Indigenous peoples to consider questions of how different knowledge systems can be understood, learning must include interpretations of their differing worldviews through a relational framing of influences in lectures, readings, and discussions. Intentional pedagogy can frame varying perspectives that lead to understanding the type of mixed hybridizations of culture, such as Latour (1997) described as a translation, as it "creates mixtures between entirely new types of beings, hybrids of nature and culture" (10). This multidimensional and, in a sense, ongoing hybridization of translation, and this divergent thinking (Anzaldúa 1987), is critical to transformational pedagogical dialogues as a pathway to increasing perceptions.

As the word "hybridity" suggests, transformational interpretations about the various topics occurs through the potential blending of influences that can result from social interactions and experiences. For instance, non-Indigenous peoples who do not identify with the notion of landforms as spiritually or culturally significant, are often called upon to make land management decisions about them that, as history demonstrates, does not always result in the best interest of tribes. However, if Indigenous peoples are invited to the public consultation process to openly discuss the cultural and spiritual significance of a location, inevitably, any change in thinking that occurs from these testimonies produces variance, one way or the other. In that flexible space located in between what was previously known or unknown, exchanges begin to result in a hybrid perspective. The presentation of real-world scenarios can be, in this sense, conduits of transformative cultural exchange.

In teaching about Indigenous peoples, my intentional pedagogy does not focus on past injustices, but it does not overlook them. It is based on a planned trajectory of empowerment. As a geographer, it is significant to engage with understandings of place and human interactions. Teaching within a historical context is necessary if we are going to gain a better comprehension of the present. Although a course topic might be focused on modern-day challenges, learning about and knowing how we got to where we are today is critical to fully understanding the present in order to be able to envision a better future.

Advancing Twenty-First-Century Curricula

Over the centuries, the almost complete genocide of Indigenous populations around the globe was driven by ignorance and a denial of their humanity. By continuing to tell about them, we can lift the veil of ignorance, which can lead to addressing instances of social injustice that Indigenous peoples continue to encounter today. What we must be asking ourselves is how and why the invisibility of their human experience prevails in twenty-first-century education curricula? If students have only Walt Disney to thank for their spare knowledge of Native America, for example, we have to question standardized education curriculum for its failure to not teach about Indigenous peoples, except for casting conciliatory historic bread crumbs for reference. Is this absence of history about Indigenous peoples an attempt to not have to deal with the atrocities that were committed against them? If this is the case, how can nations begin to dismantle dysfunctional power relationships that exist and begin to truly heal? As Freire (2000 [1970]) wrote,

> Whereas the violence of the oppressors prevents the oppressed from being fully human, the response of the latter to this violence is grounded in the desire to pursue the right to be human. As the oppressors dehumanize others and violate their rights, they themselves also become dehumanized. As the oppressed, fighting to be human, take away the oppressors' power to dominate and suppress, they restore to the oppressors the humanity they had lost in the exercise of oppression. (56)

By giving back to our research participants by continuing to tell about them, is it possible, then, to (re)mind the state of the violence they continue to perpetuate against their Indigenous populations by silencing their voices and experience in our curricula? The act of giving back is a strike against the walls of injustice and silence that continues to hinder us from really knowing and learning about each other.

The power of giving back is that the stories will not and cannot be forgotten. Intentional pedagogy in the classroom becomes an act of resistance against oppression and suppression. It creates an opportunity for changes to occur in dominant Western worldviews that have been historically reticent to accept Indigenous epistemologies and ontologies (Cajete 2000; Fixico 2003; LaDuke 2005; Wilson 2008). This change in worldview can begin to construct a bridge that spans the cultural divide that separates us from knowing the potential multiple meanings inherent in other knowledge systems. Not only are the voices of the past liberated and finally able to speak, we all are liberated and have the freedom to learn other truths. We can then resist what continues to divide us. bell hooks (2003) said it best when she observed that, "while it is a truism that every citizen of this nation is, white or colored, is born into a racist society that attempts to socialize us from the moment of our birth to accept the tenets of white supremacy, it is equally true that we can choose to resist this socialization" (56). This kind of awareness and resistance can be the beginning of the end of those uncomfortable classroom surprises when students are learning about Indigenous peoples for the very first time.

Conclusion: Continuing

Thinking back to that time, those many years ago, when I first interviewed Elder Celeste, I did not know then precisely where my life path would lead me. After talking with her, I later went to the reservoir and stood looking down at water that had flooded over 156,000 acres of some of the most highly productive agricultural lands on the Missouri River in the 1950s. I had gained a sense for the memories she had shared with me of her homeland. I wondered about the cottonwood trees that were no longer there. Elder Celeste had told me that the spirits of her ancestors were believed to have dwelled among them. With the flooding of the historic river for the reservoir, the cottonwoods had either been cut down or their skeletal remains were slowly rotting away just below the surface. Still, I felt them there, and I reached out for those spirits and for what they had to teach me.

When I meet others who, like Elder Celeste, are literally fighting for their lives and for the future of their nations, I continue to renew the promise to tell their stories, as I did again in my meeting with Attawapiskat Chief Theresa Spence at the beginning of the Idle No More movement in Canada during late December 2012 and early January 2013. It was then that the Idle No More protest movement was begun by First Nations, and others, in Canada to protest changes in laws that were passed with the support of the government of then Prime Minister Stephen Harper in December 2012 (Ornelas 2013). The changes affected water protections and tribal treaty rights without the free, prior, and informed consent of First Nations as required under the 2007 United Nations Declaration on the Rights of Indigenous Peoples, which Canada agreed to support in 2010. Chief Spence and Grand Elder Ray Robinson had begun a hunger strike after the December vote in protest of what they perceived to be a threat to their treaty rights and sovereignty. Ultimately, the hunger strike lasted forty-three days before a thirteen-point declaration was developed by First Nations leadership. The declaration, "First Nations: Working for Fundamental Change," was believed to be a positive next step in fostering better communication and transparency with the Canadian government (Canadian Progressive 2013; CBCN 2013).

When I looked into Chief Spence's eyes and I held onto her hands, I promised to tell what I had learned about her, and she thanked me for telling of her fight outside of Canada. To Chief Spence, to Elder Celeste, and to Elder Ray, I will continue to tell them about you and to give back to those who have given me so much more in return.

Chapter 10 References

Anzaldúa, Gloria E. 1987. *Borderlands / La Frontera: The New Mestiza.* San Francisco: Spinsters / Aunt Lute.

———. 2002. "now let us shift . . . the path of conocimiento . . . inner work, public acts." In *This Bridge We Call Home: Radical Visions for Transformation,* edited by Gloria E. Anzaldúa and AnaLouise Keating, 540–576. New York: Routledge.

Archibald, Jo-Ann. 2008. *Indigenous Storywork: Educating the Heart, Mind, Body, and Spirit.* Vancouver: University of British Columbia Press.

Cajete, Gregory. 2000. *Native Science: Natural Laws of Interdependence.* Santa Fe, NM: Clear Light.

Canadian Progressive. 2013. "Chief Theresa Spence Ends 43-Day Hunger Strike with Declaration 'Towards Fundamental Change.'" January 25. http://www.canadianprogressiveworld.com/2013/01/25/chief-theresa-spence-ends-43-day-hunger-strike-with-declaration-towards-fundamental-change/.

CBCN. 2013. "Chief Theresa Spence to End Hunger Strike Today." January 23. http://www.cbc.ca/news/canada/story/2013/01/23/attawapiskat-spence-hunger-strike.html.

Day, Richard J. F. 2010. "Angry Indians, Settler Guilt, and the Challenges of Decolonization and Resurgence." In *This Is Not an Honor Song: Twenty Years Since the Blockades,* edited by Leanne Simpson and Kiera L. Ladner, 268. Winnipeg: Arbeiter Ring.

Deloria Jr., Vine. 2003. "Sacred Lands and Religious Freedom." In *Sacred Lands Reader,* edited by Marjorie Beggs and Christopher McLeod, 15–25. Berkeley, CA: Earth Island Institute.

Fixico, Donald L. 2003. *The American Indian Mind in a Linear World.* New York: Routledge.

Fortier, James. 2013. *Gifts from the Elders*. DVD. Directed by James M. Fortier. London, ON: Western University.

Freire, Paulo. 2000 [1970]. *Pedagogy of the Oppressed*. New York: Seabury Press.

———. 2004 [1992]. *Pedagogy of Hope: Reliving Pedagogy of the Oppressed*. London: Continuum.

Harvey, David. 1996. "The Environment of Justice." In *Justice, Nature, and the Geography of Difference*, 366–402. Oxford: Blackwell.

hooks, bell. 2003. *Teaching Community: A Pedagogy of Hope*. London: Routledge.

Kovach, Margaret. 2009. *Indigenous Methodologies: Characteristics, Conversations, and Contexts*. Toronto, ON: University of Toronto Press.

Kübler-Ross, Elisabeth. 1969. *On Death and Dying*. New York: Macmillan.

LaDuke, Winona. 2005. *Recovering the Sacred: The Power of Naming and Claiming*. Cambridge, MA: South End Press.

Latour, Bruno. 1997 [1991]. *We Have Never Been Modern*. Cambridge, MA: Harvard University Press.

Lawson, Victoria. 2013. "Geographies of Hope Symposium 2: What Exactly Are Geographies of Hope? What Is Hope?" Discussion at the Association of American Geographers Annual Meeting, Los Angeles, April 10.

Murton, Brian. 2012. "Counterpoint: Have We Broken Out of the 'Hall of Mirrors' Yet?" *Journal of Cultural Geography* 29 (1): 15–18, doi:10.10 80/08873631.2012.646888.

Ornelas, Roxanne T. 2013. "International Treaties Models for Transparency in Governance." *Public Administration Times* 36 (1): 5.

Pulido, Laura. 1998. "The Sacredness of 'Mother Earth': Spirituality, Activism, and Social Justice." *Annals of the Association of American Geographers* 88 (4): 719.

Shaw, Wendy, RDK Herman, and G. Rebecca Dobbs. 2008. "Encountering Indigeneity: Re-imagining and Decolonizing Geography." *Geografiska Annaler* 88B (3): 267–276.

Student. 2014. "Comments." Course Evaluation (Spring), Miami University.

Tsosie, Rebecca. 2006. "going HOME again." *Native Peoples Magazine* 19 (1): 46–51.

UNSR. 2012. "Sacred Places." *Report of the Special Rapporteur on the Rights of Indigenous Peoples, James Anaya*. http://unsr.jamesanaya.org/docs/countries/2012-report-usa-a-hrc-21-47-add1_en.pdf.

Wilson, Shawn. 2008. *Research Is Ceremony: Indigenous Research Methods*. Halifax, NS: Fernwood.

PART 4

Advocacy and Beyond

11

Embedded within (Aboriginal) Redfern in Inner Sydney, Australia

WENDY S. SHAW

I**N THIS CHAPTER, I REFLECT** on the idea of the researcher as sequesterer and proprietor of knowledge and decisions made around the extent to which "data" is shared or given back to the communities worked with, and often mined, in a one-way knowledge exchange. I draw here on a history of my own engagements with the kind of research for which questions must be asked about the doing and taking during the research process. In a previous publication, I commented on researcher tendencies—including my own—to take *more* than data while working in "dangerous" highly exoticized locations, such as Papua New Guinea. I linked a tendency in the foreign, "Western" research process, which includes taking and an all too easy default to simplified and racialized caricatures and cultures of fear, particularly of the exoticized Other (Shaw 2011). The same can be said for the inner Sydney suburb of Redfern, Australia, which has a long-standing narrative as an ever-evolving fear-scape, proffered and reinforced over decades by media and government agencies because of the presence there of an impoverished Aboriginal neighborhood known as The Block (Shaw 2007). Recently, Redfern has become an icon of urban change, of built heritage-led gentrification, which assumes that the Aboriginal neighborhood and community of The Block will either disappear, or be reimagined (see Teece-Johnson 2015).

I draw here on my experiences of living, working, and carrying out research in and around Redfern to provide an example of a perhaps more complex researcher position than simply occupying the roles of "taking" and "giving back." I do not want to labor a semantic to point out a logic about giving back, which assumes that something was taken. This was certainly the case with Aboriginal lands in Australia, which were indeed taken, and, in this case, a small parcel of land was given back to the Redfern Aboriginal community. I want to offer the idea that although "taking" can be obvious—such as the seizure of lands during invasion—it can also include complex exchanges. The complexity of "giving back," in the case of Aboriginal Redfern, demonstrates that this concept needs to be considered carefully, and perhaps reimagined away from the simple taking and giving (back) binary.

My rationale is that although the lands that now constitute Australia were indeed taken, with little redress, in the case of the ongoing struggle for Aboriginal Redfern, particularly The Block, many have *given* to the cause—many Aboriginal and non-Aboriginal actors. The recent history of the Aboriginal presence in Redfern is one of struggle: to maintain The Block from threats of subsumption and for recognition that it is indeed Aboriginal land—a fact that many forget or choose not to acknowledge. The act of giving this land back to Aboriginal people has not been straightforward either. This "gift" (and how can giving back something that was taken constitute a gift?) has been plagued by controversy, which has not boded well for the Aboriginal community in this highly urbanized and increasingly wealthy location. In this chapter, I consider the tricky and vexed positionings of giving and taking in the context of the Aboriginal settlement in Redfern, Australia. This discussion closes with the idea that although such constructs can be fraught, they can certainly benefit from a process of remaining open to healthy critique. Here, I have drawn on Indigenism, or Indigenous epistemologies, in this process.

Personal Involvement, as Resident, Activist, and Researcher

I lived around the corner from The Block from the mid-1990s until 2008 and have written on contemporary struggles associated with the effects of gentrification and whiteness on the Aboriginal residents in the area. Given my embeddedness in this place for well over a decade (and as with the aforementioned paper on researchers working in Papua New Guinea), I include myself as a research subject in this process of reflection and reflexivity that also engages a process of autoethnography. So

I build on earlier work on autoethnography (Shaw 2013a) wherein my researcher-self is enabled to speak as a research participant (Butz and Besio 2009; Bullough and Pinnegar 2001; Ellis and Bochner 2000; Fuchs 2002; and Moss 2001). Autoethnography can be defined as "a qualitative research method that utilizes data about self and its context to gain an understanding of the connectivity between self and others" (Ngunjiri, Hernandez, and Chang 2010, 2).

As with others (Coffey 1999; Holt 2003), I am wary of the potential for overemphasizing the self at the expense of rigor (Shaw 2013a), so I tend to use autoethnography to fill in gaps in the public or scholarly record (triangulated, of course) and to provide leads to other details. Autoethnography does tend to polarize. There is "realist" ethnography versus "alternative" ethnographic practice. The latter, according to Ngunjiri and colleagues (2010, 3–4) comes "from the heart." My version is a little of both but influenced by the extended logics enabled through engagement with Indigenous worldviews and an ongoing commitment to the project of decolonizing scholarship (Shaw, Herman, and Dobbs 2006; Smith 1999). As a Cree scholar (Wilson 2001)from Canada noted,

> One major difference between [dominant and Indigenous] para-
> digms … is that [the former] build on the fundamental belief that
> knowledge is an individual entity: the researcher is an individual
> in search of knowledge, … something that is gained, and therefore
> … may be owned by an individual. (176–177)

From a non-Indigenous knowledge perspective then, the concept of giving back means that something has been taken, and then owned by the researcher. By this logic it must be assumed that the idea of "giving back" is, in essence, not particularly an Indigenous perspective. Rather, "An Indigenous paradigm comes from the fundamental belief that knowledge is relational … shared … not just with the research subjects … but with all … the cosmos … animals … plants … with the earth that we share this knowledge" (Wilson 2001, 177). Wilson does, however, acknowledge that appropriation of knowledge and cultures has taken place, "when proper relationships have not been established and honoured between researchers and their subjects" (177).

This chapter draws on several previous publications but specifi-cally builds on empirical examples listed in *Redfern as the Heart(h): Living (Black) in Inner Sydney* (Shaw 2013b). My intention here is to demonstrate that while I fully acknowledge the neocolonial politics of taking—information, secrets, "data," or even a good story—the power and agency of people who are often thought of as "the researched," should also never be underestimated. I think it is epistemologically appropriate to demonstrate that moving beyond a blanket notion, a binary of "taking" and "giving (back)," provides capacity to unearth richer cultural complexities and formations that also serve to unsettle notions of, for instance, black and white, that dominate this Sydney location. By revisiting my previous work of gathered memories, as well as recent recollections, I offer up processes of activism and action-based research that do not fit neatly into the concept of "giving back." While this is not denied or, indeed, forgotten, in this case of Redfern a different banner might be better described as an ongoing *politics of collaboration and sharing* among all involved. Redfern is widely imagined to consist of "black" and in-decline spaces (the high-profile Aboriginal community known as The Block), and "white" (gentrifying) spaces, but I seek to highlight the more nuanced and inclusive politics of collaboration and sharing that manifested decades ago. In so doing, I defer specifically to the expertise of Indigenous scholars who speak of relationality over binaries. Therefore, in the spirit of the decolonization of research, I am guided by a politics and epistemology of "Indigenism [that] must overcome the dichotomies in scientific thought such as object/subject, rational/irrational and white/black" (Rigney 2001, 7).

My worldview then, guided by Indigenism, utilizes "storytelling and . . . personal narratives [that] fit the epistemology because when you are relating a personal narrative, you are getting into a relationship with someone" (Wilson 2001, 176–177). Although such relationships develop in situ, they are also offered between the author and the reader—albeit a more difficult relationship to develop, which I fully acknowledge. This is, of course, a problem of publication, and the domination of the written word over the oral (Grossman 2013). Nevertheless, within this constraint, the stories I offer here are a blurring between the personal and the professional, as well as between taking and giving.

Below I provide a short social history of the Redfern story and the formalization of Aboriginal land, and The Block. I also weave stories of collaboration that have been integral to the ongoing survival of The Block, but have often remained largely unacknowledged. I do this to demonstrate that giving and taking are not clear-cut but slippery and unpredictable. I conclude with a discussion on the current status of The Block and a final comment about "giving back."

Giving Back to Aboriginal Australia

In 1973, the Australian federal government granted funds for the purchase of a small urban site of approximately seventy Victorian terraced houses, rented at that time by Aboriginal people seeking accommodation in what was a blighted, and otherwise largely abandoned, industrial inner city of Sydney. With the purchase of these houses, the Aboriginal community of The Block was formalized, and the site became Aboriginal land (Anderson 1993). This land was handed "back" to Aboriginal Australia on behalf of a radical and highly progressive Labor federal government, under the leadership of the charismatic and popular prime minister, Gough Whitlam, as a gesture to return a small parcel of lands stolen during invasion and colonial settlement. Although hard-fought-for and of extreme importance to Aboriginal Australians, particularly at that time, this act of recognition has served to feed ongoing claims that Aboriginal people in Australia are incapable welfare recipients who expect to be looked after rather than providing for themselves. Moreover, The Block is a troubled and stigmatized place and, since the 1970s at least, the focal point of populist media representations and government policy that continue to undermine its ongoing existence.

As is often the case with stigmatized locations, the ongoing narrative of decline serves to mask the rich diversity of urban Aboriginal life, and the social and cultural capitals that have been established over time. The ongoing representations that describe racially divided urban spaces certainly do not reflect the history of engagement between Aboriginal and non-Aboriginal actors and activists who are part of the ongoing story and politics of place.

Yet, the damaging script referred to as the "myth of privilege" (Mickler 1998) continues to demonize the community in Redfern, which is held up as an exemplar of how such giving (back) has failed. The ensuing discourse of decline is dangerously linked to this notion of giving (back) and has provided fuel to arguments against support for initiatives for Australian Aboriginal people, who are not faring particularly well in contemporary Australia. According to the 2016 "Closing the Gap" report, Aboriginal Australians are still likely to die ten years earlier than their non-Indigenous counterparts. Employment gaps have increased, rather than narrowed, since the 2008 report, and education measures such as school attendance, literacy, and numeracy rates are also trailing well behind (Commonwealth of Australia 2016). The story of the evolution of Aboriginal Redfern and The Block settlement provided a focus for Aboriginal politics in Australia. Although not the first place of struggle,[1] the struggle for Redfern has not abated and has remained pivotal to Aboriginal politics being voiced, and sometimes heard. Redfern has been recognized as an Aboriginal place, regardless of the ongoing pressures against its existence that have increased with recent gentrification and associated escalation in housing prices.

History of Aboriginal Redfern, Sydney, Australia

Prior to invasion and settlement by the British more than two hundred years ago, the Gadigal people and others of the Eora Darug occupied the place where the city of Sydney now stands. For a range of reasons mostly associated with changing employment arrangements, in the 1930s Aboriginal people started to migrate from rural and "outback" areas, to which they had sometimes fled, from coastal regions (Anderson 1993). Bunjalung and Dunghutti people from the North, and others from all over New South Wales, came to Redfern (Kohen 2000).

Aboriginal people tended to settle in otherwise-ignored parts of inner Sydney. Others had fled industrialisation to live in the ever-expanding suburbs. While urban Aboriginal people had remained mostly separate from the wider settler society—and therefore were generally unseen—they had moments of political visibility. One event was the "Day of Mourning" protest in 1938 that marked the sesquicentenary of invasion (DMP 1938). This quiet presence was awakened in the 1960s, when Redfern became notorious as the site of Aboriginal activism, and by the 1970s, this had resulted in the establishment of its identity as Aboriginal urban space. Now, the inner city suburb of Redfern is one of the fastest gentrifying locations in Sydney. It is located just a few kilometers and but one train station away from the central business district. Yet, it has remained notorious because of The Block. Its resilience to mounting pressures is testament to the ongoing strength and tenacity of the local Aboriginal community and its supporters.

Significant collaborations between non-Aboriginal actors—whether organisations or individuals—has contributed to the ongoing presence of The Block. Organisations such as the Builders Labourers' Federation (BLF) have been instrumental in ensuring an ongoing Aboriginal presence in Redfern. In the early 1970s, the BLF declared a ban on all work associated with the redevelopment of the site of small Victorian terraced houses that was to become The Block. This work ban leveraged the sale by the landholding developer that enabled its purchase, and then status, as Aboriginal land (Anderson 1993). Aboriginal medical, legal, and welfare services were established at that time (Gilbert 1971; Waltha 1971), as was the Redfern Aboriginal Land Council (1972) and the Aboriginal Housing Company (1973), which is the governing body for The Block.

The establishment of the Aboriginal Medical Service included the input of a high-profile (non-Aboriginal) eye surgeon (Gilbert 1971). Similarly, with collaborative efforts, the Aboriginal Legal Service began in 1971 (Waltha 1971), with support by the Law Society and the Bar Council. Other collaborative efforts were behind the advent of community welfare services, such as The Aboriginal Children's Service (1975) and educational and child-care facilities, including The Settlement (mid-1920s), an after-school care and welfare facility (Molesworth 2006), and Murawina preschool, an early childhood nursery established in Redfern in 1972. Such services have strengthened the Aboriginal identity of Redfern, as have sporting organisations such as the Tony Mundine Gym (1985) (SBS 2010). The tertiary education facility Eora TAFE College opened its doors in 1987, and Mudgin-Gal women's place was established in the early 1990s (S.H. nd). In 2010, the National Centre for Aboriginal Excellence (NCIE nd) was opened by the then prime minister, Kevin Rudd.

Personal Experiences of Collaboration—Institutions

Along with high-profile trade unions, and medical and legal professionals, many ordinary non-Aboriginal people have shown ongoing support for the Aboriginal community in inner Sydney. Around the corner from where I lived from the mid-1990s until 2008 sits an education facility known as The Settlement, which is one of the oldest community welfare agencies in the Redfern area. In the 1920s, it provided welfare services to the local working-class residents (Molesworth 2006; see also http://www.thesettlement.org.au/history.html) but by the 1970s, with support from a range of non-Aboriginal individuals, including academics from Sydney University (which is less than a kilometer away), its mandate had changed to the provision of care and services for the local Aboriginal community.

Of course, local non-Aboriginal people have mounted their own pressures against the ongoing Aboriginal presence (Shaw 2007). My experiences of living and carrying out research in the local area include crossing paths with a range of motivations. The next example illustrates how a group of "well-meaning" non-Aboriginal residents created pressure for the Aboriginal community.

I became a member of The Settlement's management committee in the late 1990s. I had been asked to join by members of The Block's extended community, who wanted an ally on the committee—which had become increasingly gentrifier-oriented. Although I was also a homeowner, my friends thought that I might bring the focus of the settlement back to its Aboriginal agenda, which was being eroded. I became involved in a range of community initiatives and activities, and general running of the organization, which I enjoyed for several years. However, I found that the fears of my associates from The Block were justified, and I ended up having to resign from the committee over a management dispute. Despite my efforts, and support from a few others on the committee, the mostly non-Aboriginal committee members, at that time, did not to listen to the voices of the Aboriginal staff, or The Block community members. It was simply too difficult to continue being part of a committee that I suspected was more interested in the capital gains of real estate than in the community. In 2006, I had learned of the plan to sell the property, which justified what I had feared had been a long-term agenda. I was elated to find out that Aboriginal elders from The Block then mounted a legal challenge, which was successful. The Settlement remains to this day (The Settlement 2016).

Eora College of Technical and Further Education

When Eora College opened its doors in 1987, it instantly became a landmark in Aboriginal (tertiary) education. "Eora takes its name from the Gadigal language of the Aboriginal nation that originally inhabited the Port Jackson area around Sydney Harbour" (Eora College nd). According to the college director, Darryl Griffin,

> Eora was the culmination of ideas by Aboriginal people . . . [and] is dedicated to re-establishing lost pride in Aboriginal culture through the Arts and Access Education programs [within] an environment more accustomed to Aboriginal learning styles. . . . Eora is also committed to helping educate the wider community in Aboriginal culture . . . [and] to establish[ing] a national and international profile where Aboriginal people throughout the world can share their culture, knowledge and visions for the future. (Eora College nd)

The intent of Eora is to educate Aboriginal people, but it also demonstrates the theme of collaborative politics of sharing in that it seeks to give to non-Aboriginal Australia in a mutually constitutive maneuver that also assists Aboriginal Australia.

I joined Eora in 1995 as a teacher in a new training course in community welfare, designed to "hand over" community welfare services to Aboriginal people by training Aboriginal community "welfare" workers. The use of the term "giving back," in this instance, is useful in that it assumes that Aboriginal people have had something taken, which has surely been the case. Successive Australian governments established organizations that were designed *to take responsibility* for Aboriginal welfare, largely against the will of Aboriginal people. For instance, The Aborigines Welfare Board went to great lengths to institutionalize the concept of welfare for a group of people that were believed to be "a dying race."[2] Another related initiative was the now-infamous policy of taking Aboriginal children that passed as "white":

> Between 1910–1970, many Indigenous children were forcibly removed from their families as a result of various government policies. The generations of children removed under these policies became known as the Stolen Generations. The policies of child removal left a legacy of trauma and loss that continues to affect Indigenous communities, families and individuals. . . . The forcible removal of Indigenous children from their families was part of the ideology of Assimilation . . . [that] was founded on the assumption of black inferiority and white superiority, which proposed that Indigenous people should be allowed to "die out" through a process of natural elimination, or, where possible, should be assimilated into the white community. (Australians Together nd)

The need to "hand back" community welfare services and, in the case of the Eora initiative, to train community welfare workers, is clear. However, the Eora initiative was discontinued a year into the first of the two-year programs because of a perceived "replication of provision" by the wider TAFE organizational management. Some of the Eora students made the uneasy transition to the mainstream college—but the point had been lost. The "handing back" had been taken back.

However, during the Eora phase, I was fortunate to be able to connect to the local Aboriginal community in more meaningful ways. Mutual trust-building resulted in the establishment of connections, friendships, and collaborations that continue to this day. One of the students I met at Eora worked at The Settlement, which was how I became involved (as detailed above), and through this connection, other networks within Aboriginal Australia opened to me.

The original idea—to hand over welfare provision for Aboriginal people to Aboriginal welfare professionals—was finally realized when Eora simply *took control* and established its own courseware, titled "Aboriginal Studies for Professional and Community Practice Course Details," which is open to all. This Diploma of Aboriginal Studies for Professional and Community Practice is

> a course for both Aboriginal and non-Aboriginal people. It provides Aboriginal specific cultural literacy and competence by developing high level understanding of Aboriginal Cultures and Knowledge systems, complex socio/historical issues, and skills and knowledge for practical application in a workplace, community or academic context. (TAFE NSW nd)

Having taught in mainstream community welfare courses, I think this course should be the mandatory course for all so-called community welfare students. It demonstrates also that Aboriginality is alive and thriving in the Redfern area. As well, it provides an exemplar of "giving" something back—in this case, to the wider community, in a politics of collaboration and sharing. Eora has taken responsibility for changing the face and focus of what used to known as "community welfare," which is now professional and community practice.

Personal Experiences of Living in a Community, and Some Collaborative Politics

My involvement with Eora, The Settlement, and The Block community more generally included—and still includes—socializing. Having moved away from the area, I miss Friday nights at a local venue where everyone would dress up and dance to country music. Occasionally, Aboriginal celebrities would just turn up and perform, but overall everyone was welcome to "have a go." Over the years, I have attended many events, such as birthday parties, weddings, and funerals. Such invitations reinforce friendships and a sense of inclusion that reaches well beyond research.

I did continue to carry out research on the politics of whiteness and gentrification in the area. There was plenty of data, after all.

In the next few examples of collaborative politics, I turn to personal stories about attending political rallies. At one gathering, an elder told me that something special would happen. Suddenly, an enormous kangaroo was unearthed from hot coals. I was then offered a piece of the tail in a gesture of friendship. On another occasion, I was part of a group that was about to head off around the corner to a rally on The Block. Just before departure, I was told of a "change of plan," which resulted in my attending the rally alone, without my comrades who were heading to play Koori golf (Koori is the Aboriginal collective noun for Indigenous inhabitants of the eastern part of Australia). This group of men was happy for me (as a "sister") to represent them at the rally. But I was not particularly happy about this arrangement. The Koori golf day was a statewide competition that happened to clash with the rally. These golf tournaments were significant events in mentoring boys and young men from all over the state of New South Wales. It certainly challenged some of my preconceptions about the meanings of collaborative politics, but I eventually realized the significance of the event.

On another occasion, at another rally in support of the ongoing existence of The Block, a man I vaguely knew threw a beer bottle at me. He had not recognized me, as I was dressed more formally than usual, particularly for a rally. He had thought I was a government official. Fortunately, another (Aboriginal) man intervened and quickly pulled me out of the way of the flying bottle. I did not know this man who pulled me away, but he apologized profusely, even though he had saved me. Tensions were high that day, and rallies on The Block had become volatile in the past. On this occasion, several elders wrested control, and the bottle-thrower, realizing I was someone he knew, apologized unreservedly. Later, I would see my acquaintance (unnamed for anonymity), and he always sang out, "Hello sis[ter]." This man was not particularly well, generally living "rough" but well-cared-for by his community. Many who lived on The Block have lived "rough" for decades because of the demolition of houses; in particular, a tent occupation was set up as a deliberate and visual reminder that this community prevails, with or without houses.[3] This story serves as a reminder that not all "giving" (back) is necessarily wanted, and in this case, there was hostility to the presence of a "gubba" (white person/from the government). Had I not had a long-term association with The Block, the outcome might have been quite different.

My final story about collaborations (not always wanted, as noted above) is highly memorable and has retained a media focus ever since. This event was part rally, part memorial. It occurred after the death of a young man in 2004, which resulted in the so-called Redfern Riots (Shaw 2009). The young man had been killed while pedaling away from police on his bicycle. He died when he hit a fence, and although police were cleared of any wrongdoing, answers are still sought by the young person's family and the community more broadly. The death remains controversial to this day (see Barrett 2014).

Relations between young Aboriginal people in and around Redfern and police already had a history of tension. At this time, tensions were high. Funnell (2005, np, following Cunneen 2001) states, "The tensions between Indigenous Australia and police represent a greater fissure stemming from the lack of autonomy, self-government and self-determination that defines the Indigenous political struggle in Australia." Although I slept through the actual "riot"—it was a very small event by riot standards—it was international news.[4] I recall the scenes from the next few days, of the bricked-in windows at the railway station, a burnt-out car, and other debris, but most importantly, the memorial service/rally on The Block. Support arrived from near and far. It was a somber event of extreme sadness at what was clearly seen to be a reinforcement of the distinction between "black" and "white." The glaring reality was how different the incident would have been treated had the young person been "white." The event also reiterated the message that, regardless of the sense of removal from the world beyond, the small Aboriginal community of The Block might be beholden to forces that are beyond its control, but it does not give up the fight for survival.

Conclusion: Giving Back?

I have presented my role as a supporter of the staff at The Settlement, my experience as a teacher at Eora, and my research and general embeddedness in Redfern daily life to demonstrate the blurring of otherwise highly reinforced and racialized divisions in urban space. By remaining vigilant to an episteme of Indigenism, I hope, too, to have demonstrated a necessary blurring of several binaries: between the researcher and the researched, as well as between seemingly separated activisms based along urban lines of racialized segregation. The twist in the case of my ongoing research project in this place has been that I have taken details, "data," mostly from the dominant or empowered group: my ongoing critique is of processes of whiteness and gentrification. This has occurred, however, within the context of my overt and ongoing commitment to Indigenous geographies, particularly in this important location. I have therefore studied my "own kind" in this context, and by standard identity definitions. However, the boundaries between "white and gentrifying" and "black and in decline" are not nearly as clear-cut as Redfern's reputation would indicate. I know Aboriginal as well as non-Aboriginal gentrifiers, and non-Aboriginal as well as Aboriginal renters. The split between homeowner and renter is also not clear-cut in one of the world's most expensive cities to find housing. So the tangible assets of my research are not clear-cut. The processes of living, working, and doing research have included giving and taking. If I have given anything back, it has not been directly to the research participants as such (unless they are interested in the racializing process in which they are immersed, and some have shown interest). My efforts in living, working, and researching have included relationships with the group affected by such processes. But in reality, living in Redfern meant immersion within the whole community—I was fortunate to be included within Aboriginal worlds.

My Redfern life certainly contributed to my scholarly development in tangible ways, whereas my "giving back" remains less clear. Even though questions remain about mutual benefits that should not be shied away from, they remain somewhat immeasurable. Moreover, an epistemology of Indigenism tends also to not be bounded by the hegemony of the written word.

It must be remembered that a well-meaning, and sometimes useful, presence is not automatically welcomed—as in any social and/or professional arrangement, as my experience of the bottle-throwing at a rally exemplified. When the bottle-thrower realized that I was someone he knew from the area, and not from the government (and if I had been, I still might have been a supporter), he apologized. Yet, on that day, the presence of an "outsider" was unwanted, even though I was an invited guest. These collaborations are not always predictable.

My experiences of place include the uncanny realities of being a non-Aboriginal gentrifier (of sorts) and of occasions of participation with Redfern's Koori worlds. My insider/outsider perspective includes moments of participation in these worlds that exist, and are messy, yet survive and sometimes thrive regardless of wider pressures, and have done so regardless of my presence and what I might have written about them. In Redfern, many stories of worlds within worlds demonstrate that there are daily contexts that are Aboriginal but where others are, at times, welcomed. And for those who have built trusting relationships, research is sometimes welcomed as well. Moreover, as an elder said to me when I talked about whiteness, "We love it when you mob turn your microscopes onto yourselves."

Yet, such collaborations have remained marginal to the discourses that clamour to reinforce and exacerbate lines of distinction between "black" (Indigenous) and "white" (gentrifier) Redfern. This common populist focus continues to reinforce the belief that the "gift" to Aboriginal Australia was squandered, that "they" have been "given" too much. The Block carries the stigma as a "failed human experiment" in Aboriginal self-determination (Anderson 1993; Shaw 2007). It has provided ammunition for developers in the march toward gentrification. This rhetoric continues to try to erase the existence of The Block. However, recent success by the Aboriginal Tent Embassy in Redfern demonstrate that members of the community, and its supporters, do not give up the struggle for The Block. As a result of the refusal of members of The Block community to leave the site, and then living in tents because houses had been demolished, the Australian federal government has promised $5 million, as part of a $70 million deal, for the construction of sixty-two new houses for Aboriginal people. As a well-known elder, and founder of the Tent Embassy, asserted, "My teachers taught me the principles of our resistance—we never ceded our land to anyone. . . . The embassy has demonstrated that for our people, resistance is the only way to go" (McNally and Staff 2015).

The "giving back" in this instance is probably better characterized as an example of Indigenous people "taking back."

Chapter 11 References and Recommended Reading

Anderson, K. 1993. "Place Narratives and the Origins of Inner Sydney's Aboriginal Settlement, 1972–73." *Journal of Historical Geography* 19:314–335.

Australians Together. nd. "The Stolen Generations." http://www.australians together.org.au/stories/detail/the-stolen-generations (accessed February 16, 2016).

Barrett, Rebecca. 2014. "Thomas 'TJ' Hickey's Family Seeks Apology on 10th anniversary of Teenager's Death in Redfern Riot." ABC News, February 13. http://www.abc.net.au/news/2014-02-14/tj-hickey-death-tenth-anniversary-march/5258958.

BBC News. 2004. "Sydney Riots over Aborigine Death." February 6. http://news.bbc.co.uk/2/hi/asia-pacific/3491299.stm.

Butz, D., and K. Besio. 2009. "Autoethnography." *Geography Compass* 3 (5):1660–1674.

Bullough Jr., R. V., and S. Pinnegar. 2001. "Guidelines for Quality in Autobiographical Forms of Self-Study Research." *Educational Researcher* 30 (3): 13–21.

Cairns Post. 1946. "The Aboriginal Australian: A Dying Race." August 29, p. 3. http://trove.nla.gov.au/newspaper/article/42508269.

Coffey, P. 1999. *The Ethnographic Self*. London: SAGE.

Commonwealth of Australia, Department of the Prime Minister and Cabinet. 2016. "Closing the Gap: Prime Minister's Report." http://closingthegap. dpmc.gov.au/assets/pdfs/closing_the_gap_report_2016.pdf.

Correy, Joseph. 2006. Rebuilding The Block: Tent Embassy Comes to Redfern. *South Sydney Herald*, July 1. http://www.redwatch.org.au/media/060701sshg/.

Cunneen, C. 2001. *Conflict, Politics and Crime: Aboriginal Communities and the Police*. Crows Nest, NSW: Allen and Unwin.

DMP. 1938. Our Historic Day of Mourning and Protest, Aborigines Conference. *The Abo Call* April. *https://aiatsis.gov.au/sites/default/files/catalogue_resources/20373.pdf.*

Ellis, C. S., and A. Bochner. 2000. "Autoethnography, Personal Narrative, Reflexivity: Researcher as Subject." In *The Handbook of Qualitative Research*, edited by Norman Denzin and Yvonna Lincoln, 733–768. Thousand Oaks, CA: SAGE.

Eora College. nd. http://Eora.net/default03.htm (accessed 17 February, 2016).

Funnell, N. 2005. "Non-Lethal Intelligence: Strike Force Coburn and the Police Response to the Redfern Riot." *Indigenous Law Bulletin* 17; 6 (10).

Fuchs, M. 2002. "Autobiography and Geography: Introduction." *Biography* 25 (1): ix–xi.

Gilbert, C., ed. 1971. *New Dawn: A Magazine for the Aboriginal People of New South Wales* 2 (4): 3–4.

Grossman, M. 2013. *Entangled Subjects: Indigenous/Australian Cross-Cultures of Talk, Text, and Modernity*. Amsterdam: Rodopi B.V.

Holt, N. L. 2003. "Representation, Legitimation, and Autoethnography: An Autoethnographic Writing Story." *International Journal of Qualitative Methods* 2 (1): 18–28.

Kohen, J. 2000. "First and Last People: Aboriginal Sydney." In *Sydney: The Emergence of a World City*, edited by John Connell Melbourne, 75–95. Oxford: Oxford University Press.

McGregor R. 1997. *Imagined Destinies: Aboriginal Australians and the Doomed Race Theory, 1880–1939*. Carlton: Melbourne University Press.

McNally, Lucy, and Staff. 2015. "Redfern Tent Embassy Claims Victory with Aboriginal Housing Deal." ABC News, August 26. http://www.abc.net.au/news/2015-08-27/redfern-tent-embassy-claim-victory-after-aboriginal-housing-deal/6728342.

Mickler, S. 1998. *The Myth of Privilege: Aboriginal Status, Media Visions, Public Ideas*. South Fremantle, Western Australia: Fremantle Arts Centre Press.

Molesworth, R. 2006. "A Settlement at the Crossroads." *Sydney Alumni Magazine* (Spring): 24–25.

Moss, P., ed. 2001. *Placing Autobiography in Geography*. Syracuse, NY: Syracuse University Press.

NCIE. nd. National Centre for Indigenous Excellence. http://www.ncie.org.au/index.php/about/who-are-we.html (accessed September 7, 2011)

New South Wales Government. 2016. "Archives in Brief 42—Aborigines Welfare Board, 1883–1969." https://www.records.nsw.gov.au/state-archives/guides-and-finding-aids/archives-in-brief/archives-in-brief-42 (accessed February 15, 2016).

Ngunjiri, F. W., K. C. Hernandez, and H. Chang. 2010. "Living Autoethnography: Connecting Life and Research." *Journal of Research Practice* 6 (1): Article E1. http://jrp.icaap.org/index.php/jrp/article/view/241/186.

Redfern Aboriginal Tent Embassy Community. nd. (Facebook page). https://www.facebook.com/Redfern-Aboriginal-Tent-Embassy-249063975290466/timeline?ref=page_internal.

Rigney, L. 2001. "A First Perspective of Indigenous Australian Participation in Science: Framing Indigenous Research towards Indigenous Australian Intellectual Sovereignty." *Kaurna Higher Education Journal* 7:1–13.

SBS, 2010. The Block—Anthony. http://www.sbs.com.au/theblock/anthony.html#/ anthony/.

S. H. nd. *Seeding Hope, Mudgin-Gal Aboriginal Corporation*. www.redfernfoundation.org.au/mudgingal.pdf.

Shaw, W. S., RDK Herman, G. R. Dobbs. 2006. "Encountering Indigeneity: Re-Imagining and Decolonizing Geography." *Geografiska*

Annaler B: Human Geography 88 (3): 267–276. http://dx.doi. org/10.1111/j.1468-0459.2006.00220.x.

Shaw, W. S. 2007. *Cities of Whiteness*. London: Blackwell-Wiley.

Shaw, W. S. 2009. "Riotous Sydney: Redfern, Macquarie Fields, and (My) Cronulla." *Environment and Planning D: Society and Space* 27 (3): 425–443. http://dx.doi.org/10.1068/d8707.

Shaw, W. S. 2011. Researcher Journeying and the Adventure/Danger Impulse. *Area* 43 (4): 470–476.

Shaw, W. S. 2013a. "Auto-Ethnography and Autobiography in Geographical Research. *Geoforum* 46:1–4.

Shaw, W. S. 2013b. "Redfern as the Heart(h): Living (Black) in Inner Sydney." *Geographical Research* 51 (3): 257–268. http://dx.doi. org/10.1111/1745-5871.12000.

TAFE NSW—Sydney Institute. nd. "Diploma of Aboriginal Studies for Professional and Community Practice." http://sydneytafe.edu.au/ future-students/eora-college/course-finder/10225NAT-01V01/ diploma-of-aboriginal-studies-for-professional-and-community-practice#results (accessed February 16, 2016).

Taipei Times. 2004. "Racial Riot Rocks Sydney." February 17. http://www. taipeitimes.com/News/world/archives/2004/02/17/2003099081.

Teece-Johnson, Danny. 2015. "At Redfern's The Block, Spirits Lifted after Tent Embassy Win." NITV, August 27. http://www.sbs.com.au/nitv/ article/2015/08/27/redferns-block-spirits-lifted-after-tent-embassy-win.

The Settlement. 2016. http://www.thesettlement.org.au/ (accessed February 17, 2016).

Smith, Linda Tuhiwai. 1999. *Decolonising Methodologies: Research and Indigenous Peoples*. London: Zed Books.

Waltha, C., ed. 1971. "Aboriginal Medical Service." *New Dawn: A Magazine for the Aboriginal People of New South Wales* 2 (8): 6–8.

Washington Times. 2004. "Aborigines Riot, Set Rail Station Afire." February 16. http://www.washingtontimes.com/news/2004/feb/16/ 20040216-094803-6107r/.

Wilson, S. 2001. What Is Indigenous Research Methodology? *Canadian Journal of Native Education* 25 (2): 175–179.

Notes to Chapter 11

1. For example, the William Barak story, http://www.cv.vic.gov.au/stories/ aboriginal-culture/william-barak/william-barak-king-of-the-yarra/.

2. See *Cairns Post*, "The Aboriginal Australian: A Dying Race," and McGregor (1997).

3. The story of the Redfern Aboriginal Tent Embassy is beyond the scope of this chapter, but for details see Correy (2006) and Redfern Aboriginal Tent Embassy (nd).

4. See BBC News 2004, the *Washington Times* 2004, and the *Taipei Times* 2004.

12

Returning Research Results

A Means for Giving Back and Advocating beyond the Academy

CATRINA A. MACKENZIE, JULIA CHRISTENSEN,
AND SARAH TURNER

S CIENTISTS HAVE LONG recognized academic journals as the premier means by which to validate their work, establish their reputations, and share their results with fellow academics and (in theory) the public (Guedon 2001). While upward of fifty million academic journal articles have been published since the seventeenth century (Jinha 2010), subscription costs limit the ability of the general public, researchers, nonprofit organizations, and governments in the Global South to access scientific findings (Guedon 2001). Despite the advent of open access journals, research remains "a conversation of 'us' with 'us' about 'them'" (Cahill and Torre 2007, 196). Kindon, Pain, and Kesby (2007, xxiii) aptly note, "In this era of neoliberal politics and funding, many academics feel pressured by the ambitions and needs of their universities to prioritize rapid publication of theoretical research in high status academic journals." Researchers thus often find it difficult to find meaningful ways to "give back" to communities—frequently from lack of time or funding, or pressure to publish (Castleden, Sloan-Morgan, and Lamb 2012). The journal article itself, as a means of giving back and as a form of communication to reach research participants, is often unsuitable and ineffective, underscoring the power differential between the academic ivory tower and local communities (Sidaway 1992). And as Herman points out in chapter 1, extractive research in Indigenous and Global South communities has for decades—if not centuries—demonstrated little attempt to give back by sharing results with the populations under scrutiny or upon whose lands or jurisdictions research takes place, leading many local peoples to distrust and resent social science researchers (Smith 1999).

Drawing on our fieldwork in northern Indigenous Canada, Uganda, and Vietnam, we move beyond journal articles to examine other avenues to meaningfully give back relevant research results to the communities with which we work, and to other interested parties. Ideally, we are aiming for a "partnership of knowledge systems" (Chilisa 2012, 297) that situates results within local contexts, in native languages, and in formats useful for participants and academics alike. The benefits of such partnerships are considered widespread: opening communication, showing respect for study participants, and building trust with participating communities. Moreover, these partnerships enable researchers to validate their work with participants, provide a venue to respond to questions, facilitate future collaboration by increasing communities' willingness to participate, and, most significantly, offer a means to advocate for change on behalf of participant and similar communities in the Global South (cf. Cahill and Torre 2007; Wilcox, Harper, and Edge 2013).

We start this chapter examining the tactics we have drawn upon as we work toward this partnership ideal, focusing on how we have made our communication of research results as relevant as possible for local communities. We highlight our difficulties finding appropriate audiences and also scrutinize the different ways in which we have struggled with self-censorship. Finally, we discuss our concerns managing the expectations of the communities we work with, as well as our own expectations regarding the ability of our research to catalyze positive change for marginalized groups. All along, as three white female academics, we are well aware of our privileged position when working in these research sites. From conversations with other social scientists, we know that we are not alone in struggling with how to give back meaningfully. There are many ways one might achieve this, as exemplified by the diversity of approaches presented in this book; in this chapter we focus on how returning relevant research results can be an effective strategy, while honoring the Indigenous research principles introduced in chapter 1.

Strategies for Giving Back via Relevant Research Results in the Global South

Our research contexts lie within the area broadly categorised as the Global South. Though the inclusion of Northern Canada under this umbrella may seem strange at first glance, several scholars have drawn parallels among the socioeconomic, environmental, and political dynamics in arctic and Indigenous community contexts, and communities in the more "mainstream" Global South (see Schroeder, Martin, and Albert 2006; Young 1995). Uniting these contexts is a common experience of researchers "parachuting" into communities and leaving without reporting back on results (Brant Castellano 2004; Caine, Davison, and Stewart 2009; Sidaway 1992). In an attempt to counter this extractive pattern, we outline how each of us has attempted to give back research results through strategic channels in the communities where we work.

Catrina

I use qualitative, quantitative, and geographic information science methods in and around protected areas in sub-Saharan Africa to understand how conservation policies affect local communities, and whether the gains and losses accrued influence conservation attitudes and behaviors. Since 2008, I have worked in twenty-five communities on the edge of Uganda's Kibale National Park, a protected habitat for chimpanzees and other primate species. The Uganda Wildlife Authority (UWA) uses exclusion policies in tandem with community outreach programs to manage the park; such outreach includes negotiated access to nonthreatened park resources and using a portion of tourism revenues to fund community projects. Most of my research participants are subsistence farmers from the Batooro or Bakiga tribes. Crop raiding by park-protected animals, for which no direct compensation is available, is the most substantial loss that these farmers accrue as a result of living next to the park.

I use research to advocate for effective conservation incentives that both benefit local communities and mitigate conservation-based losses. My efforts to give back via returning relevant information fall primarily into three strategic channels: advocacy, policy recommendations, and supporting nongovernmental organizations (NGOs). First, by sharing results with local government officials, I argue for the use of shared tourism revenue to support crop raiding defences and income-generating activities. Second, I recommend policy changes to the UWA in an effort to make their revenue-sharing process more equitable and relevant for local communities, and as a result I have been asked to comment on newly developed legislative guidelines for the process. Third, since boys are preferentially held back from school to guard crops against park-protected animals (MacKenzie, Sengupta, and Kaoser 2015), I conduct voluntary research to support NGOs trying to improve primary education near the park. My efforts to give back by communicating research findings have been met with gratitude that I respect my study participants enough to return with the results, an action that is unfortunately rare based on comments from village chairpersons: "You are the first researcher to return and provide results to the village, even though many researchers have worked in this village."

Julia

I was born and raised in Canada's Northwest Territories and have conducted research there since 2003. In many ways, I feel a personal obligation to maintain open lines of communication and knowledge transfer stemming from my emotional connection with my collaborators, research participants, and the community as a whole. Both personal and professional links with the territory have encouraged me to ensure that my research produces relevant outcomes for northern communities, including Inuvialuit, Dene, and Métis. In the Canadian North, questions about the causes and results of homelessness have only recently received attention from policy makers and academics. The vast majority of northern residents who experience a lack of shelter are Indigenous peoples. In order to attend to what many front-line workers, social advocates, and Indigenous organizations see as an urgent social concern, I focus my research around Indigenous experiences of home, homelessness, and housing. This research began in 2006 at the outset of my PhD, through which I sought to investigate the social, cultural, and health geographies of Indigenous homes and homelessness in the Canadian North, and situate them within the larger context of colonialism in Canada.

Guiding my research approach are the three main strategic foci of policy, sharing, and advocacy, which I employ in an attempt to give back to communities and individual participants and to facilitate a research-policy-practice chain. During early consultations in my research projects, community groups and research participants identify policy-related expectations and goals for action. For example, for my doctoral research, I was asked by community groups to submit yearly progress reports that highlighted emerging themes, organize a series of feedback workshops to discuss preliminary findings, maintain a dialogue with community advisers, and write a final policy report (see Maiter et al. 2013). I shared my results outside the communities directly involved in my PhD research through public presentations at the outset and culmination of the project, choosing a style and medium that maximized the accessibility and applicability of my findings. In an effort to further contribute to the community, I also gave several lectures on conducting social science research at local college campuses, touching on topics like qualitative methods, northern housing, and social determinants of health. Once my PhD research had concluded, homeless research participants requested I advocate on their behalf by delivering my findings to local media outlets and politicians that they felt would benefit from information regarding their experiences. I am also a member of the Yellowknife Homelessness Coalition and meet regularly with municipal and territorial leadership as well as support agencies, serving as an advocate and maintaining communication channels to disseminate research findings from both my PhD and ongoing research. The primary objective of my continuing research is to inform and encourage social change and improvements in the lives of research participants and their communities.

Sarah

I have been conducting research in upland northern Vietnam since 1999, and in southwest China since 2009, especially among the Hmong (Miao) and Yao ethnic minorities. The Chinese and Vietnamese socialist state authorities have long considered this a frontier region where "inconsequential peoples" lag behind the majority in socioeconomic development (World Bank 2009). My work focuses on livelihoods, food security, and environmental decision making in these uplands, aiming at better understanding the activities, interactions, and power relations among upland minorities, majority Kinh (lowland Vietnamese) and Han Chinese residents, and government officials. By investigating the livelihood adaptations and forms of resistance upland residents have adopted in a context of antagonistic political circumstances and some suspect development policies, I try to produce research with my collaborators and graduate students that raises broader awareness of local sustainable livelihood practices and helps shape relevant policy.

Focusing here on Vietnam, I attempt to give back to the communities where I undertake research through sharing results, advocacy, and mentoring. In upland villages, I work to support ethnic minority research informants by sharing information potentially relevant to their household livelihoods and well-being. I also assist a local Hmong-run social enterprise that provides job training and education to ethnic minority youth. I provide help with gaining international funding for this enterprise, through drafting applications and budgets, sharing information, and liaising with an advisory group of overseas volunteers. In addition, I disseminate research results at Hanoi-based research institutes and universities. There, I also teach qualitative methods to interested local students and professors, while engaging in discussions regarding the ethics of social science research among ethnic minorities. I mentor a number of students from Vietnam pursuing social science degrees at research institutions both in Vietnam and overseas. Apart from my immediate goal to give back to the local communities with whom I work, my other approaches have developed rather organically as opportunities have presented themselves.

Who Should and Can Receive Results?

In addition to choosing from a plethora of strategies by which to give back by disseminating relevant results, each of us is sensitive to the many different *audiences* to which research findings can be aimed. We have found returning results to be a sharing, iterative activity with a broad range of participants (cf. Maiter et al. 2013). We believe that our success in using research to advocate for participants is meaningful only if we listen carefully to their advice on how best to represent their needs and with whom to share results (Cahill 2007; Minkler 2004). Furthermore, the degree to which research is collaborative, community-based, and grounded in an Indigenous methodological framework, has a significant impact on the appropriateness, accessibility, and usefulness of our research findings.

Catrina

I returned to Kibale National Park in 2012 to present my PhD results to UWA and the communities that participated in my study. I gave my thesis, published papers, and a presentation to UWA wardens and rangers, and planned to return to all twenty-five research communities to convey my results. In the first two village meetings, this information was well received. Village members commented that "there is good alignment between what we told you and what is in your report." However, as I was preparing to speak in one of the villages, I overheard women complaining that they would rather be in the fields than at the meeting. I also observed that though most people indicated afterward by a show of hands that the presentation was interesting, less than half actually seemed to be listening. Many of the villagers' comments focused on distrust of sub-county government, leading to questions like, "How can you help us get our revenue sharing money instead of it being taken by higher levels of government?" In post-presentation discussions, the audience suggested that presenting to the sub-county council could allow the findings to guide local government decisions that might benefit the people and was more important than presenting the results to the villagers because, they argued, the results already accurately reflected what they had said.

Based on similar feedback from two village meetings, I turned my presentation material into a bound report with versions in English, Ratooro, and Rakiga. With my interpreter, Peter, we delivered and discussed the report with each village (twenty-five), sub-county (eleven), and district (three) council chairperson. All of them thanked us for providing answers for their community members who had been asking what had become of the researchers, and for listening to their interpretations of the results. Leaders at the village and sub-county levels were particularly pleased to receive a paper copy in their own language that they could keep and continue to use. One village chairperson said, "I will use this report with my sub-county chief," and a sub-county chairperson commented, "I will take the report and call a meeting with all the village chairmen to discuss." Although it had not been my original goal, by returning written reports where the villagers wished them to go, I was able to help local voices be heard by government officials.

Julia

When I was a PhD student, I felt as though there was a persistent tension between the time requirements of my graduate program and the expectations of the research participants and community groups with whom, and for whom, I worked. Nurturing important local relationships requires time and active engagement, something that can clash with university demands when it threatens to extend the timeline to completion of proposal approval, candidacy exams, thesis writing, and so on. In the end, I completed my thesis on time, but I felt as though I was constantly juggling two opposing sets of expectations. In the same vein, conventional (Anglo-Western) academic culture does not prioritize writing policy reports and delivering community feedback to nearly the same degree as having peer-reviewed journal articles and conference presentations (see Kindon, Pain, and Kesby 2007).[1] A senior scholar once advised me to save public engagements until after securing tenure, since my efforts should be focused on the academic currency of peer-reviewed articles in high-impact journals. Now that I have completed my graduate studies and am an assistant professor in a geography department, I feel this pressure even more acutely; having a high number of peer-reviewed articles often sets apart the most successful applications for external funding.

I find deciding who the most relevant groups are to receive research results a complex challenge. As communities are multifaceted entities (see Pain 2004), delivering results should be a multifaceted process. In the case of my research with homeless men and women, the community leaders nominally tasked with bestowing community approval are usually not the community members with the most at stake in the research. Rather, my research tends to have the greatest bearing on community organizations involved in providing services and advocating for homeless people, and of course the homeless individuals themselves. It is important, however, that I inform community leaders of my research findings in order to further the goals of both my research and those of my partner organizations to create greater awareness and increase public support for public funding of home-lessness intervention programs. I therefore try to develop multiple strate-gies that take into account as many different needs as feasible to ensure that my research makes as positive a contribution to the community as possible. Some strategies I have attempted include conducting informal feedback dis-cussions with homeless shelter residents, sharing and performing creative reproductions of research findings with research informants and the wider public (see Christensen 2012), holding workshops with support providers and advocacy groups, and delivering policy recommendations through conventional research reports to NGOs and government policymakers.

Sarah

Officially authorized fieldwork in Vietnam requires the acquisition of a host of permissions, including a research visa and a variety of "red stamps" obtained through a state research institution or local university (see Turner 2013). I have attempted to give back to these sponsoring organisations by holding research seminars and mentoring local students. But because Vietnamese professors and state researchers are paid low salaries ($250–$400 US per month) compared with what they might receive in the private sector, they frequently find themselves on a funding treadmill, depending on private tutoring and external funding and contracts to make ends meet (see Zink 2013). Often this means they do not have the time, energy, or academic incentive to discuss results outside of specific contracts. Unfortunately, I find the seminars I hold to discuss my findings remain a rather one-way delivery of results. Given their education and background, Vietnamese students find voicing opinions that are at odds with a more senior academic, or putting forth their own interpretations and experiences, difficult. Nonetheless, as the state relaxes controls over study at international universities and overseas conference trips, local scholars are increasingly able to access non-state-endorsed interpretations and participate in more meaningful dialogues. Though time-consuming, one-on-one conversations with students, and commenting on their written work, also allows for more open discussions and are a crucial part of establishing two-way information flows.

Returning results to NGOs working on upland projects is rather more difficult. After initial enthusiasm from international and local NGO staff, my attempts to share findings seldom lead to follow-up discussions. Like local academics, NGO workers face significant pressure to complete fieldwork, churn out reports, and apply for funding, all usually on short-term contracts. For instance, an international NGO working in the province where I have been doing fieldwork initially seemed keen to have a master's student supervised by me involved with their food security agenda; however, once the NGO director's short-term contract was complete, no follow-up occurred. A local NGO also seemed enthusiastic to have me talk to staff about research methods, but the NGO's other deadlines interfered, and they never ended up scheduling a meeting. Clearly, being an overseas researcher in the field for a limited time each year adds to these challenges to forming meaningful engagements.

Finding relevant ways to present results directly to Hmong and Yao research participants is something I find particularly challenging. Written reports are of little use to individuals who are illiterate, and can expose communities to unwanted official scrutiny (see below). One well-received strategy has been to hold discussions with ethnic minority farmers about other comparable villages' livelihood experiences and opportunities—for instance, exchanging information about the success or failure of hybrid seeds in certain locations, or the availability of health care. But I still struggle to give back in more meaningful ways.

Managing Messages and Self-Censorship when Giving Back

Research findings are not innocent, neutral bodies of interpretations; they are subjective and politicized. We have found that significant care must be taken in deciding what to say, to whom, and when.

Catrina

I struggle with ethical dilemmas rooted in the nature of my research, especially in balancing what to say with what not to say. I agree with Minkler (2004, 693) that, "although many academics argue that scientists have a duty to make all of their findings public, the value base underlying CBPR [community-based participatory research] suggests that our primary responsibility is to the community." In testing the effectiveness of conservation incentives to foster improved conservation behaviors, the data I have collected have become a record of illicit resource extraction from the park. As such, when returning results, I need to protect participating villages from possible prosecution. I also worry that if one village realizes the extent of another's resource extraction, they might be tempted to increase their own extraction and potentially cause further damage to the park's protected habitat. This has led me to not identify participating villages in any presentations, reports, or journal articles, and to use a more generalized scale of park areas as having high, medium, or low illegal extraction. This trade-off protects local people, but the necessary aggregation and smoothing of data weakens the UWA's ability to spatially target management strategies to reduce poaching. Given that my passion for wildlife conservation was the reason I chose this field of research, this data-masking leaves me ethically conflicted.

Julia

The small population of the Northwest Territories and the ease with which research participants' anonymity might be compromised in research outputs presents its own ethical dilemmas regarding self-censorship. In my PhD research, I had to give significant thought to how to describe homeless research participants' experiences while keeping them anonymous—easier said than done when the populations of my study communities were as low as three thousand (Inuvik) and nineteen thousand (Yellowknife) people. My participant pool of individuals accessing emergency shelter services is even smaller, making it easy to identify subjects despite using pseudonyms. Such identification could possibly harm research participants or cloud community members' responses to the results because of preexisting personal biases. My strategy therefore involved selecting interview quotes that did not identify participants, as well as changing certain details that, together, could reveal someone's identity. The trade-off was that overall portraits of individual experiences were weakened. To counter this, I complemented interview excerpts with aggregated experiences common to several homeless men and women in a process of "research storytelling" (Christensen 2012), using creative writing to fictionalize shared "pathways" (Fitzpatrick 1999). This way, I could give policy makers a sense of the structure-agency linkages that existed among the homeless while leaving out participants' identifying details. This approach also respects the significance of narrative within the local Indigenous cultural context (see Louis 2007). I have further developed this practice since my PhD and continue to apply it in my research today.

Sarah

State officials frequently investigate the private affairs of ethnic minorities in the Sino-Vietnamese borderlands, and government interference can seriously impact land rights and livelihood practices. Given the scope of state intervention, researchers in Vietnam (and socialist Asia as a whole) walk "in the footsteps of the Communist Party" (Hansen 2006, 82). In this context, my access to local voices crucially depends on trust and respect. I have been repeatedly humbled by Hmong and Yao elders noting, "You're not like the others [state officials] who come here, you listen to us." These individuals' expressions of frustration with their lack of power drive me to try to represent their opinions and interests in both academic and nonacademic contexts. I am well aware, however, of how careful I must be while doing so. Over many visits, I have cultivated long-standing relationships with individuals ranging from official authorities to Hmong and Yao interviewees. The trust established through these connections allows me to gain a broad spectrum of insights into the livelihoods of ethnic minorities (cf. Michaud 2010). Only after many informal conversations, shared meals, and visits to the marketplace did I begin to hear locals' complex concerns and struggles. Minorities' distrust of state market officials, the impacts of bans on opium cultivation and tree felling, their concerns about cross-border kidnappings and other sensitive topics did not emerge in our discussions until a great deal of rapport had been established. However, as an overseas researcher, I must balance my need to follow official procedures to maintain field access with my desire to voice the concerns of local respondents criticizing that same government. Findings critical of government policy can easily end up in the hands of a senior official, making future field access—for myself, my associates, or other foreign scholars—all the more difficult (see Salemink 2013). I also find it rather difficult at times to distinguish between what counts as "sensitive" and what does not; things that may not initially appear controversial, such as a sampling strategy or visiting a certain village, can suddenly gain importance as political and economic interests change. Vietnamese researchers also face consequences if they collaborate on and publish critical research. These situations all result in self-censorship, and I need to remain hyper-aware of my audiences and when it is better to dampen certain critiques.

Managing Numerous Expectations and the Role of Advocacy

Having examined our tactics to make our communication of research results as relevant as possible in local contexts, our difficulties finding appropriate audiences, and how we have struggled with self-censorship, the question remains how to balance the expectations communities have of us, as well as our own expectations. Into this equation also comes the potential role of advocacy.

Catrina

Villagers in Uganda are usually most focused on what I can do to improve their lives. Concrete goals like the installation of crop-raiding defences, and more general aims to improve livelihood opportunities around Kibale National Park, lie beyond my own financial resources. Alternatively, by advocating for change in meetings with UWA, NGOs, and various levels of government in Uganda, I feel able to help local communities. I am wary, however, of whether I have the right, as an "outsider," to speak on behalf of villagers (Alcoff 1991). What keeps me going is the feedback I receive in local council meetings: "Your findings show what people truly face next to the park. You and the chairman can always find the ones who lose most. UWA should be using you instead of going through the sub-county [to decide on revenue sharing projects]." Repeatedly, the councils have authorized me and my assistant, Peter, to speak for them in meetings with UWA and higher levels of government, validating my aim to effect positive change.

In all, I am satisfied with the ways I have returned my research results, and UWA has considered my findings when developing management policies. Yet, I am also discouraged by the likelihood that other economic and political pressures will quickly overshadow my concerns once I am no longer in the field to actively keep crop-raiding and revenue-sharing front and center on local and regional government agendas. While I question whether my work can ever really effect change (Cahill 2007), I am glad to get feedback indicating that the people I work with in Uganda consider me a partner: "You got the books and we people who stay close have got the experience. I saw the elephant and you recorded it and produced this report. You are not like those who, say, discovered Lake Victoria. What about the ones who were staying there? What about the ones who took them there?"

Julia

In my research and social activities, I often hear from individuals who take a dim view of social science research, given past difficulties in the Canadian North with researchers who "dropped in" to conduct research of their own design, only to leave and never return with results for the community (see Castleden, Sloan-Morgan, and Lamb 2012). Meanwhile, as marginalized members of their own communities, men and women experiencing homelessness are rarely approached for their perspectives by researchers or the media. In contrast to the research scepticism I have witnessed from some parts of the community, at times I have felt overwhelmed by homeless research participants' hopes and expectations. Research participants place an enormous amount of trust in me by sharing their stories and perspectives, so I feel a deep responsibility to ensure that their experiences are communicated to those in positions of greater power. Though I can act at the very least as a facilitator of in-person meetings with politicians and policy makers, I am often disheartened by politicians' preoccupation with funding and jurisdiction. While research participants often express their hopes that my research could have tangible results, my findings are ultimately subject to political negotiation. Even so, I see my work as inherently valuable insofar as it connects people who feel excluded to those in positions of greater power.

Advocacy workers and providers of social services tend to be overworked, and their other responsibilities must, understandably, come before their participation in academic studies. Likewise, homeless individuals, facing exceptional challenges in their own relationships, health, and personal lives, must spend a significant amount of time seeking out and benefiting from support services. Therefore, I have often been forced to reevaluate my goals for participatory community-based research (Caine, Davison, and Stewart 2009). Community groups and homeless people directly inform my research objectives and are continually consulted throughout the process, yet I often take responsibility for designing methodology, carrying out fieldwork, and interpreting data. Returning relevant research results also provides an additional avenue for participant input because it serves as a form of participant validation, with participants having the opportunity to provide their own additional insights into the data analysis (see Turner and Coen 2008). My emphasis on policy is a form of advocacy research that meshes action-oriented goals with community-grounded research while also taking into account individuals' limited time and resources.

Sarah

I am confronted in the field with expectations ranging from financially supporting a hospital visit to assistance with grant applications to student mentoring. However, ethnic minority research participants generally expect little. Though they seem to appreciate my attempts to give back through gifts and information-sharing, they remain pragmatic about the discriminatory, political environment of the socialist state in which they live. Locals are acutely aware that directly and vocally confronting state development agendas or agricultural policies is self-defeating and ultimately not in their interest. The everyday politics that upland ethnic minorities navigate involves overt compliance with state directives, while covertly maintaining decades-old agricultural techniques, traditional ecological knowledge, and educational practices (Turner 2012). For my research into upland livelihood coping strategies, true participatory action research is potentially dangerous in the current political climate, running the risk of exposing households to unwanted attention and possible sanctions by state officials. This means that my expectations of how I can usefully return results have to be carefully molded to local concerns. Yet, like Catrina, I frequently ask myself, who am I to come into this environment and advocate on behalf of others? The sole reason I continue to pursue the advocacy that I do is because individuals continue to ask me to do so. I look forward to a future in which these communities feel empowered to advocate on their own behalf, having gained far greater freedom of expression (see Alcoff 1991).

Conclusion: The Struggles of Giving Back via Communicating Relevant Research Results

In documenting our various struggles with communicating relevant research results to local communities, several interesting themes emerge about this approach to giving back. Across our experiences in the Global South, we find that the process of returning results is multifaceted, involving short- and long-term strategies that target different groups in different ways. As Staeheli and Mitchell have observed, "relevance [when returning results] is not easily measured, and it may not be directly observable" (2005, 357). We have seen that a long-term commitment, and the maintenance of local relationships over time, is crucial to actualizing the researcher-advocate's potential. We have all developed strategies to give back to communities after seeking feedback to make sure that local community members value our research and approaches. This process of returning results also brings to our attention the heterogeneous nature of "communities," and no single approach is appropriate for every community member. Rather, we create strategies that target different sectors of communities, to make sure that our research can have a positive effect on the broadest swath of individuals, in the most relevant ways. This can entail the careful management of our messages and even self-censorship to ensure that participants are protected.

In addition, it has become clear that, just as research and interpretation are dynamic processes (Maiter et al. 2013), so too is disseminating results. All three of us have noted that effectively communicating results requires the researcher to avoid a unidirectional approach by extending the dialogue-based model of qualitative research. We try to tailor the dissemination of our findings to be locally relevant by soliciting feedback on what participants wish to gain from our research and to whom results should be returned. The process of presenting our findings also gives us a chance to have our analyses evaluated and validated by the community, with fresh insights and new research ideas continually emerging.

Finally, our experiences illustrate that returning results is an effective means of "giving back." Our fears regarding the failure of our research to have positive impacts have been allayed by communities who see our efforts to return results as a significant step in the right direction. While institutional barriers within academia as well as within research communities and contexts still create limitations to our effectiveness, we gain motivation when the community members whose stories we seek to tell consider us allies. Our positions as researcher-advocates stem from being asked officially or unofficially to use our findings to advocate on behalf of the individuals and communities with whom we work. The support of community members gives our attempts to give back by returning research results true meaning and legitimacy. In our three diverse settings, we have noted that finding appropriate avenues to return relevant research results complies with many of the Indigenous research principles outlined in chapter 1: we attempt to deliver benefits through advocacy, we show respect for and engage in open dialogue with participating communities, our research communities perceive us as partners, and we deliver results in multiple forms and forums that best align with the cultural values of the Indigenous people with whom we work.

Acknowledgments

We sincerely thank our participants, field assistants, and collaborators for their time, energy, and knowledge. Thank you to Thomas Kettig for editing assistance on this chapter.

We acknowledge funding support from the International Polar Year Canada; the Social Sciences and Humanities Research Council, Canada; and the Trudeau Foundation.

Chapter 12 References

Alcoff, L. 1991. "The Problem of Speaking for Others." *Cultural Critique* 2:5–32.

Brant Castellano, M. 2004. "Ethics of Aboriginal Research." *Journal of Aboriginal Health* 1 (1). http://www.naho.ca/jah/english/jah01_01/journal_p98-114.pdf.

Cahill, C. 2007. "Repositioning Ethical Commitments: Participatory Action Research as a Relational Praxis of Social Change." *ACME: An International E-Journal for Critical Geographies* 6 (3): 360–373.

Cahill, C., and M. E. Torre. 2007. "Beyond the Journal Article: Representations, Audience, and the Presentation of Participatory Action Research." In *Participatory Action Research Approaches and Methods*, edited by S. Kindon, R. Pain, and M. Kesby, 196–205. Abingdon, Oxon: Routledge.

Caine, K. J., C. M. Davison, and E. J. Stewart. 2009. "Preliminary Field-Work: Methodological Reflections from Northern Canadian Research." *Qualitative Research* 9 (4): 489–513.

Castleden, H., V. Sloan-Morgan, and C. Lamb. 2012. "'I Spent the First Year Drinking Tea': Exploring Canadian University Researchers' Perspectives on Community-Based Participatory Research Involving Indigenous Peoples." *Canadian Geographer* 56 (2): 160–179.

Chilisa, B. 2012 *Indigenous Research Methodologies.* Los Angeles: SAGE.

Christensen, J. 2012. "Telling Stories: Exploring Research Storytelling as a Meaningful Approach to Knowledge Mobilization with Indigenous Research Collaborators and Diverse Audiences in Community-Based Participatory Research." *Canadian Geographer* 56 (2): 231–242.

Fitzpatrick, S. 1999. *Pathways to Independence: The Experience of Young Homeless People.* Edinburgh: Scottish Homes.

Guedon, J-C. 2001. *In Oldenburg's Long Shadow: Librarians, Research Scientists, Publishers, and the Control of Scientific Publishing.* Washington, DC: Association of Research Libraries.

Hansen, M. 2006. "In the Footsteps of the Communist Party: Dilemmas and Strategies." In *Doing Fieldwork in China*, edited by M. Heimer and S. Thøgersen, 81–95. Honolulu: University of Hawai'i Press.

Jinha, A. 2010. "Article 50 Million: An Estimate of the Number of Scholarly Articles in Existence." *Learned Publishing* 23 (3): 258–263.

Kindon, S., R. Pain, and M. Kesby. 2007. *Participatory Action Research Approaches and Methods: Connecting People, Participation and Place.* London: Routledge.

Louis, Renee Pualani. 2007. "Can You Hear Us Now? Voices from the Margin: Using Indigenous Methodologies in Geographic Research." *Geographical Research* 45 (2): 130–139.

MacKenzie, C. A., R. R. Sengupta, and R. Kaoser. 2015. "Chasing Baboons or Attending Class: Protected Areas and Childhood Education in

Uganda." *Environmental Conservation* 42 (4): 373–383. doi:10.1017/S0376892915000120.

Maiter, S., A. Joseph, N. Shan, and A. Saeid. 2013. "Doing Participatory Qualitative Research: Development of a Shared Critical Consciousness with Racial Minority Research Advisory Group Members." *Qualitative Research* 13 (2): 198–213.

Michaud, J. 2010. "Fieldwork, Supervision and Trust." *Asia Pacific Viewpoint* 51 (2): 220–225.

Minkler, M. 2004. "Ethical Challenges for the 'Outside' Researcher in Community-Based Participatory Research." *Health Education and Behavior* 31(December): 684–697.

Pain, R. 2004. "Social Geography: Participatory Research." *Progress in Human Geography* 28 (5): 652–663.

Salemink, O. 2013. "Between Engagement and Abuse: Reflections on the 'Field' of Anthropology and the Power of Ethnography." In *Red Stamps and Gold Stars: Fieldwork Dilemmas in Upland Socialist Asia,* edited by Sarah Turner, 241–259. Vancouver: University of British Columbia Press.

Schroeder, R. A., K. S. Martin, and K. E. Albert. 2006. "Political Ecology in North America: Discovering the Third World Within?" *Geoforum* 37 (2): 163–168.

Sidaway, J. D. 1992. "In Other Worlds: On the Politics of Research by 'First World' Geographers in the 'Third World.'" *Area* 24 (4): 403–408.

Smith, Linda Tuhiwai. 1999. *Decolonizing Methodologies: Research and Indigenous Peoples.* London: Zed Books.

Staeheli, L. A., and D. Mitchell. 2005. "The Complex Politics of Relevance in Geography." *Annals of the Association of American Geographers* 95 (2): 357–372.

Turner, S. 2012. "Making a Living the Hmong Way: An Actor-Oriented Livelihoods Approach to Everyday Politics and Resistance in Upland Vietnam." *Annals of the Association of American Geographers* 102 (2): 403–422.

Turner, S., ed. 2013. *Red Stamps and Gold Stars: Fieldwork Dilemmas in Upland Socialist Asia.* Vancouver: University of British Columbia Press.

Turner, S., and S. E. Coen. 2008. "Member Checking in Human Geography: Interpreting Divergent Understandings of Performativity in a Student Space." *Area* 40 (2): 184–193.

Wilcox, A. C., S. L. Harper, and V. L. Edge. 2012. "Storytelling in a Digital Age: Digital Storytelling as an Emerging Narrative Method for Preserving and Promoting Indigenous Oral Wisdom." *Qualitative Research* 13 (2): 127–147.

World Bank. 2009. *Country Social Analysis: Ethnicity and Development in Vietnam.* Washington, DC: World Bank.

Young, E. A. 1995. *Third World in the First: Development and Indigenous Peoples.* London: Routledge.

Zink, E. 2013. *Hot Science, High Water: Assembling Nature, Society and Environmental Policy in Contemporary Vietnam.* Copenhagen: NIAS Press.

Notes to Chapter 12

1. This differs according to academic context. For example, in Denmark there is a long-standing tradition in university departments of placing community reports on a par with peer-reviewed journal articles. However, in recent years, this equal standing has been eroded significantly with the introduction of neoliberal policies that prioritize peer-reviewed publishing requirements and ranking systems that do not recognize non-peer-reviewed publication outputs.

13

Sovereignty-Driven Research

JOHN R. WELCH

THIS BOOK IS TESTIMONY that academic research, especially initiatives to create and mobilize knowledge in Indigenous settings, continues to become more diverse, more attentive to ethical standards, and more attuned to the possibilities of not only doing no harm but of also doing some good. The information, perspectives, and recommendations provided by the scholars whose work appears here stand as practical and conceptual tools for researchers to use, combine, and refine in their collaborations with Indigenous people and communities.

My approach to the subject of ethical research engagements with Indigenous people includes a few premises best stated at the outset. I distinguish between academic and community researchers. Academic researchers are generally trained to apply Western scientific principles and methods to expand the reach of Western science and to identify and fill gaps in knowledge and understanding. Academic research proceeds regardless of practical or societal need or relevance, though these criteria are increasingly recognized as meritorious. Academic researchers are not alone, however, in our quests to create and mobilize knowledge. Like people around the world, Indigenous people do research, daily and hourly, usually for the direct and practical benefit of their lives, communities, and territories. Academic researchers' estimable technical, disciplinary, organizational, and analytic capabilities are often matched by the sophistication of Indigenous people's abilities to gather observations, identify factors responsible for observed phenomena, and apply knowledge in practical and otherwise consequential ways (Chilisa 2012; Cajete 1994, 2000; Johnson and Murton 2007). This truth leads me to distinguish between academic research driven by disciplinary and other external (to communities) interests, on the one hand, and community-based research driven by interests and perceived needs internal to Indigenous communities (see Yellowhorn 2002). While academic research most often derives from and serves a diffuse and imagined academic collegium, observations and analyses by Indigenous people typically serve the immediate needs of families, communities, and ecosystems. I leave aside the many issues associated with a third category, industrial researchers, for others to grapple with (see Kamau and Winter 2009).

I perpetuate the academic/community distinction because the two different sets of research drivers and audiences significantly affect my work and that of many other researchers, academic as well as internalist. I situate myself as a liaison, a non-Indigenous, academically trained anthropologist and archaeologist with a career commitment to community-based cultural heritage research and stewardship. I have worked with many Indigenous communities and, in the case discussed below, as an appointed representative for the White Mountain Apache Tribe, a sovereign nation recognized by the US government. Other chapters in this book show how researchers trained in diverse fields have also worked along privileged boundaries among Indigenous and non-Indigenous societies, geographies, and ways of learning, knowing, and taking care of territory and community (see also Colwell-Chanthaphonh and Ferguson 2008).

It is important to acknowledge that most of the best tools and rules for research engagements among academics and community representatives—notably beneficence and the "four Rs" of respect, relevance, reciprocity, responsibility (Kirkness and Barnhart 1991)—derive not from academic research but from Indigenous ways of sustaining relationships, communities, and ecosystems (Chilisa 2012; Smith 2012). My experience as a tribal official heightened my sensitivity to academic research that, however well-intentioned, often leaves Indigenous communities either with scraps from academic and industrial feasts or with recommendations—often theoretical, sometimes technical, seldom practical—for repairing colonialism's massive and still-unfolding damages to Indigenous territories, communities, rights, and traditions. In this regard my fingers point both ways. Much of my work to rehabilitate heritage sites damaged by excavations and to publish findings from excavations by archaeologists who never got around to it fits into the category of indirect and possibly inconsequential atonement for past failures to meet the ethical obligations at the time (see, for example, Welch 2009, 2013, 2015; Welch, Riley, and Nixon 2009).

Still, there are many reasons to try to make academic research relevant and broadly beneficial. Indeed, the proof is in your hands (or on your reading screen) that the time has arrived for giving back and for broader aspirations to retool academic research into activities and opportunities grounded in the Belmont Report's standards of respect, beneficence, and justice (see Herman, this volume, introduction and chapter 1; Smith 2012). Academic researchers in fields ranging from archaeology (e.g., Atalay 2012; Atalay et al. 2014) to zoology (e.g., Tidemann and Gosler 2010) are recognizing and advancing ethical mandates with respect to diverse engagements with Indigenous people and places. Efforts by liaison researchers (for example, Sakakibara, this volume), shifts in standards for ethical research (for example, Fadiman, this volume), and programs to harmonize Indigenous and non-Indigenous interests in specific research domains (for example, Howitt and colleagues, this volume) are reducing institutionalized barriers between Indigenous people and knowledge, power, capacity, and opportunity linked to academic research. Compilations of guidelines, protocols, and recommended practices organized by disciplines and regions are increasingly available to guide communities and researchers. Even the short list of resources in table 13.1 provides an indication of the momentum for academic research and researchers to collaborate with community colleagues to address and reconcile traumatic colonial legacies and to author, by and through their varied research practices, new and more broadly beneficial histories for and with Indigenous peoples. It is now more possible and more important than ever to craft research practices that embrace Indigenous values and preferences, Herman's nine potent principles (this volume, chapter 1), and broad mandates for free, prior, informed consent (FPIC), as promulgated through the UN Declaration on the Rights of Indigenous Peoples (Ward 2011).

Welcome as well as timely, *Giving Back* and other recent explorations of the meanings and values of reciprocity in research (for example, Tobias, Richmond, and Luginaah 2013) nonetheless prompt questions about whether giving back is enough. Disparities between Indigenous communities and academic researchers with respect to access to knowledge, power, perspective, and money require that researchers working in

Table 13.1: Seven Online Sources of Information and Perspective on Community-Based Participatory Research (CBPR) Involving Indigenous People and Communities

1. Alaska Native Knowledge Network, http://www.ankn.uaf.edu/

2. Community Guide to Protecting Indigenous Knowledge, Simon Brascoupé and Howard Mann, Research and Analysis Directorate, Department of Indian Affairs and Northern Development, Canada, 2001, http://publications.gc.ca/collections/Collection/R2-160-2001E.pdf

3. Heritage Toolkit, First Peoples' Cultural Council, 2015, http://www.fpcc.ca/culture/heritage-toolkit/

4. The Intellectual Property in Cultural Heritage Project, 2015, http://www.sfu.ca/ipinch/

5. Knowledge Translation (KT) for Indigenous Communities: A Policy Making Toolkit, P. Gaye Hanson, Janet Smylie, and the Indigenous KT Summit Steering Committee, 2006, http://ahrnets.ca/files/2011/02/KT_Policy_Toolkit_Indigenous_Communities_IPHRC.pdf

6. Research and Ethics resource page, Inuit Tuttarvingat and the National Aboriginal Health Organization (NAHO), Canada, 2012, http://www.naho.ca/inuit/research-and-ethics/

7. Toolbox of research principles in an aboriginal context, First Nations of Quebec and Labrador Health and Social Services Commission, 2015, http://www.cssspnql.com/docs/default-source/centre-de-documentation/tab_existing_protocols_initiatives_eng.pdf?sfvrsn=2

Indigenous settings consider the extent to which our research designs, methods, and outcomes comport with the values and interests of affected people and communities. What can academic researchers do to benefit Indigenous communities, and what should we do? Who is to say how much benefit is enough? Under what conditions is giving back appropriate and sufficient? Under what conditions it is possible and useful to go beyond giving back, beyond FPIC, even beyond balanced reciprocity to research engagements that prioritize Indigenous interests and goals?

Are local circumstances and relationships the main or only bases for answering these questions, or should national and international organizations continue to develop broadly applicable yet sufficiently detailed standards for academic researchers to use in avoiding adverse effects and boosting beneficial effects in Indigenous settings?

As an initial and incomplete foray into these questions, this chapter does not offer concrete answers. Instead, based mainly on my participation in and discussions about Indigenous research initiatives, I provide a rationale and framework for researchers to take advantage of opportunities to go well beyond giving back. In this sense, the chapter stands as an invitation to academic researchers to step outside the confines of disciplinary thought and to adopt community-based, internal reference frames for planning and implementing research programs with Indigenous collaborators and organizations. I proceed by describing some of my professional engagements with the White Mountain Apache Tribe in Arizona. The brief chronicle highlights some factors that affect the levels and types of benefits that flow from research into Indigenous communities. It also underscores the potential, in certain circumstances, of what I refer to as sovereignty-driven research. I define sovereignty-driven research as the creation and mobilization of knowledge to serve collective interests in establishing and maintaining rights and responsibilities to govern, provide for, represent, and pursue desired futures on behalf of people and associated territory. After discussing the sovereignty-driven approach in more detail, I apply the framework to analyze ongoing research and management projects conducted on behalf of the White Mountain Apache Tribe at the Fort Apache and Theodore Roosevelt School National Historic Landmark. My conclusions speak to the benefits of sovereignty-driven research in settings where it is appropriate and embraced by academic and community partners.

Research Modes: Extractive, Balanced, Sovereignty-Driven

My collaborations with Indigenous communities have traversed three dominant modes of practice, glossed here as *extractive, balanced,* and *sovereignty-driven* (figure 13.1). I came of academic age in the early 1980s working in an extractive mode as an archaeologist in Belize and Arizona. Academic questions and professional networks were the driving forces behind the research designs and the selection of project locations and partners. Authorizations for conducting excavations and removing ancestors and their belongings for research and curation came primarily from central state governments. Though the leaders of the projects I worked on sincerely solicited permission from local community representatives, there were no institutional means for engaging our local hosts in planning research designs or outcomes. The projects advanced the careers of dozens of archaeologists, including my own; local benefits were generally limited to short-term employment of wage laborers (Welch 2015).

By the mid-1980s, at least in where I was doing research, things began to balance out. I settled in to doctoral studies at the University of Arizona centered on the Grasshopper archaeology project, led by Jeff Reid (see Reid and Whittlesey 1999, 2005). The White Mountain Apache Tribe, upon whose land the Grasshopper project was located, is the governing body for about thirteen thousand tribal citizens and 1.6 million acres of trust (reservation) lands in the upper reaches of Arizona's Salt River watershed. As the tribe began to assert interests and values regarding research through feedback from the tribe's elected leaders and local community

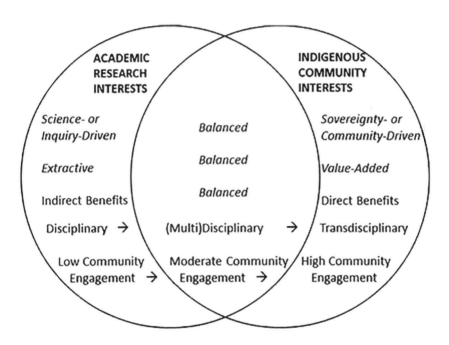

FIG. 13.1 Scheme for boosting overlap and harmony among academic and Indigenous community interests.

representatives, Reid responded professionally and humanely. He ended intentional excavations of human remains, committed to a "buy local" program for supplies, and engaged many Apache citizens in research activities ranging from basic heritage site prospecting to long-range research planning that included early forays into Apache archaeology (Reid and Whittlesey 1999, x; Reid and Whittlesey 2005, 143–144). With collegial bridges into the Apache community still under construction, Reid and I worked to find ways to balance out the tribe's many substantial contributions to archaeology and anthropology. This led to incremental shifts away from discipline-driven research and toward new uses of archaeological data, sites, and perspectives to address issues the tribe was confronting in land and resource management, notably looting, environmental change, and heritage tourism (see table 3 in Welch 2015).

Inevitable only in retrospect, my next career move involved further distancing myself from academic research to work directly for the tribe. While completing my graduate studies, and for a decade afterward, I served as the tribe's archaeologist (1992–2005) and tribal historic preservation officer (1996–2005). The experience gave me access to knowledge and perspectives relating to legal, political, economic, cultural, and social challenges and opportunities addressed by tribal leaders and US Bureau of Indian Affairs officials. Several of these leaders supported and guided my work to facilitate research, management, and training partnerships with Apache citizens and representatives of neighboring tribes to address heritage site rehabilitation, repatriation, and cultural perpetuation initiatives. Most of the work has employed heritage sites and landscapes as contexts for reclaiming, enhancing, and expanding local knowledge systems, capacities, economies, and institutions (Welch 2000, 2013; Welch and Ferguson 2007).

Service as a tribal official also gave me the opportunity to participate in detailed discussions regarding proposed research, publication, and other projects that carried potentials to affect heritage sites and values important to the tribe and its citizens (see Welch et al. 2009). The discussions revealed that, for many Apaches, history since sustained contacts with Westerners is often viewed as a relentless sequence of deletions— of losses in places, objects, traditions, rights, powers, and relationships (Welch 2000; Welch and Riley 2001). I also learned that these losses are experienced by Apaches, on personal and collective levels, as harmful and continuing results of non-Apache miners, loggers, cowboys, labor contractors, and researchers looking to Apache people and lands as means for advancing non-Apache interests (Mills et al. 2008, 44–46; Welch in Nicholas, Welch, and Yellowhorn 2008, 281–282; Welch 2009).

Living and working on White Mountain Apache territory made it clear that the colonial histories of the nineteenth and early twentieth centuries continue to translate into daunting suites of real and pressing problems. These problems include low educational attainment, employment and income levels, and life expectancies, coupled with high rates of substance abuse, violence, and ecological dis-integration. Already pushed to the political, economic, cultural, and ecological margins, and already obliged to operate within externally imposed legal, political, and economic institutional arrangements, Indigenous people are also dealing with unprecedented environmental and climate changes, population dislocations, militarism, and new pulses of environmental and cultural conservation initiatives. There is no sugar-coating the reality that these problems plague White Mountain Apaches (Wagner 2014) and other Indigenous people across North America (Dunbar-Ortiz 2014; Hoover et al. 2012) and around the world (UN Permanent Forum on Indigenous Issues 2015). Colonial impositions and reverberations encumber Indigenous capacities to govern territories and populations while also impeding broader national and international progress toward intercultural reconciliation and the consensus definition and pursuit of desired futures.

Sovereignty-Driven Research in General

The shifts from extractive to balanced to sovereignty-driven engagements in my research reflect broad changes in societal values relating to Indigenous peoples. The 1990 enactment in the United States of the Native American Graves Protection and Repatriation Act and the 2007 adoption by the UN General Assembly of the right of free, prior, and informed consent (FPIC) as part of the UN Declaration on the Rights of Indigenous Peoples (UNDRIP) are major milestones in Indigenous research ethics (Ward 2011). Changes in national and international law and policy continue to prompt ethical advances on disciplinary and organizational scales directly relevant to researchers. In the Philippines, for example, the Indigenous Peoples Rights Act explicitly includes the right to FPIC for bioprospecting and archaeological explorations within Indigenous territories (Office of the President, National Commission on Indigenous Peoples, Administrative Order No. 1, Rules and Regulations Implementing Republic Act No. 8371; see also Kamau and Winter 2009).

Researchers—academic, industrial, and other—working with Indigenous peoples in the post-UNDRIP world have ethical and often legal obligations to conduct their work in accord with FPIC and in pursuit of reciprocal relations. On the other hand, not all academic researchers understand FPIC discussions as means for learning about community values, interests, and preferences or for sharing knowledge, perspectives, and capacities that may be useful or relevant to communities. Not all approach ethical mandates as opportunities to understand the challenges communities face and to identify ways to make academic research processes and outcomes relevant and useful to affected communities. Not all are willing to build collaborations with an eye toward integrating academic imperatives to publish and obtain grants with Indigenous community imperatives to insist that all activities affecting their territories and people create local benefits in proportion to external benefits. Not all are willing to consider going beyond giving back and toward partnering up, to pursue synergies by and through the cocreation of research that embraces community as well as academic values, interests, and goals. These issues in community-based participatory research direct attention to some basic questions, including these: What do Indigenous people want? What do researchers want? What might be done to integrate or co-advance those interests? (See figure 13.1.)

In some cases, addressing such questions means identifying standards and criteria that academic researchers and community representatives agree are likely to foster mutually satisfying research engagements. The issue with specific guidelines or with applying lessons learned in one setting to another is that every academic-community research engagement is distinctive and dynamic. On the other hand, all or most Indigenous people and communities share interests in shedding colonial impositions, improving the lives of their citizens and the powers of their governing institutions, and assuring the vitalities of their territories and cultural traditions. Indigenous people have been notably consistent in asserting that what they want from researchers is the same thing they desire from businesspeople, governmental representatives, missionaries, and others who come to "help." Although many terms describe these interests and desires, I think the best single term is *sovereignty*, defined here as control over territory and associated people.

Specific definitions aside, for many or most Indigenous communities, sovereignty means restoring that which colonialism has degraded and usurped. Sovereignty means crafting cultural, economic, and political institutions tailored to unprecedented circumstances as well as tethered to treasured traditions. The research reports on nation-building (Norman and Kalt 2015) and lists of Honoring Nations–award recipients associated with the Harvard Project on American Indian Economic Development (www.hpaied.org) reveal a wide spectrum of initiatives designed by US tribes and their research partners to further sovereignty. These projects, and hundreds of similar, sovereignty-enhancing initiatives in North America and other world regions, indicate that one good way to understand sovereignty in specific contexts is by asking questions of and collaborating with those who know how to enact it and have been working to exercise more of it (see, for example, Willow 2013). Sovereignty is, in this sense, what sovereigns *do*.

My experience working at the interface of sovereignty and the stewardship of cultural and biophysical heritage is the basis for suggesting that sovereignty, in Indigenous settings and elsewhere, rests on and is enacted through five interconnected "pillars" and pursuits:

1. Self-sufficiency—creation and maintenance of sustainable supplies of the food, water, shelter, and human relationships essential for people to survive and thrive
2. Self-determination—policies and practices that foster futures concordant with long-standing and emergent community values and interests
3. Self-governance—internal capacities to pursue and sustain self-determination
4. Self-representation—first-person portrayals of cultures, histories, and aspirations
5. Peer Recognition—establishment of government-to-government and other peer relationships based on legitimate authority over territory, citizens, and resources

This general framework provides a basis for encouraging researchers and community representatives to discuss and potentially act to exercise and advance sovereignty in specific contexts. Reframing research as a means for understanding and strengthening the constituents of sovereignties offers a lens for analyzing research initiatives and for (re)designing or reforming such programs to better serve Indigenous community interests. Academic researchers willing or obligated to try to create benefits for Indigenous people and communities, either in general or in the context of specific collaborations, may find the framework to be a good tool for identifying the constituents of sovereignty and exploring ways that academic knowledge, perspectives, and capacities might assist the people who are assisting or hosting their research. As a constructive response to colonial histories and to feminist and Indigenous scholars' critiques of extractive research and resource management, sovereignty-driven research has the potential to engage diverse academic and local community colleagues in blazing and traveling paths toward culturally and situationally appropriate economic and community development, among other goals.

Sovereignty-Driven Research at Fort Apache

The research and management collaborations with the White Mountain Apache Tribe I have facilitated since leaving my job there in 2005 illustrate aspects of the sovereignty-driven approach. Working closely with the tribe's Heritage Program and the Fort Apache Heritage Foundation, a tribally chartered nonprofit organization I helped the tribe establish in 1997, we have provided technical and financial support for site conservation and cultural perpetuation initiatives. Most of the work has focused on preserving and redeveloping the Fort Apache historical site, the hub of colonial domination that the tribe has worked to transform into a place of pride and opportunity—a hub for decolonization. Our partnership has created ongoing employment for about ten Apaches and provided the impetus for a successful research initiative to obtain recognition for Fort Apache and the Theodore Roosevelt School as a US National Historic Landmark (Welch 2011). In 2007, following a protracted legal battle, the US government transferred the property (350 acres and twenty-six historic structures) and $12 million in litigation settlement funds to the tribe (Welch and Brauchli 2010). More recently, and in keeping with the tribe's decolonizing vision for Fort Apache, the property has served as a proving ground for education—including a field school dedicated to the community-based production of a Western Apache cultural atlas (Hoerig et al. 2015)—entrepreneurship (Welch 2018), and community-authored historical research (Welch 2016). Table 13.2 lists the initiatives undertaken at Fort Apache as elements of a sovereignty-driven approach to research, conservation, and community development. Our work at Fort Apache is formally reviewed annually by the tribe's chief governing body and maintains an informal "social license to operate" through continuous and responsive engagements with all interested parties, including the Theodore Roosevelt School Board, neighbors, building tenants, and programming partners, most notably the Johns Hopkins Center for American Indian Health (2018).

Conclusion: Beyond Giving Back

The issues raised and examples put forward in this chapter stem from my hope that this volume and discussions about reciprocity in the context of researcher access and benefits sharing are points of departure rather than destinations. The concept and practice of sovereignty-driven research constitutes a call for collaborative planning and acting to build researcher-local community relationships imbued with respect, beneficence, and justice and committed to FPIC in both letter and spirit. This invitation humbly acknowledges that every research relationship is distinctive and that the terms of negotiation must be meaningful and useful to the affected parties. The sovereignty-driven approach I employ and offer explicitly recognizes that research engagements with Indigenous people are fraught and encumbered with historical and ongoing imbalances in material and political conditions of existence and other divisive dynamics. Factors external to communities—including the lack of funding and professional incentives available to researchers interested in community-based work and the resistance on the part of national governments—impede serious challenges to colonial institutions. Internal factors—institutional, disciplinary, interpersonal, and the like—often influence and even determine research engagements' intended processes and desired outcomes. For these reasons, some Indigenous communities have uncritically rejected what appear to be broadly beneficial research proposals; other communities have embraced research proposals having few if any reasonably foreseeable benefits except for academic researchers and disciplines. This means that, in at least some situations, giving back may be sufficient or all that is possible. In other situations, including the White Mountain Apache Tribe context described above, two decades of diligent and multifaceted efforts to provide local research benefits equal to or greater than those experienced by academic researchers has revealed important possibilities while barely scratching the surface of community needs.

One thing is for sure: other than as a basic precondition for academic/community engagements, good researcher intentions are insufficient. The myriad challenges faced by the world's most structurally and historically disadvantaged communities and nations are not likely to be

Table 13.2: Sovereignty-Driven Research and Management at Fort Apache

	PEOPLE	PLACE	MEMORY	PLANS
Self-sufficiency	Develop internal capacities to steward lands, water supplies, buildings, grounds, collections, and traditions	Rehabilitate the Fort Apache and T.R. School farm fields, orchards, and irrigation systems	Train Apache citizens to collect and conserve oral traditions, photographs, documents, and objects	Use Fort Apache as an enterprise zone to boost local commerce and reduce reliance on off-reservation businesses
Self-determination	Support T.R. School Board interests in creating an immersion school focused on instruction in Apache language and culture arts and traditions	Collaborate with the Johns Hopkins Center for American Indian Health in harnessing youth entrepreneurship to expand the Internet café in Building 103	Build existing object and document collections into a world-class center for research and interpretation	Set aside Fort Apache's riparian corridors and other areas of high ecological integrity as tribal preserves
Self-governance	Host the local school district's Junior Leadership Academy, a four-week summer program for Apache middle schoolers	Manage the Nohwike' Bágowa Museum Store to become the premier retail outlet for Apache artists and for raising funds to promote Apache arts	Build the Apache National Archives to boost administrative solvency as the destination for tribal government records	Transition the Foundation Board of Directors to (even) fuller control by White Mountain Apache citizens
Self-representation	Assure the primacy of Apache voices in the interpretation of local and regional history and culture	Host each May the annual Ndee Ła' Ade (Gathering of the People) Fort Apache Heritage Celebration and Apache Song and Dance Competition	Maintain respectful separations between interpretations of the Apache community history and those of Fort Apache and T.R. School history	Privilege Apache values, interests, and preferences in policies and practices, including in board recruitment and decision making
Peer recognition	Provide staff and board members as trainers for workshops on tribal museum and tribal historic preservation officer operations	Host the only Arizona Office of Tourism Local Visitor Information Center located on tribal lands	Sponsor additional intercultural reconciliation processes for representatives of groups linked to Fort Apache and T.R. School history	Maintain and grow public- and private-sector partnerships; attract federal, state, and private investments to support all of the above

effectively addressed by open hearts or modest gifts. Institutional and power dynamics embedded in colonial governmental and academic institutions operate to reify divides separating Indigenous people from outsiders in general and from Western academic researchers in particular. The burdens—legal, ethical, and practical—are on academic researchers to either use our knowledge, perspectives, capacities, and privileges to address these inequities and decrease these divides or face the truth of deriving personal and professional benefits from participation in institutions that perpetuate research at the expense of Indigenous peoples and territories. Most Indigenous peoples and communities need much, much more than spin-off research benefits. Despite the fine efforts represented in this book and elsewhere, we have barely begun the essential tasks of scoping out what can and should be done to create local benefits from and through our research—to go beyond giving back.

Because researchers have been part of the colonial problem, and because we control funds of power, money, and networks applicable to reducing and reversing colonialism's adverse effects, we must be part of the solutions, however incomplete. Academic and some for-profit research programs and paradigms are redefining the terms of reference for engagements with host and source communities (see table 13.1). Responsible and ethical shifts have been made from engaging Indigenous people as subjects to treating them as full partners. The next step, obvious in some cases, like Fort Apache, is to reposition Indigenous people and communities as the beneficial owners of research initiatives (figure 13.1). Many academic researchers, myself included, are in positions to facilitate the development of research agendas authored by and for Indigenous communities. Such agendas promise to transform Indigenous communities from sources and hosts for researchers into research clients and managers.

Offering as it does a practical antidote to colonial trauma and a potent guide to the consideration of "real-world" values and interests as drivers for academic research in many Indigenous settings, sovereignty-driven research deserves consideration and experimental application. I think many national and local governments share Indigenous communities' suspicions regarding the costs of globalization and hierarchy. At multiple sociopolitical and geographical scales people and organizations are following the leads of Indigenous quests to enhance and expand sovereignty by boosting collective, nonauthoritarian controls over food, fiber, air, water, and energy supplies and by embracing cultural traditions that emphasize human-ecosystem integrations (see, for example, Welch et al. 2011). It bears mention in this regard that quests for sovereignty are by no means limited to American Indian tribes and other Indigenous groups. Many issues relating to Indigenous settings apply to some extent to other local, place- and culture-based communities. As is the case for many Indigenous communities, some non-Indigenous communities maintain mutualistic, intergenerational dependencies with territories (see, for example, Garcia 2000). Such communities should not be forsaken as sources of knowledge and perspective comparable to Indigenous communities. Nor should they be approached as contexts for research with bars to entry that are lower than those for Indigenous contexts. FPIC should serve as a baseline for negotiating research access and benefits-sharing with all people affected by academic research activities.

The authors of this book are in the business of opening minds, project designs, and collaborative opportunities to the possibilities of creating new and better benefits from research engagements with the Indigenous and place-based communities who have helped build so many academic research careers and curricula vitae. By crafting partnerships purposefully designed to strengthen local sovereignties, and by insisting on balanced reciprocity in both inputs and benefits, research engagements with Indigenous and local communities provide contexts for conserving cultural, educational, economic, political, and scientific values embedded in objects, places, and traditions. Through creative and altruistic efforts to reconcile imbalances between researchers and our host and source communities, this volume is a testament to and champion for new forms and levels of ethical research practices focused on providing benefits to people who deserve and need them. In speaking truth to power imbalances that have defined the landscapes of research just as surely as these imbalances have shaped the landscapes of resource extraction and commodification, these chapters offer glimpses of critically important new directions. Research partnerships that are open-eyed as well as open-minded beckon. I am heeding the call and encourage others to do so.

Chapter 13 References

Atalay, Sonya. 2012. *Community-Based Archaeology: Research with, by, and for Indigenous and Local Communities*. Berkeley: University of California Press.

Atalay, Sonya, Lee Rains Clauss, Randall H. McGuire, and John R. Welch, eds. 2014. *Transforming Archaeology: Activist Practices and Prospects*. Walnut Creek, CA: Left Coast Press.

Burnette, Catherine E., Sara Sanders, Howard K. Butcher, and Jacki T. Rand. 2014. "A Toolkit for Ethical and Culturally Sensitive Research: An Application with Indigenous Communities." *Ethics and Social Welfare* 8 (4): 364–382.

Cajete, Gregory A. 1994. *Look to the Mountain: An Ecology of Indigenous Education*. Durango, CO: Kivaki Press.

—————2000. *Native Science: Natural Laws of Interdependence*. Santa Fe, NM: Clear Light.

Chilisa, Bagele. 2012. *Indigenous Research Methodologies*. Thousand Oaks, CA: SAGE.

Colwell-Chanthaphonh, Chip, and T. J. Ferguson. 2008. *Archaeological Practice: Engaging Descendant Communities*. Walnut Creek, CA: AltaMira Press.

Dunbar-Ortiz, Roxanne. 2014. *An Indigenous Peoples' History of the United States*. Boston: Beacon Press.

Garcia, Paula. 2000. "Community and Culture vs. Commodification: The Survival of Acequeias and Traditional Communities in New Mexico." *Voices from the Earth* 1 (2): 5–6.

Hoerig, Karl A., John R. Welch, T. J. Ferguson, and Gabriella Soto. 2015. "Expanding Toolkits for Heritage Perpetuation: The Western Apache Ethnography and Geographic Information Science Research Experience for Undergraduates." *International Journal of Applied Geospatial Research* 6 (1): 60–77.

Hoover, Elizabeth, Katsi Cook, Ron Plain, Kathy Sanchez, Vi Waghiyi, Pamela Miller, Renee Dufault, Caitlin Sislin, and David O. Carpenter. 2012. "Indigenous Peoples of North America: Environmental Exposures and Reproductive Justice." *Environmental Health Perspectives* 120 (12): 1645–1649. doi:10.1289/ehp.1205422.16.

Johns Hopkins Center for American Indian Health. 2018. "Fort Apache." http://caih.jhu.edu/locations/fort-apache.

Johnson, Jay T., and Brian Murton. 2007. "Re/Placing Native Science: Indigenous Voices in Contemporary Constructions of Nature." *Geographical Research* 45 (2): 121–129.

Kamau, Evanson C., and Gerd Winter. 2009. *Genetic Resources, Traditional Knowledge and the Law: Solutions for Access and Benefit Sharing*. London: Earthscan.

Kirkness, V. J., and R. Barnhardt. 1991. "First Nations and Higher Education: The Four R's—Respect, Relevance, Reciprocity, Responsibility." *Journal of American Indian Education* 30 (3): 1–15.

Mills, Barbara J., Mark Altaha, John R. Welch, and T. J. Ferguson. 2008. "Field Schools without Trowels: Teaching Archaeological Ethics and Heritage Preservation in a Collaborative Context." In *Collaborating at the Trowel's Edge: Teaching and Learning in Indigenous Archaeology*, edited by Stephen W. Silliman, 25–49. Tucson: University of Arizona Press.

Nicholas, George P., John R. Welch, and Eldon C. Yellowhorn. 2008. "Collaborative Encounters." In *Archaeological Practice: Engaging Descendant Communities*, edited by Chip Colwell-Chanthaphonh and T. J. Ferguson, 273–298. Walnut Creek, CA: AltaMira Press.

Norman, Dennis K., and Joseph P. Kalt, eds. 2015. *Universities and Indian Country: Case Studies in Tribal-Driven Research.* Tucson: University of Arizona Press.

Reid, J. Jefferson, and Stephanie M. Whittlesey. 1999. *Grasshopper Pueblo: A Story of Archaeology and Ancient Life.* Tucson: University of Arizona Press.

———. 2005. *Thirty Years into Yesterday: A History of Archaeology at Grasshopper Pueblo.* Tucson: University of Arizona Press.

Smith, Linda Tuhiwai. 2012. *Decolonizing Methodologies: Research and Indigenous Peoples.* New York: Zed Books.

Tidemann, S., and Andrew G. Gosler. 2010. *Ethno-Ornithology: Birds, Indigenous Peoples, Culture and Society.* London: Routledge/Earthscan.

Tobias, Joshua K., Chantelle A. M. Richmond, and Isaac Luginaah. 2013. "Community-Based Participatory Research (CBPR) with Indigenous Communities: Producing Respectful and Reciprocal Research." *Journal of Empirical Research on Human Research Ethics* 8 (2): 129–140.

UN Permanent Forum on Indigenous Issues. 2015. *State of the World's Indigenous Peoples.* Vol. 2. http://www.refworld.org/docid/55c89dac4.html.

Wagner, Dennis. 2014. "Apaches Approach Crossroads." *Arizona Republic.* February 2. http://www.azcentral.com/news/articles/20140106white-mountain-apaches-crossroads.html.

Ward, Tara. 2011. "The Right to Free, Prior, and Informed Consent: Indigenous Peoples' Participation Rights within International Law." *Northwest Journal of International Human Rights Law* 10 (2): 54–84. http://scholarlycommons.law.northwestern.edu/njihr/vol10/iss2/2.

Welch, John R. 2000. "The White Mountain Apache Tribe Heritage Program: Origins, Operations, and Challenges." In *Working Together: Native Americans and Archaeologists*, edited by Kurt E. Dongoske, Mark

Aldenderfer, and Karen Doehner, 67–83. Washington, DC: Society for American Archaeology.

———. 2008. "Places, Displacements, Histories and Memories at a Frontier Icon in Indian Country." In *Monuments, Landscapes, and Cultural Memory,* edited by Patricia E. Rubertone, 101–134. Walnut Creek, CA: World Archaeological Congress/Left Coast Press.

———. 2009. "Reconstructing the Ndee Sense of Place." In *The Archaeology of Meaningful Places,* edited by Brenda Bowser and M. Nieves Zedeño, 149–162. Salt Lake City: University of Utah Press.

———. 2011. "National Historic Landmark Nomination for Fort Apache and Theodore Roosevelt School." Washington, DC: National Park Service. US Park System Advisory Board. http://www.nps.gov/nhl/news/LC/spring2011/FortApache.pdf.

———, ed. 2013. *Kinishba Lost and Found: Mid-Century Excavations and Contemporary Perspectives.* Arizona State Museum Archaeological Series 206. Tucson: University of Arizona.

———. 2015. "The Last Archaeologist to (Almost) Abandon Grasshopper." *Arizona Anthropologist* (Centennial Edition):107–119.

———, ed. 2016. *Dispatches from the* Fort Apache Scout: *White Mountain and Cibecue Apache History through 1881,* by Lori Davisson, Edgar Perry and the Original Staff of the White Mountain Apache Cultural Center. Tucson: University of Arizona Press.

———. 2018. "Conserving Contested Ground: Sovereignty-Driven Stewardship by the White Mountain Apache Tribe and the Fort Apache Heritage Foundation." In *Environmentalism on the Ground: Processes and Possibilities of Small Green Organizing,* edited by Jonathan Clapperton and Liza Piper. Edmonton: Athabasca University Press.

Welch, John R., Mark K. Altaha, Karl A. Hoerig, and Ramon Riley. 2009. "Best Cultural Heritage Stewardship Practices by and for the White Mountain Apache Tribe." *Conservation and Management of Archaeological Sites* 11 (2): 148–160.

Welch, John R., and Robert C. Brauchli. 2010. "'Subject to the Right of the Secretary of the Interior': The White Mountain Apache Reclamation of the Fort Apache and Theodore Roosevelt School Historic District." *Wicazo Sa Review* 25 (1): 47–73.

Welch, John R., and T. J. Ferguson. 2007. "Putting Patria into Repatriation: Cultural Affiliations of White Mountain Apache Tribe Lands." *Journal of Social Archaeology* 7:171–198.

Welch, John R., Dana Lepofsky, Megan Caldwell, Georgia Combes, and Craig Rust. 2011. "Treasure Bearers: Personal Foundations for Effective Leadership in Northern Coast Salish Heritage Stewardship." *Heritage and Society* 4 (1): 83–114.

Welch, John R., and Ramon Riley. 2001. "Reclaiming Land and Spirit in the Western Apache Homeland." *American Indian Quarterly* 25 (1): 5–12.

Welch, John R., Ramon Riley, and Michael V. Nixon. 2009. "Discretionary Desecration: American Indian Sacred Sites, Dzil Nchaa Si An (Mount Graham, Arizona), and Federal Agency Decision Making." *American Indian Culture and Research Journal* 33 (4): 29–68.

Willow, Anna J. 2013. "Doing Sovereignty in Native North America: Anishinaabe Counter-Mapping and the Struggle for Land-Based Self-Determination." *Human Ecology* 41: 871–884.

Yellowhorn, Eldon C. 2002. Awakening Internalist Archaeology in the Aboriginal World. PhD diss., Department of Anthropology, McGill University, Montreal.

CONTRIBUTORS

Jennifer Carter is an associate professor and geography discipline leader in the School of Social Sciences at the University of the Sunshine Coast, Australia. She has more than twenty years of research experience with Indigenous Australians in many regions of northern and eastern Australia. Her research has explored how environmental research projects could be more collaborative, inclusive, and equitable for Aboriginal Australians, working with Iwaidja, Eastern Kunwinjku, Rembarrnga, Gun-nartpa/ Burarra, Gurr-goni, Ndjébbana, Nakkara, and Kunbarlang language groups in Arnhem Land, Australia. She has also researched community forestry initiatives with Wik peoples and sustainable microenterprise development with Kaanju peoples, in Cape York Peninsula. More recently, she worked with Wakka Wakka, Butchulla and Kabi Kabi language groups on the Sunshine Coast exploring structures and processes that better enable Indigenous peoples involvement in governance, particularly with respect to the mosaic of cultural landscapes that occur in regional and urbanizing areas. She obtained her PhD from Charles Darwin University, and BA, BS, and BS (Hons first class in geography) from the University of Queensland. She is a member of the Institute of Australian Geographers, the Australian Institute of Aboriginal and Torres Strait Islander Studies, and is co-leader of the Indigenous studies research theme at the university's Sustainability Research Centre.

Julia Christensen is an assistant professor in geography and Canada Research Chair in Northern Governance and Public Policy at Memorial University, Canada. Her research is based primarily in northern Canada and Greenland. Most recently, Julia has led research on the dynamics of rural-urban migration, homelessness, and health in Greenland, as well as research on Indigenous conceptualizations of home and homelessness in the Canadian Arctic. Recent publications include *No Home in a Homeland: Indigenous Homelessness in the Canadian North* (University of British Columbia Press, 2017) and a coedited volume, *Activating the Heart: Storytelling, Knowledge Sharing, and Relationship* (Wilfrid Laurier University Press, 2018), with Christopher Cox and Lisa Szabo-Jones. Julia was born and raised in the Canadian north and maintains close collaborative working relationships with community-based organizations across the north. She is also a fellow at the Institute for Circumpolar Health research in the Northwest Territories, Canada.

Claire Colyer completed her PhD in human geography at Macquarie University, Sydney, in 2014. She has more than thirty years' experience in a variety of research, media, editorial, and consultancy roles with Indigenous organizations, government agencies, and the not-for-profit sector in Australia, most recently providing support for Aboriginal inputs to the Royal Commission into the Protection and Detention of Children in the Northern Territory. She completed postdoctoral work with Janice Monk and Richie Howitt in 2015–2016.

David Crew is a PhD candidate in the Department of Geography and Planning, Macquarie University, Sydney, as well as the manager of the Yarkuwa Indigenous Knowledge Centre Aboriginal Corporation. David qualified as an archaeologist from the University of Sydney in 1985 and has worked for twenty-five years as a consultant and community developer with Aboriginal communities in several areas of New South Wales. In the 1990s, David worked with the Banbai Aboriginal Nation to declare the first Indigenous Protected Area in NSW, and in 2003 was involved in establishing Yarkuwa Indigenous Knowledge Centre Aboriginal Corporation in Deniliquin in southern NSW in the traditional lands of his wife, Jeanette.

Erica A. D'Elia is currently working as the assistant archaeology lab director with Fairfax County Park Authority. She previously worked as the lab manager at James Madison's Montpelier. Erica earned her MA in archaeology at Western Michigan University. She has been actively engaged in public outreach and education at Poplar Forest, Montpelier, Fairfax County, and with the Fort St. Joseph Archaeological Project. She is particularly interested in incorporating archaeology as a teaching tool in K–12 school curricula.

Maria Fadiman is an associate professor in the Department of Geosciences at Florida Atlantic University. She was named one of National Geographic's Emerging Explorers in 2006. Dr. Fadiman works with the human/environmental aspect of conservation. She received her PhD in geography at the University of Texas at Austin, an MA from

Tulane University, and a BA from Vassar College. Her research focuses on ethnobotany, the study of the relationship between people and plants. She works primarily in rural areas with Indigenous people and subsistence agriculturalists; the majority of her research is in the rainforests of Latin America. She has also researched alternative livelihoods through sustainable wood carving in Africa, house construction from natural materials in the Philippines, Maori utilization of the Kauri tree in New Zealand, and Tibetan children's plant knowledge while also teaching them to record their own ethnobotanical traditions and doing the ethnobotanical aspect of the creation of a cultural sanctuary in Bhutan. She is currently working on a global-scale cross-cultural study of how people's use of plants can act as larger ecosystem preservation incentives.

RDK Herman is senior geographer for the Smithsonian National Museum of the American Indian (NMAI). At the Smithsonian, he has served as chair of the Smithsonian Institutional Review Board (IRB) for Human Subjects Research, and chair of the Smithsonian Congress of Scholars. He holds a doctorate in geography from the University of Hawai'i, and, in addition to his work at NMAI, he is the director of *Pacific Worlds*, a web-based Indigenous-geography education project for Hawai'i and the American Pacific. He has served in various roles with the Indigenous Peoples Specialty Group of the Association of American Geographers since 2001, and has organized over 150 conference sessions on Indigenous geography. His publications include "Approaching Research in Indigenous Settings: Nine Guidelines" (2015), and his current research foci include Indigenous conflict resolution. He serves on the board of the journal *IK: Other Ways of Knowing*.

Richard Howitt recently retired as professor of human geography, Department of Geography and Planning, Macquarie University, Sydney. His research is generally concerned with the interplay across scales of social and environmental justice, particularly in relation to Indigenous rights and well-being in local communities of diversity. He advocates deep integration of social, environmental, and economic dimensions of justice into local governance systems. His current research explores issues of land, resources, and human rights of Indigenous groups in East Asia and Australasia, as well as ongoing work on engagement of the not-for-profit sector with Indigenous welfare, urban social justice, and community development.

Stephanie Hull graduated from the Applied Finance Program, majoring in statistics and demography at Macquarie University, Sydney. She has worked in academic teaching and research positions and in the government and private sectors in demography. She currently works in retail research. She was research assistant on Jan Monk and Richie Howitt's "Looking Forward—Looking Back" project.

Gwyneira Isaac is curator for North American ethnology at the Smithsonian National Museum of Natural History. Her research investigates knowledge systems and relationships societies develop with their past, especially as to how this is expressed through material culture and museums. Central to this study is her ethnography of a tribal museum in the Pueblo of Zuni, New Mexico, where she examined the difficulties faced by Zunis operating between Zuni and Euro-American approaches to knowledge. Through the book *Mediating Knowledges: Origins of a Museum for the Zuni People* (2007), she explores how the Zuni museum reconciled different approaches to knowledge both within its own constituency and cross-culturally and, consequently, how it took on the role of mediator between internal and external expectations about Zuni history. She is currently the director of the Smithsonian Recovering Voices initiative, through which a diverse group of researchers and communities are developing collaborative methodologies as a means to understand the role of museums and collections in interdisciplinary research on endangered language and knowledge.

Chris Jacobson is a senior research fellow with the Sustainability Research Centre at the University of the Sunshine Coast, Australia, and a research associate with Kā Rakahau o te Ao Tūroa—Centre for Sustainability, University of Otago, Aotearoa-New Zealand. Her research focuses on the intersections among community learning processes and adaptive governance and management arrangements in natural resource management, with a particular interest in cross-cultural contexts. She completed her undergraduate and postgraduate studies in New Zealand before moving to Australia in 2006. She has researched co-management, evaluating its effectiveness, the contentious issue of whose knowledge informs it, and how governance structures affect knowledge exchange. This includes working on Mahinga Kai (food resources), protected areas and freshwater management in Aotearoa-New Zealand (with Ngāi Tahu), on protected area management in Australia (with Great Sandy Biosphere Reserve and Booderee National Park) and Canada (Auyuittuq National Park), and community-based adaptation and agricultural development in Southeast Asia and the Pacific Islands.

Meredith Luze is a NAGPRA regional coordinator at the Peabody Museum of Archaeology and Ethnology at Harvard University. She is a former archaeology field coordinator at James Madison's Montpelier, where she worked intensively with the African American descendant expedition in 2015. She earned her MA in historical archaeology from the University of Massachusetts Boston, with a thesis exploring how the Wampanoag Indigenous Program at Plimoth Plantation, a living history museum, incorporates and engages with archaeology in its exhibits. She first began focusing on community outreach and engagement with descendant communities during her time at University of Massachusetts Boston, particularly through her involvement in archaeology with the Eastern Pequot Tribal Nation in Connecticut. She is interested in promoting the accessibility of museum and archaeological collections to descendant groups as well as scholars.

Catrina A. MacKenzie is an affiliated member of the Geography Department at McGill University, Canada, an adjunct lecturer in the Department of Geography at the University of Vermont, United States, and a collaborating researcher with Population, Environment, and Climate in the Albertine Rift (PECAR). She received her PhD in geography from McGill University. Her mixed methods research is focused on the relationship between conservation policy and human livelihoods in communities bordering protected areas in Sub-Saharan Africa. For the last ten years she has worked with communities bordering national parks in the Ugandan Albertine Rift to understand how incentives and socioeconomic conditions influence conservation attitudes and behaviors of local people, with a particular focus on tourism revenue sharing, loss compensation, resource extraction, and environmental justice. To give back in the villages where she works, she volunteers her time to study primary school enrollment and academic achievement of children living near protected areas and tries to understand the influence that integrated conservation and development projects have in the primary schools they support.

Lea S. McChesney is curator of ethnology at the Maxwell Museum of Anthropology, research assistant professor in the Department of Anthropology, and director of the Alfonso Ortiz Center for Intercultural Studies at the University of New Mexico. Her research interests include comparative perspectives on material, visual, and expressive culture; representation and inscription; indigeneity, gender, and identity; and the legacy of museum collections to ongoing cultural heritage in Indigenous communities. She examines the relationship of Native North American communities historically and contemporaneously to Euro-American institutions through their material culture. Her research addresses the historical processes and social contexts that have transformed Native arts through time, spanning collections-based research and multi-sited ethnographic fieldwork, and restoring an ethnographic dimension to museum collections through linking cultural resources with their descendant communities. She is the editor of *Museum Anthropology* and is also a research associate of Harvard University's Peabody Museum and a core member of the Hopi Pottery Oral History Project under the Recovering Voices initiative of the Smithsonian's National Museum of Natural History and in collaboration with the Hopi Tribe's Cultural Preservation Office. Lea has conducted collaborative ethnographic research in the Hopi First Mesa community for over two decades.

Kendra McSweeney, professor of geography at Ohio State University, is a geographer specializing in the study of human-environment relations through the interdisciplinary lens of political ecology. She received her PhD from McGill University in Montreal. She has worked for more than two decades in Latin America, particularly in collaboration with Indigenous federations in Honduras and Ecuador. Her research interests include rural livelihoods, agrarian change, uneven development, and socioecological resilience. She has documented the population resurgence and mobility of Amazonian indigenous populations and the theoretical and policy implications of that growth for indigenous territoriality. Most recently, she has been researching how cocaine smuggling through Central America is profoundly changing rural landscapes and livelihoods. Her research projects have been supported by the Open Society Foundations, the National Geographic Society, and the National Science Foundation's Dynamics of Coupled Natural and Human Systems Program. Her work has appeared in more than twenty-five journals, including *PNAS* and *Science*.

Janice Monk earned her BA (Hons) at the University of Sydney and PhD at the University of Illinois. She is research social scientist emerita in the Southwest Institute for Research on Women, research professor in the School of Geography and Development at the University of Arizona, and adjunct professor in the Department of Environment and Geography, Macquarie University, Sydney. In 2017 she was named as fellow of the American Association of Geographers. She has long engagement with research on issues of diversity, especially gender themes, and on practices in geography in higher education. Her involvement with Indigenous studies began in the 1960s with dissertation research on Aboriginal communities in small towns in New South Wales. Her field materials from that project are archived at the Australian Institute of Aboriginal and Torres Strait Islander Studies (Canberra) and serve as basis for current collaboration with Richard Howitt and David Crew, including attention to ethical aspects of work with archival materials.

Roxanne T. Ornelas is an associate professor in the Department of Geography at Miami University, Ohio. Her research includes a focus on the geographies of Indigenous peoples and their sacred lands, Indigenous women and water activism, and environmental policy and leadership. Dr. Ornelas has had numerous opportunities to visit sacred places on the North American continent, as well as some of the most polluted and environmentally degraded "sacrifice zones." Her field research experience has led her to travel thousands of miles in support of water protection with Indigenous women water walkers and other water protectors. Her method of research is direct in-the-field qualitative ethnographic methodology in search of the answers she seeks. At the core of her work is a belief that all Earth is sacred and must be preserved and protected for the seventh generation from today.

Tristan Pearce is a senior research fellow in geography with the Sustainability Research Centre at the University of the Sunshine Coast (USC) and adjunct faculty in the Department of Geography at the University of Guelph, Canada. His research takes place at the interface between science and policy, with a strong focus on understanding what makes Indigenous communities vulnerable or resilient to environmental changes, using this understanding to identify and evaluate pathways for adaptation. This involves working closely with people in communities and drawing on both Indigenous and Eurocentric knowledge systems to understand our relationship with the natural environment and how it is changing. He is committed to building equitable community-researcher relationships and has long-term relationships with communities in the Canadian Arctic, Australia, and Pacific Island region.

Matthew Reeves is the director of archaeology at James Madison's Montpelier in Orange, Virginia. His specialty is sites of the African diaspora, including plantation and freedman period sites and Civil War sites. He grew up in Fairfax, Virginia, and received his doctorate from Syracuse University. For his dissertation, Reeves researched and excavated two early nineteenth-century Jamaican slave settlements and spent over two years living and working within the rural descendant community he was studying. Prior to Montpelier, he led archaeological projects in upstate New York, southern Maryland, and for the National Park Service at Manassas National Battlefield. In his seventeen years at Montpelier, Reeves has developed a strong public archaeology program known for its citizen science approach to research. At the heart of this program is community-based research with a heavy focus on investing descendant communities in the research and interpretation process. Most recently, his department's work on an eight-year study excavating the remains of slave homes at Montpelier has yielded very detailed information on the homes of enslaved individuals dating to the early nineteenth century and has led to their reconstruction. He has also led the archaeological discipline in devising new ways to engage metal detector hobbyists and archaeological surveys though his department's work locating the living and working sites of the enslaved community across the 2,700-acre Montpelier property. These new site discoveries hold the future for Montpelier continuing to telling the story of the enslaved community.

Chie Sakakibara is an assistant professor of environmental studies at Oberlin College. Prior to her current appointment, Chie was a postdoctoral research fellow at the Earth Institute and Center for Ethnomusicology at Columbia University (2008–2010). Her academic backgrounds are in cultural geography, art history, and Native American studies, and her teaching and research interests lie in the field of the human dimensions of global environmental change among indigenous peoples, specifically on their cultural resilience and socio-environmental justice. Her current research focuses on climate change and its influence on traditional relationships with the bowhead whale in the Alaskan Arctic, particularly among the Indigenous Iñupiaq people, who call themselves the "People of the Whales." In addition to her own research, she collaborates with Columbia University's Center for Ethnomusicology for their community-partnered Iñupiaq music heritage repatriation project. Chie also explores climate change and cultural identity among the islanders of the Azores, Autonomous Region of Portugal, in the northern Atlantic.

Wendy S. Shaw is an associate professor in the School of Biological, Earth and Environmental Sciences at the University of New South Wales, Sydney Australia. She teaches and carries out research in critical race studies, whiteness in postcolonial Australia, Indigenous geographies, and urban worlds. Her book, *Cities of Whiteness* (Blackwell-Wiley 2007) is recognized internationally as a key work on Indigenous experiences of whiteness in postcolonial urban Australia. The study of complex realities of (post)colonial life in Australia and beyond has taken Wendy's research across the Asia-Pacific region. Wendy S. Shaw is on the editorial boards of the *Annals of the Association of American Geographers, Geoforum,* and *Acme: An International E-journal for Critical Geographies.*

Sarah Turner is professor of development geography in the Department of Geography, McGill University, Canada. She has conducted fieldwork in urban Malaysia, Indonesia, and Vietnam and, for the past twenty years, with upland ethnic minority groups in rural northern Vietnam and southwest China. Her research interests span agrarian change, everyday politics and resistance, minority livelihoods, and urban informal economies. She has edited *Red Stamps and Gold Stars: Fieldwork Dilemmas in Upland Socialist Asia* (University of British Columbia Press 2013), and coauthored *Frontier Livelihoods: Hmong in the Sino-Vietnamese Borderlands* (University of Washington Press 2015). She has also published in *Annals of the Association of American Geographers, Journal of Peasant Studies,* and *Development and Change,* among others, and is an editor of *Geoforum.* Her commitment to giving back to the communities where she works includes a long-term involvement with a local ethnic minority-run social enterprise in the Vietnam uplands, Sapa O'Chau.

John R. Welch is an applied archaeologist who has spent more than three decades facilitating research and outreach partnerships with tribes in upland Arizona and New Mexico, as well as First Nations in coastal British Columbia. Against a backdrop of ongoing reassessments of what to conserve in the face of global change, Welch coordinates the mobilization of Indigenous knowledge and the advancement of Indigenous community agendas for stewardship of sociocultural and biophysical legacies. Welch served as the archaeologist and historic preservation officer for the White Mountain Apache Tribe from 1992 to 2005, and continues on the board of the Fort Apache Heritage Foundation, a tribally chartered nonprofit he helped found in 1998. Welch authored the 2011 nomination of the Fort Apache and Theodore Roosevelt School district as a US National Historic Landmark. He edited *Dispatches from the Fort Apache Scout: White Mountain and Cibecue Apache History through 1881* (University of Arizona Press 2016), a compendium of newspaper articles from the 1970s prepared by Lori Davisson, with Edgar Perry and the original staff of the White Mountain Apache Cultural Center. Welch's current research involves locating and following old Apache foot trails to places of intercultural conflict and reconciliation.

INDEX